The Ultimate

PANINI PRESS

Cookbook

More than 200 Perfect-Every-Time Recipes
for Making Panini—and Lots of Other Things—on Your
Panini Press or Other Countertop Grill

KATHY STRAHS

THE HARVARD COMMON PRESS
BOSTON, MASSACHUSETTS

The Harvard Common Press
www.harvardcommonpress.com

Printed in China
Printed on acid-free paper

Library of Congress Cataloging-in-Publication Data
Strahs, Kathy Lipscomb.
The ultimate panini press cookbook : more than 200 perfect-every-time recipes for making panini—and lots of other things—on your panini press or other countertop grill / Kathy Strahs.
pages cm
Includes index.
ISBN 978-1-55832-792-4 (pbk. : acid-free paper)
1. Panini. I. Title.
TX818.S77 2013
641.7'6--dc23
2013001298

Special bulk-order discounts are available on this and other Harvard Common Press books. Companies and organizations may purchase books for premiums or resale, or may arrange a custom edition, by contacting the Marketing Director at the website above.

10 9 8 7 6 5 4 3 2 1

For Grandma

CONTENTS

PREFACE

I knew what was inside the box from my sister the moment it arrived on my doorstep.

Ever since Oprah Winfrey raved about a panini press as one of her "Favorite Things" that year, I had been on the hunt to buy one—as a holiday gift for my sister-in-law, actually. But, as tends to happen, once this particular panini press received the green light from Oprah it sold out in stores immediately. I looked all over, but I couldn't find one anywhere. I ended up buying my sister-in-law a different model, which she tells me she likes.

And then this package arrived.

After all the effort that my sister put into procuring this panini press for me, I felt as though I'd better do something good with it. It would be a shame to see it collect dust on the upper, out-of-reach shelves in my pantry, which had been the fate of too many other small appliances. Not this time. I wanted to see what this thing could really do.

Then I had the idea to start a blog. I would create and share recipes for the panini press with others who, like me, were looking for ways to get the most out of this machine. I put up my first post on PaniniHappy.com on January 14, 2008, and thus began a panini-grilling odyssey that's brought me more creative challenges and triumphs than I ever could have imagined.

One of my favorite stories about my early days in the kitchen takes place in a cooking class my sister Julie and I attended one summer, when I was twelve and she was almost nine. Our assignment one day was to bake chocolate chip cookies, a task we'd helped our mother with countless times at home (my mom devoted several years to perfecting her chocolate chip cookie recipe—it's the best). Rather than bake the two dozen cookies that the recipe called for, we opted to ratchet up the fun meter at our cooking station and produce six gigantic cookies instead—six gigantic cookies that turned out raw in the center and burnt around the edges. Judging from the stern talking-to we got, the teacher didn't appreciate our creativity, but Julie and I couldn't have been more pleased with ourselves. We may not have "gotten it right," but it was exciting to push the limits. For me, this is where the true thrill of cooking exists.

To this day, I view food with a passion for discovery. What will this taste like? How can I make that? Why didn't it come out right? Experimenting in the kitchen from an early age, taking the opportunity to taste all kinds of foods as often as I can, and becoming part of a vibrant community of food enthusiasts (let's not say "foodies," okay?) through blogging have not only made me a better cook but also given me a forum to share this opportunity for discovery with others.

My parents' basement is full of handicrafts from my childhood—the Garfield the cat "piggy" bank I carved and painted in seventh-grade wood shop class, the medieval costumes I sewed for my Cabbage Patch Kids, latch-hook pillows, the papier-mâché model of Bernarda Alba from the book we had to read in Spanish my senior year of high school. I have always loved to make stuff. I think I get that from both sides of my family. My mom taught me to knit and crochet when I was a little kid, and she always kept my two sisters and me supplied with arts and crafts materials. The walls of my grandma's house are adorned with decades' worth of elaborate needlepoint and quilt projects. My dad has become a self-taught oil-paint artist in recent years, finding plenty of inspiration in the colors of desert sunsets. My own two preschoolers are proving to be budding visual artists as well, if the profusion of construction paper hats around our living room and chalk murals on the backyard patio are any indication. "Making stuff" is what we do in my family.

Today I look at the panini press in the same way I viewed the pasty strips of my childhood papier-mâché projects—what will I make with this? My goal is to create recipes that I not only can grill on the panini press, but that I should make on this machine because it tastes better or cooks faster or frees up space in the oven or saves me from having to heat up the entire house—or all of the above.

This cookbook is for everyone who wants to put their panini press—or George Foreman grill or any other type of indoor grill—to work. I will show you the simple techniques for grilling restaurant-quality panini as well as a huge variety of non-sandwiches—meats, vegetables, desserts, and breakfasts that will become go-to recipes for your everyday cooking. Let your creativity soar and see where it takes you.

ACKNOWLEDGMENTS

I am beyond thankful to everyone who has supported me and cheered me on during this nearly two-year cookbook creation process.

My PaniniHappy.com readers are those for whom I first began creating panini press recipes, and they continue to encourage and inspire me week after week. Thank you for proving to me and to the world that a blog about sandwiches wasn't such a crazy idea after all.

I can hardly begin to thank my husband, Mike, for his unwavering support for me, whether I am behind a corporate desk or a panini press. I may have been the author of this book, but he was the chief taste tester, crazy idea generator, child wrangler, dish washer, photo evaluator, and kind word giver throughout the project. Thank you for making this possible for me. Love you more.

Mike and I have been blessed with the two sweetest little kids we could have ever asked for. Their verve and enthusiasm motivate me every day to reach higher, live a little louder, and find fun in every day. Mommy loves you so much, buddies!

Thanks to Jo Arazi for dress-up, puzzles, crafting, and trains, making it possible for me to carve out time to write this cookbook. My little guys thank you, too!

If my sister Angela hadn't given me that first panini press as a Christmas gift, none of this would have ever happened. Look what you started! My entire family has taken part in this cookbook project; they helped me test recipes, came up with chapter titles, and provided a steady stream of inspiration. I'd especially like to thank my parents, James and Nancy Lipscomb, for their unconditional love and support. I love you all!

I'll always be grateful to The Harvard Common Press for the opportunity to branch out from the blogosphere into the print world. Special thanks to my editor, Dan Rosenberg, for never saying "No," but rather "Let's talk about it." I've appreciated every piece of wisdom and thoughtful advice you've shared with me. Thanks also to Bruce Shaw, Adam Salomone, Roy Finamore, Virginia Downes, Pat Jalbert-Levine, and Karen Wise for all of the decisions, designs, and notes that have made my first cookbook one of which I am truly proud.

Many thanks to my literary agent, Stacey Glick, for being my sherpa through this entire process. Your guidance, diligence, and openness have been invaluable to me.

I'm proud to belong to a large, supportive community of bloggers and other food folks, with whom I have the opportunity to exchange ideas, triumphs, and challenges on a daily (hourly?) basis. There are far too many of you to name, but you know who you are. Thank you for everything. I'm honored to call you my friends.

Speaking of friends . . . I'm thrilled to finally share this cookbook with my "real life" friends who have been there for me every day as I steadily cooked and photographed for what seemed like forever. Whether we are catching up at preschool drop-off, playgroup, the gym, girls' night out, or via text, you have continually encouraged and supported me all along the way. Know that your friendship means the world to me.

A stellar team of family, friends, and Panini Happy readers helped me test the recipes in this book. Thank you all so much for your insightful feedback and for being an instrumental part of this process: Nancy Lipscomb, Julie Atkinson, Angela Lipscomb, Susan Strahs, Colleen Strahs, Melissa Black, Brooke Russell, Alex Ota, Anthony Mannarino, Patti Aretz, Eleni Mavromati, Marie Tran-McCaslin, Brenda Thompson, Dick Bennett, Tricia Kenny, Rebecca Jackson, Dawn Gibian, Roxana Payton, Lauren Hall, Isla Globus-Harris, Danielle and Chris Houser, Heather Zimmerman, Amanda Richard, and Yusef Joyner.

PANINI AND PANINI PRESSES

The Basics

Panini Presses—The Ins and Outs

The panini press is, of course, named for the Italian pressed sandwiches that have become so popular here in recent years. You will sometimes see a panini press called simply a "sandwich maker" or an "indoor grill." For the purposes of this book, when I say "panini press" I'm referring to any countertop appliance—including a George Foreman grill—that can heat food between two grates.

That said, as with any appliance, not all panini presses are the same. Some come with a myriad of features and are large enough to accommodate a family's worth of steaks, while others are very basic and designed to fit comfortably in a college dorm room. They're available at all price points, ranging from as little as $20 for a very simple model with a single heat setting to upwards of $300 for one with an LCD screen and removable plates.

People often ask me which type of panini press I recommend. My response is usually "Well, what do you plan to use it for?" I suggest examining five key features to help you determine which panini press meets your needs and your budget:

- Adjustable thermostat
- Grill surface area
- Drainage
- Removable plates
- Adjustable height control

ADJUSTABLE THERMOSTAT

An adjustable thermostat allows you to control the amount of heat you're grilling with. Some panini presses allow you to set a specific cooking temperature (350°F, for example), some come with "high," "medium," and "low" settings; some give an adjustable range between "panini" and "sear"; and others are built with a simple on/off switch and no ability to adjust the heat level at all.

If you're planning to grill mainly sandwiches, a panini press without an adjustable thermostat will likely suit your needs. However, the ability to control the temperature is key when grilling certain foods. For my Grilled Rib-Eye Steak (page 151), for instance, I turn the heat up high to get a nice, crusty sear on the meat. To slowly render the fat and crisp the skin on my Grilled Duck Breasts (page 71), I use a medium-low setting. And for my Mini Yellow Layer Cake with Chocolate Buttercream (page 325), which involves baking, I need to set the thermostat exactly to 350°F.

In general, the more heating options, the more expensive the panini press will be. You can buy a press without an adjustable thermostat for as little as $20 or $30; presses with adjustable thermostats typically cost $70 and up.

GRILL SURFACE AREA

Some folks prefer a smaller grill due to space constraints in their kitchen or dorm room, or if there are just one or two people in the household. Small grills are also more portable, making them a great option for those who like to bring their panini press on vacation. A large grill surface area is especially beneficial to those who want to make a lot of panini or other foods for a whole family at once—it can be a real timesaver not to have to cook in batches.

Panini presses with large surface areas, accommodating four panini or more, are pricier than small models and usually offer other premium features. They typically range between $70 and $300.

DRAINAGE

If you plan to use your panini press to grill meats, poultry, and other foods beyond panini, it's important to choose a press with drainage features. The grill plates on many panini presses and other indoor grills are designed to drain excess fat, which can make them a healthier cooking alternative. On some models, you can adjust the plates to tilt forward to allow the fat to flow into a drip pan, while others remain flat and drain via the back of the grill.

Some no-frills panini presses do not have any drainage features at all—you'll notice that the lower plate stays flat and there are no cutouts or sloped edges to allow fat to roll away. Models like these are intended mainly for grilling panini and shouldn't be used for raw meats.

Feature Comparison

You'll find panini presses on the market with features and price points to suit all needs. Here is a rundown of what you can expect to find at the basic, midrange, and premium levels of the panini press spectrum.

BASIC ($20–$50)
Pros: Compact size; cooks quickly; affordable
Cons: No adjustable thermostat, drainage feature, removable plates, or adjustable height control; small to medium grill surface area; may not be suitable for grilling raw meats (refer to the manufacturer's instructions)

MIDRANGE ($50–$80)
Pros: May have an adjustable thermostat and drainage feature; larger grill surface area; greater grilling versatility, including raw meats
Cons: Not likely to have removable plates or adjustable height control

PREMIUM ($80–$300)
Pros: Adjustable thermostat; large grill surface area, with drainage feature; may have removable plates; may have adjustable height control; greatest grilling versatility
Cons: Requires more counter space; less portable; less affordable

REMOVABLE PLATES

Melted and cooked-on bits are a fact of life with the panini press. If your grill has removable plates, cleanup is much easier. You can just pop off the plates and scrub them in the sink or dishwasher. But if your grill doesn't have removable plates, don't despair—I've got helpful cleaning tips for you on page 4.

ADJUSTABLE HEIGHT CONTROL

I regularly use the adjustable height control feature on my panini press to give me greater flexibility in terms of the types of foods I can grill. This feature allows me to position the upper plate to hover above open-faced sandwiches, make very light contact with soft foods like tomatoes and French toast, and regulate the amount of pressure applied to panini so that the ingredients don't squeeze out. Most panini presses come with a floating hinge, which allows for a degree of pressure control, but very few offer fully adjustable height control.

Whether your panini press comes with all of these features or just one or two, nearly any model will make grilling sandwiches and other foods an easy task.

How to Use a Panini Press

Most panini presses are very easy and straightforward to operate. Here are my tips for getting the best results when it comes to heating, grilling, and cleaning.

HEATING

Each panini press model heats differently—some you just plug in, while others have specific heat settings. As you can imagine, this poses quite a challenge for me when it comes to developing recipes that each of you can accurately follow with whichever type of panini press you might have. "High" on one grill might be "sear" on another, and still others have no option to set a heat level at all.

For the vast majority of the recipes in this cookbook, I've suggested setting your panini press to "medium-high" heat. That's a level that's not the highest, but not the lowest—somewhere in between, leaning toward the higher side. (Note: Panini presses with simple on/off heating tend to run on the hotter side, so your cooking time may be shorter with these machines.) The good news is that, for most recipes, the exact temperature won't really matter. Just look at the food you're grilling and decide whether it looks done to you or not. If it's a meat dish, I highly recommend using a meat thermometer (see more discussion on meat thermometers on page 13) to monitor doneness.

GRILLING

Notice that I called this section "Grilling." I didn't call it "Flattening" or "Leaning Into the Panini Press to Make Sure the Sandwich Gets Good and Flat." I'm not sure where the practice of pressing down hard on a panini press originated. I see evidence of it over and over again in photos, but it's not what I'd recommend unless you happen to like really flat food. Today's panini presses are designed to provide the right degree of pressure, without any need for you to press down—or flatten—your food.

My recommendation, whether you're making sandwiches or other foods, is that you *grill* them. That is, you place the food on the grates, close the lid so that it's resting on top of the food, and wait until it's done. If you're grilling panini, the sound of melted cheese sizzling on the grates is a good indication that it's time to take the panini off the grill. For meats, I always use a meat thermometer that beeps when the desired temperature has been reached.

CLEANING

As I've mentioned before, if your panini press comes with removable plates, cleanup is relatively easy. Once the grill has cooled down, you just unsnap the grates from the base and wash them in the sink or dishwasher. But what about grills without removable plates? Truth be told, the grill I use most often doesn't have removable plates. No big deal—here's how I get it as clean as new.

SCRAPE IT WHILE IT'S HOT. More often than not there's melted cheese remaining on the grates after I've grilled panini. It comes with the territory. Thanks to the nonstick coating on the grates, cheese scrapes off easily with the help of the plastic grill scraper that came with my panini press (if yours didn't come with its own grill scraper, see my recommendation for a silicone grill brush on page 13) and a clean cloth. For more stubborn stuck-on food—which often happens when I grill meat, especially with sweet marinades—I unplug the grill and, while it's still hot, I (very carefully) try to loosen and lift off as many bits as possible with the grill scraper. Then I let the grill cool completely. *Safety note:* Make sure the unplugged power cord is resting next to the grill, not dangling where it could accidentally be pulled and drag the panini press off the table or counter. And never use an abrasive pad on the grill as it may damage the nonstick coating.

TAKE IT TO THE SINK. Once the grill has cooled, I bring it over to the counter adjacent to the kitchen sink (let me reiterate—the grill *must be unplugged* before you bring it anywhere near water). I position the grill so that the front edge is just above the bowl of the sink. Then I squirt on some dish soap and wash the lower plate with a wet sponge and use a silicone grill brush to get to those hidden places between the grates. Once it's clean, I use the pull-out faucet to rinse off the plate and then dry it with paper towels (just in case I missed any bits of blackened cooked-on food that would stain my nice kitchen towels). If your sink doesn't have a pull-out faucet, you can also rinse with a very wet sponge. *Safety note:* As with all electrical appliances, don't ever let the electrical connection get wet and never submerge any part of the panini press itself in water.

TURN IT UPSIDE DOWN. And what about that upper plate, you ask? Cleaning that had been a challenge for me until I discovered an easy solution—I turn the entire machine on its end so that the upper plate lies flat on the counter over the sink. Then I can clean it just as I did with the lower plate. Just be aware that with this new distribution of weight—the upper plate is typically much lighter than the lower plate—the press may be less stable, so work carefully.

REMEMBER THE DRIP TRAY. Some panini presses come equipped with a drip tray that is so well concealed that it's easy to forget about it. Especially after grilling meats and vegetables, it's important to clean out any fat or juices that may have accumulated.

Ingredients for Perfect Panini

"You don't have to cook fancy or complicated masterpieces—just good food from fresh ingredients."—Julia Child

BREAD

Bread, the traditional foundation of most panini, can take many forms—loaf slices, rolls, baguettes, flatbreads, and so on. When I'm deciding which type of bread to use for a sandwich, I take a lot into consideration:

- Will my fillings hold up well on sliced bread, or will I need something more substantial, like a baguette?
- Do I want the bread itself to contribute flavor to the sandwich—such as with an olive or rosemary bread—or should it play more of a neutral supporting role?
- Are there specific breads that match the cultural heritage of my sandwich, such as a *telera* roll for a Mexican torta or ciabatta for a sandwich with lots of Italian meats?
- What kind of bread do I have in my house at this moment?

Choice of bread can have a real impact on the structure, texture, and flavor of your panini. Often it's easiest just to use what you happen to have on hand, but to get the very best results when grilling sandwiches, here are some thoughts to keep in mind.

KEEP IT DENSE (MOSTLY). Generally speaking, denser bread is best when it comes to grilling panini. Throughout this book you'll see me suggesting that you use rustic breads "sliced from a dense bakery loaf." This isn't me just being all fancy-pants food snob (for the most part). There is a practical reason that I specify denser bread and advocate slicing it yourself. Dense bread—such as the freeform loaves you find in the bakery section of your grocery store—will hold its shape better than soft, pre-sliced sandwich bread when it gets between the two grates (see the photo below).

Now, with every rule, there is an exception: I do use softer breads from time to time. Two examples are my Brie, Nutella, and Basil Panini (page 314), which is grilled on brioche, and my Grilled French Toast (page 293), which calls for challah. In these instances, I cut the slices extra-thick to accommodate some compression during grilling. They still retain some of their

The Bakery Loaf vs. Sliced Sandwich Bread

I grilled the sandwich on the left on a country *levain* from my local grocery store. I sliced the bread myself, about ½ inch thick. As you can see, the bread maintained its thickness, for the most part, and didn't get soggy. On the right is the same sandwich grilled on regular pre-sliced sandwich bread. The soft, airy bread—which is normally very desirable for cold sandwiches—flattened to nearly a cracker. The weight of the panini press plates is simply too much for softer breads. Dense is the way to go.

airiness, which I want in these recipes. So if you're an especially big fan of softer breads and really want to grill with them, I'd advise cutting thicker slices.

THINK OUTSIDE THE BREAD. We tend to focus on the fillings that go inside the sandwich, but for the best sandwiches you should flavor the outside as well.

In many panini recipes throughout this book, you'll see that I call for spreading butter or olive oil on the outside of the bread prior to assembly. Your sandwich will come out fine if you omit this step—it's not required to prevent sticking, as most panini presses have a nonstick coating on the grates—but a little swipe of butter or oil will add flavor and a bit of crunch to the bread, as well as more defined grill marks (which are a nice aesthetic touch).

Another way to flavor the outside of the bread is through crusting. You can crumble all sorts of different foods—tortilla chips, nuts, and cookies, to name a few—and mix them with softened butter to create spreads that will turn into crunchy, flavorful crusts on the outside of your sandwiches when they're grilled. See my Jalapeño Popper Grilled Cheese Panini (page 251), Honey Walnut–Crusted Aged Cheddar Panini (page 246), and Nutella S'mores Panini (page 315) for examples of these crusts in action.

VENTURE BEYOND THE BAGUETTE. Lastly, I encourage you to think beyond the traditional types of breads that we use for sandwiches and play around with other creative options: pound cake, banana bread, tortillas, zucchini bread, corn bread—whatever you can possibly "sandwich." After a while, nearly everything in your fridge and pantry will start looking like a great candidate for grilling on your panini press!

MEAT

The meats I typically use for panini fall into three categories: deli, leftovers, and panini-grilled.

DELI MEATS. Good-quality sliced deli meats are often the most convenient meats to use in panini. You can buy anything from turkey to roast beef to prosciutto pre-sliced and packaged in any grocery store. However, I've found that it's usually less expensive to grab a number at the deli counter and have the butcher slice exactly the amount I need.

LEFTOVERS. My mother-in-law taught me to appreciate the versatility of leftovers. With a little creativity, you can transform leftovers into a new dish that will rival—and just might out-shine—the original. Especially around the holidays, when we tend to cook larger roasts, it's a great time to pull out the panini press and start reinventing. Throughout this cookbook I've highlighted recipes that are particularly suitable for repurposing the cooked chicken, turkey, beef, lamb, and pork you already have on hand.

PANINI-GRILLED MEATS. Depending on the grill you own (see the Feature Comparison box on page 2), you can often use it to prepare your fillings as well as the sandwiches themselves! It takes just a few minutes to grill chicken breasts or steak that you can then build into panini. In most cases you will want to unplug the panini press, cool it, and clean the grates between grilling the meat and grilling the sandwiches. The time isn't wasted, however, because your meat needs a chance to rest anyway.

CHEESE

I grill panini with all types of cheese. Of course, I go for the easy melters most often—cheddar, mozzarella, and Gruyère are among my favorites. But I also choose cheeses like feta, blue cheese, and goat cheese, whose intense flavor more than makes up for their lack of meltability.

Explore the cheese shops in your area or get to know the folks in the cheese department at your local grocery store. They can often introduce you to interesting cheeses.

Sliced vs. Shredded

I've gone back and forth between sliced and shredded cheese for panini. I use both forms, but the best approach I've found is slicing cheese thinly by hand with a cheese slicer (see page 12). Here's why:

PRE-SLICED CHEESE
Pros: It's the most convenient. You can buy a wide variety of pre-sliced cheese, and the slices are ready to go.
Cons: It can take a while for thick pre-sliced cheese to melt, sometimes too long. The bread may start to burn before the cheese has had a chance to melt completely. A way around this problem is to grill at a lower heat for a longer time.

SHREDDED CHEESE
Pros: Shredded cheese melts the fastest and the most evenly.
Cons: When you're assembling a sandwich, corralling cheese shards can be a messy task. They have a tendency to fall out of the sandwich, which is bothersome. Also, pre-shredded cheeses often have anti-caking agents that prevent them from melting as smoothly as we might like.

HAND-SLICED CHEESE
Pros: These thinner slices not only melt quickly but also lie flat on your sandwich, making for easy assembly. In addition, a block of cheese usually costs less per pound than pre-sliced cheese.
Cons: It takes an extra few minutes to slice the cheese yourself (but not long at all) and you need to buy a cheese slicer (but they're not expensive).

FRUITS AND VEGETABLES

Before I started grilling panini on a regular basis, the fruits and vegetables I used on my sandwiches were largely limited to lettuce, tomatoes, onions, and occasionally preserves. I still use those ingredients, of course, but far more garden and orchard treats make their way onto my bread these days.

SWEET AND TART. Apples have become a favorite panini ingredient for me—they pair well with many cheeses, as well as with pork, beef, and turkey. Depending on the flavors in the sandwich, I might choose a sweeter apple, like a Gala, or one that will bring more tartness and acidity, such as a Granny Smith. There are more than 15 recipes featuring apples in this book—check them all out!

Sweet summer peaches and nectarines are also interesting alternatives to tomatoes anytime you want to switch things up a bit.

MAKE ROOM FOR MUSHROOMS. For a substantial alternative to meat, look no further than mushrooms. These things drink up flavor like nobody's business and are quick to grill on the panini press or sauté on the stove. I use big, hearty portobello mushroom caps to make vegetarian Grilled Portobello Cheese Steak Panini (page 210) and Portobello Patty Melt Panini (page 209), and I sauté wild mushrooms with shallots and balsamic vinegar for Wild Mushroom Melt Panini (page 211) and Turkey and Wild Mushroom Panini (page 44).

LEAFY PURSUITS. Greens such as arugula, basil, watercress, and leaf lettuce bring delicate flavor and a shot of color to panini. They do, however, have a tendency to wilt under the heat of the grill. I have three good solutions for this problem:

- Consider adding greens as a final step after grilling—open up the grilled panini and stick the greens in at the end so they'll stay nice and crisp.
- Position greens toward the middle of the sandwich, where they will be exposed to less heat.
- If all else fails, embrace wilted greens—they still taste great!

EAT YOUR VEGGIES. Whether you have leftovers on hand or you opt to grill some right on the panini press (see "Grilling Beyond Sandwiches" on page 10), vegetables make wonderful panini ingredients. I love to use grilled eggplant, asparagus, zucchini, onions, and bell peppers as well as tender raw vegetables like fennel and cabbage. You can also puree cooked legumes—beans, peas, and lentils—and spread them onto your sandwiches either in addition to or as an alternative to cheese.

WATCH THE MOISTURE. Bear in mind that the juiciness that makes many fruits and vegetables so tasty and appealing can also bog down a sandwich with too much moisture. Here are a few tips to avoid soggy bread:

- Remove the seeds from tomatoes. When possible, go for plum tomatoes (I use the Roma variety), which tend to have less pulp and seeds.
- Position wetter ingredients toward the center of your panini, away from the bread. (This goes for other wet ingredients, like sauces and coleslaw, too.)
- If you're grilling panini with juicy fruits and vegetables, consider firmer, denser, crusty breads like baguettes or ciabatta, which can stand up to moisture better than sliced bread.

CONDIMENTS

Order panini at a nice café and chances are you will be treated to a fabulous condiment inside. Basil aioli, caramelized onions, wasabi mayonnaise, honey mustard—well-placed flavorful condiments often make the difference between a so-so sandwich and one worth remembering. I often make up a big batch of Slow-Roasted Tomatoes (page 135) or Caramelized Onions (page 19) and keep them in the refrigerator to add to sandwiches and other dishes all week long. But condiments don't have to be as time-intensive as those—often it's easy enough to simply mix some herbs or garlic into store-bought mayonnaise, or spread on some fig preserves straight from the jar.

Make It and Save It

Throughout this book, you'll find a slew of recipes for tasty spreads, dressings, and other condiments to dress up your panini. Some take just minutes to whip up; others require a bit longer to marinate, blend, caramelize, or roast. Trust me: the ones that take a while to prepare are well worth the wait. Most will stay fresh in the refrigerator for several days or even weeks. Go ahead and take the time to make them—you'll be glad to have them on hand.

Grilling Beyond Sandwiches

Anyone who believes that a panini press is useful only for grilling sandwiches is missing out on a whole world of possibilities. We're talking about a tool with two direct heating sources—which, by the way, heat up in under five minutes. There's really no limit to what it can grill—unless, of course, the manufacturer of your grill suggests limits. Always abide by your product's manual.

MEAT, POULTRY, AND SEAFOOD

Grilling meat, poultry, and seafood on the panini press is not only a healthy way to cook but also, with the ability to grill both sides of your food at once, a much faster technique than outdoor grilling or oven roasting. Especially in the summertime, when it's often too hot to turn on the stove or stand over a hot outdoor grill, the panini press can become your best friend when it comes to getting dinner on the table. Be sure to have a drip tray in place to collect any grease that runs off (and be sure to keep this book away from the grill to avoid the side spatter!). If your press does not come equipped with a drain and/or drip tray, I don't recommend using it for grilling raw meats.

So how long will it take to cook your meat and poultry on the panini press? I'll say it again: a meat thermometer will take all the guesswork out of determining when the food is done (see page 13). Just insert the thermometer and wait until the desired temperature is reached. The United States Department of Agriculture (USDA) recommends the following safe internal cooking temperatures:

FOOD	TEMPERATURE
Beef, pork, lamb, and veal steaks, chops, and roasts	145°F
Ground beef, pork, lamb, and veal	160°F
Poultry	165°F

You'll find a slew of recipes for grilled meats in this cookbook—everything from rib-eye steak (page 151) and bratwurst (page 116) to barbecued chicken thighs (page 61) and seared ahi (page 182).

FRUITS AND VEGETABLES

Whether I'm grilling zucchini or eggplant, bananas or peaches, it's all made easy with the panini press. I'll usually toss vegetables in a little olive oil, season with salt and pepper, and grill till they're tender. With fruit, often just a brush of melted butter is all that's needed to get those beautiful dark grill marks and a lightly crisp crust on the outside.

A real advantage to grilling fruits and vegetables on the panini press, as opposed to an outdoor grill, is the food won't fall through the grates. This means you can grill green beans, asparagus, and any other long, skinny, or tiny produce item you can think of, and everything will stay in place on the grill.

BAKING

Yes, baking. It's not the first task most people attempt with their panini press (or even the second or the third), but it's possible to do it. My secret weapon for baking on a panini press is a ramekin, a small straight-sided ceramic dish. I just fill a ramekin with my cake batter, frittata mixture, or anything else I might normally bake in the oven, close the grill lid, and wait till it's done. I've used this method to make a variety of individual-sized dishes such as frittatas (page 307) and even mini layer cakes (page 325).

Tools of the Trade

In addition to a good panini press, the following tools will make preparing and grilling panini even easier.

CHEESE SLICER. As I've mentioned, slicing your own cheese is often the best way to go from a melting and ease-of-layering standpoint. A basic cheese plane or slicer isn't expensive, typically $10 to $15. You want one that is comfortable to grip, and with a metal blade that can stand up to slicing firmer cheeses without bending itself out of shape. I use the Calphalon dual-edge cheese plane.

CHEESE GRATER. Yes, slicing your own cheese is usually best, but I do grate some cheeses, especially Parmesan and other harder cheeses that take longer to melt. You can also use the grater for zesting lemons and limes as well as for finely grating garlic and onions. I prefer a box grater for these jobs. They're available at all price points, but I have to say that I have had a much easier time grating since I upgraded to a higher-end Microplane model.

SERRATED KNIFE. A sturdy serrated knife will allow you to slice through your panini cleanly without placing undue pressure on your ingredients. Even better—although it's a bit of a

splurge—is an offset knife, which you'll often see used in panini cafés and restaurants. The offset design allows you to bring the knife all the way down to the cutting board without your knuckles getting in the way.

MEAT THERMOMETER. If you're going to grill meats on your panini press, I highly recommend using a meat thermometer. It's the easiest and most reliable way to ensure that meat is cooked to the desired temperature. With the OXO model I have, it's easy for me to set the temperature (it comes with preset USDA and chef recommendations), insert the probe into the meat I'm grilling, place the meat on the panini press, close the lid, and wait until the thermometer beeps to tell me that the meat is done. It eliminates all of the guesswork, and I don't lose any heat by having to open the lid repeatedly to check for doneness.

SILICONE SPATULA AND TONGS. Everything you place on the grill has to come off at some point. For this task, you'll want a silicone spatula and silicone tongs. They easily lift your food without causing any damage to the nonstick surface of the panini press.

SILICONE GRILL BRUSH. Many grills come equipped with their own grill scraper, but for those that don't, you will probably find a silicone grill brush very helpful when it comes time to clean your panini press. The soft-yet-firm bristles make it easy to scrape up the cooked-on bits that can get trapped between the grates without damaging the nonstick coating. OXO makes the excellent grill brush that I use.

SILICONE BASTING BRUSH. For brushing olive oil onto bread, vegetables, black bean patties, and more, a silicone basting or pastry brush is a useful tool. It distributes oil evenly and goes right into the dishwasher for cleanup.

POULTRY PERFECTION

Chicken, Turkey, and Duck
on the Panini Press

PANINI

MORE FROM THE PANINI PRESS

Chicken, Brie, Fig, and Arugula Panini

Yield: 4 panini

For the longest time I avoided adding leafy greens to my panini out of concern that they would wilt. But after a while I really started to miss arugula, basil, cilantro, and all of the other herbs and lettuces that brought such bright, fresh flavors to my non-grilled sandwiches. Then I had a "Eureka!" moment—the closer to the middle of the sandwich I layered the greens, the less likely they were to wilt, because the middle of the sandwich is the last to receive the heat. I've been freely adding greens to panini ever since. (You might say I turned over a new leaf!)

1 French baguette, cut into 4 portions, or 4 mini baguettes
½ cup fig preserves
8 ounces Brie cheese (with or without the rind), sliced

½ cup baby arugula
8 ounces carved or deli-sliced chicken breast

1. Heat the panini press to medium-high heat.

2. *For each sandwich:* Slice off the domed top of a baguette portion to create a flat grilling surface. Split the baguette to create top and bottom halves. Spread 1 tablespoon fig preserves inside each baguette half. Layer a few slices of Brie, a small handful of arugula, and a few slices of chicken on the bottom half of the bread. Close the sandwich with the top half.

3. Grill two panini at a time, with the lid closed, until the cheese is melted and the baguettes are toasted, 3 to 5 minutes.

Pulled BBQ Chicken Panini

Yield: 6 panini

God made napkins so that we could partake of sandwiches like this. Yes, it's messy, but I promise you won't mind (at least I don't). We're talking about shredded rotisserie chicken simmered in barbecue sauce, piled on Italian bread, drizzled with chili oil, and topped with fresh mozzarella and caramelized onions. That's worth a little untidiness, right? You can easily adjust the recipe, which was inspired by my favorite barbecued chicken pizza, to use up any leftover chicken you might have on hand.

Look for chili oil, a spicy condiment that's been infused with chili peppers, alongside other oils or in the Asian foods section of your grocery store.

2½ cups barbecue sauce
1 whole rotisserie chicken, skin and bones removed, meat shredded
6 Italian rolls, such as *filone* or ciabatta

1 cup Caramelized Onions (recipe follows)
12 ounces fresh mozzarella cheese, thinly sliced
Chili oil for brushing (optional)

1. In a medium-size saucepan, bring the barbecue sauce to a simmer over medium heat. Add the shredded chicken and continue to simmer for another 10 minutes.

2. Heat the panini press to medium-high heat.

3. *For each sandwich:* Split a roll to create top and bottom halves. Scoop a generous amount of pulled BBQ chicken on the bottom half of the roll, followed by some caramelized onions and several slices of mozzarella. Close the sandwich with the top half of the roll and brush a little chili oil on the surface, if desired.

4. Grill three panini at a time, with the lid closed, until the cheese is melted and the rolls are toasted, 4 to 5 minutes.

Caramelized Onions

Yield: About 1 cup

I couldn't write this cookbook without including a recipe for my all-time favorite panini ingredient, caramelized onions. They're that "something sweet" I'm always looking for when I'm creating sandwiches. It is well worth the time it takes to allow these silky onion ribbons to slowly cook down to their deep brown caramelized state.

You can use the onions right away or store them in a covered container in the refrigerator for up to a week. Consider making a double batch so you'll have plenty on hand to add to sandwiches, burgers, pizzas, pastas—anything that could use a touch of savory sweetness.

1 tablespoon extra-virgin olive oil
3 medium-size onions (white, yellow, or red), halved and thinly sliced

Coarse salt and freshly ground black pepper

1. Heat the olive oil in a large skillet over medium heat. Add the onions and cook for 10 minutes, stirring occasionally. The onions will be soft and just barely beginning to turn brown.

2. Reduce the heat to low. Season with salt and pepper and continue to cook, stirring often to prevent scorching, until the onions are soft, deep brown, and caramelized, another 40 to 50 minutes.

Mediterranean Chicken Flatbread Panini

Yield: 4 panini

Nothing feels homier to me than roasting a whole chicken on the weekend. Even though we're a family of four, the junior members of our household aren't quite old enough yet to hold up their end of the chicken-eating requirements necessary to finish off a whole bird in one meal. That means that we tend to have leftover chicken in the fridge at the beginning of the week, which is a blessing when you're someone who enjoys creating new kinds of sandwiches! Here, I've matched up shredded leftover chicken with some of my favorite Mediterranean flavors—hummus, olive tapenade, roasted red bell peppers, and feta—all grilled on toasty flatbread.

4 pita breads or other flatbreads
½ cup hummus
4 tablespoons olive tapenade
1 cup shredded cooked chicken

¼ cup sliced roasted red bell peppers
8 fresh basil leaves, roughly torn
4 ounces crumbled feta cheese

1. Heat the panini press to medium-high heat.

2. *For each sandwich:* Cut a pita in half across the diameter, creating two semicircles—these will become your top and bottom halves. Spread 2 tablespoons hummus on one pita half and 1 tablespoon olive tapenade on the other. Top the hummus with chicken, red peppers, torn basil, and feta. Close the sandwich with the other pita, tapenade side down.

3. Grill two panini at a time, with the lid closed, until the feta is softened and the pitas are toasted, 4 to 5 minutes.

Jerk Chicken Panini

Yield: 4 panini

If you like things spicy, these panini were made for you. This recipe takes leftover Jamaican-style Grilled Jerk Chicken (page 66) and matches it up with pepper Jack cheese, sweet caramelized onions, and cilantro-lime mayonnaise on a crunchy baguette.

½ cup mayonnaise
1½ teaspoons freshly squeezed lime juice
1 tablespoon chopped fresh cilantro
1 French baguette, cut into 4 portions, or
    4 mini baguettes

1 cup Caramelized Onions (page 19)
2 Grilled Jerk Chicken breasts (page 66),
    halved horizontally to create 4 cutlets
4 ounces pepper Jack cheese, sliced

1. Heat the panini press to medium-high heat.

2. In a small bowl, stir together the mayonnaise, lime juice, and cilantro until well blended.

3. *For each sandwich:* Slice off the domed top of a baguette portion to create a flat grilling surface. Split the baguette to create top and bottom halves. Spread 1 tablespoon cilantro-lime mayonnaise inside the top and bottom halves of the baguette. On the bottom half, layer some caramelized onions, a jerk chicken cutlet, and some cheese. Close the sandwich with the top half.

4. Grill two panini at a time, with the lid closed, until the cheese is melted and the baguettes are toasted, 5 to 7 minutes.

Red Chile Chicken Panini

Yield: 4 panini

It's the complex flavors in the marinade that make these spicy chicken panini so delicious. Beyond the heat from the chiles, the addition of cloves, allspice, and cinnamon brings warmth and a subtle sweetness. I have Elise Bauer from SimplyRecipes.com to thank for this and so many other flavorful recipes that have become go-to favorites in my house. She originally created this marinade for bone-in chicken on the outdoor grill, but it also works marvelously for quick grilling on the panini press.

CHICKEN
1 tablespoon extra-virgin olive oil
1¼ cups Mexican red chile sauce (see Note)
2 tablespoons distilled white vinegar or cider vinegar
1 garlic clove, minced
1 teaspoon ground cinnamon
½ teaspoon ground cloves
½ teaspoon ground allspice
¼ teaspoon ground cumin
⅛ teaspoon freshly ground black pepper
A pinch of dried oregano, crushed
4 boneless, skinless chicken thighs (about 1 pound)
½ teaspoon coarse salt

PANINI
4 tablespoons (½ stick) butter, at room temperature
8 slices sourdough bread, sliced from a dense bakery loaf
½ cup Avocado Spread (page 173) or mayonnaise
½ medium-size red onion, thinly sliced
2 plum tomatoes (such as Roma), thinly sliced and seeded
4 ounces pepper Jack cheese, sliced

1. *Chicken:* In a medium-size saucepan, heat the olive oil over medium heat. Add the chile sauce, vinegar, garlic, cinnamon, cloves, allspice, cumin, black pepper, and oregano and stir until well combined. Raise the heat to medium-high and bring the marinade to a simmer (small bubbles will begin to form around the edges of the saucepan). Let the marinade continue to simmer for 5 minutes, allowing the flavors to mix and mingle. Remove the pan from the heat and let it cool to room temperature.

2. Season the chicken thighs on both sides with salt. Put the chicken thighs in a large zipper-top plastic bag. Pour in the cooled marinade and seal the bag. Roll the chicken around in the marinade to make sure that all of the pieces are well coated. Marinate in the refrigerator at least 1 hour, and preferably overnight.

3. *Panini:* Heat the panini press to medium-high heat. If your panini press comes with a removable drip tray, make sure it is in place (see page 2). Remove the chicken thighs from the marinade and gently shake off any excess marinade (discard the marinade). Place the thighs on the grill, close the lid, and cook to an internal temperature of 165°F, 7 to 8 minutes. Unplug the grill, carefully clean the grates, and then reheat the panini press to medium-high heat.

4. *For each sandwich:* Spread butter on two slices of bread to flavor the outside of the sandwich. Flip over both slices and spread 1 tablespoon avocado spread on the other side of each. Top one slice with onion, a chicken thigh, tomatoes, and cheese and close the sandwich with the other slice of bread, buttered side up.

5. Grill two panini at a time, with the lid closed, until the cheese is melted and the bread is toasted, 4 to 5 minutes.

NOTE: You can find canned Mexican red chile sauce in the Latin foods section of your grocery store. I like the Las Palmas brand.

Can I Make Panini on My George Foreman Grill?

My blog readers ask me this question all the time. My response? "Well, of course!" Tabletop grills like the Foreman work very much like panini presses. They apply heat from both the top and bottom, which is basically all you need to grill a sandwich.

There are a myriad of different Foreman grill models with varying features, so I can't speak for all of them. But, in general, if you've got a grill that provides heat from both the top and bottom it ought to work just fine for preparing the recipes in this book.

That said, in my experience, panini do come out a little different when you prepare them on a Foreman grill rather than a panini press. The ridges on the Foreman grill cooking plates, which were mainly designed for grilling burgers and other meat, are set farther apart than on a typical panini press. As a result, the grill makes less direct contact with the panini, so the bread tends to crisp up to a lesser degree. Most people won't mind at all, but it's one difference I've noticed.

Chicken Bacon Melt Panini

Yield: 4 panini

Once I realized just how quick and easy it was to grill chicken breasts on the panini press, it opened up a whole world of chicken sandwich options that I had never explored before. These panini are among my favorites, with simple, classic comfort-food flavors.

Use Leftovers: Swap in any leftover cooked chicken you have on hand in place of grilling chicken breasts in this recipe.

2 boneless, skinless chicken breasts, halved horizontally to create 4 cutlets (about 1 pound total)
½ teaspoon coarse salt
⅛ teaspoon freshly ground black pepper
4 tablespoons (½ stick) butter, at room temperature
8 slices rustic white bread, sliced from a dense bakery loaf

½ cup Avocado Spread (page 173)
8 strips cooked bacon
2 plum tomatoes (such as Roma), thinly sliced and seeded, or 8 Slow-Roasted Tomato halves (page 135)
4 ounces Asiago or other sharp cheese, sliced

1. Heat the panini press to medium-high heat. If your panini press comes with a removable drip tray, make sure it is in place (see page 2).

2. Season both sides of the chicken breasts with salt and pepper and grill them, with the lid closed, until they're cooked to an internal temperature of 165°F, 3 to 4 minutes.

3. Unplug the grill, carefully clean the grates, and then reheat the panini press to medium high heat.

4. *For each sandwich:* Spread butter on two slices of bread to flavor the outside of the sandwich. Flip over both slices of bread and spread 1 tablespoon avocado spread on the other side of each. Top one slice with 2 bacon strips, a chicken breast, tomato slices, and cheese. Close the sandwich with the other slice of bread, buttered side up.

5. Grill two panini at a time, with the lid closed, until the cheese is melted and the bread is toasted, 4 to 5 minutes.

Chicken Parm Panini

Yield: 4 panini

Imagine my delight once I discovered that leftover pasta, with the flavorful sauce it's absorbed, is great in sandwiches. The next time you've got extra spaghetti in your fridge, go ahead and create a sandwich version of your favorite pasta dish. For this update on a chicken parm sandwich, I bread and sauté thin chicken breast cutlets and layer them with fresh basil, mozzarella cheese, and leftover spaghetti on garlic-buttered ciabatta. It's the classic dish in handheld form!

CHICKEN
2 boneless, skinless chicken breasts, halved
    horizontally to create 4 cutlets (about
    1 pound total)
½ teaspoon coarse salt
⅛ teaspoon freshly ground black pepper
½ cup all-purpose flour
1 large egg, beaten
1 cup Italian seasoned breadcrumbs (see Note)
2 tablespoons extra-virgin olive oil

PANINI
2 tablespoons butter, at room temperature
1 garlic clove, minced
1 ciabatta loaf, cut into 4 portions, or
    4 ciabatta rolls
8 fresh basil leaves
1 cup leftover cooked spaghetti, tossed in
    marinara sauce
4 tablespoons additional marinara sauce
4 ounces mozzarella cheese, sliced

1. *Chicken:* Season the chicken with salt and pepper on both sides. Set up a dredging station with the flour, beaten egg, and bread crumbs each in its own separate shallow bowl. In a large skillet, heat the olive oil over medium-high heat. Dredge each piece of chicken in the flour, then the egg, then the bread crumbs, and place it carefully in the skillet. Cook the chicken for 3 to 4 minutes on each side. Transfer the chicken to a wire rack or a paper towel–lined plate to drain.

2. *Panini:* Heat the panini press to medium-high heat.

3. Mix the butter and garlic in a small bowl until they're well combined.

4. *For each sandwich:* Split a ciabatta portion to create top and bottom halves. Spread a few teaspoons of garlic butter inside each ciabatta half. On the bottom half place 2 basil leaves, some spaghetti, a chicken breast, 1 tablespoon marinara, and a few slices of cheese. Close the sandwich with the other ciabatta half.

5. Grill two panini at a time, with the lid closed, until the cheese is melted and the ciabatta is toasted, 4 to 5 minutes.

NOTE: Alternatively, you can use 1 cup plain bread crumbs, mixing in ½ teaspoon *each* coarse salt, dried parsley, dried basil, and garlic powder and ¼ teaspoon *each* onion powder, freshly ground black pepper, and dried oregano.

Chicken Cordon Bleu Panini

Yield: 4 panini

I t's time to take things a little retro. Chicken cordon bleu (which translates to "blue ribbon") may not have actually originated at the famed French cooking school, but it was nonetheless a winning dish for many American families in the 1960s and '70s. The key components—breaded chicken breast, cheese, and ham—transform easily into a sandwich, along with a sweet kick of honey mustard.

CHICKEN
2 boneless, skinless chicken breasts,
   halved horizontally to create 4 cutlets
   (about 1 pound total)
½ teaspoon coarse salt
⅛ teaspoon freshly ground black pepper
½ cup all-purpose flour
1 large egg, beaten
½ cup plain bread crumbs
2 tablespoons extra-virgin olive oil

PANINI
¼ cup honey
¼ cup Dijon mustard
4 tablespoons (½ stick) butter, at room
   temperature
8 slices rustic white bread, sliced from a
   dense bakery loaf
4 ounces sliced ham
4 ounces Swiss cheese, sliced

1. *Chicken:* Season the chicken with salt and pepper on both sides. Set up a dredging station with the flour, beaten egg, and bread crumbs each in its own separate shallow bowl. In a large skillet, heat the olive oil over medium-high heat. Dredge each piece of chicken in the flour, then the egg, then the bread crumbs, and place it carefully in the skillet. Cook the chicken for 3 to 4 minutes on each side. Transfer the chicken to a wire rack or a paper towel–lined plate to drain.

2. *Panini:* Heat the panini press to medium-high heat.

3. Whisk together the honey and Dijon mustard in a small bowl.

4. *For each sandwich:* Spread butter on two slices of bread to flavor the outside of the sandwich. Flip over both slices and spread 1 tablespoon honey mustard on the other side of each slice. Top one slice with a breaded chicken breast, followed by ham and cheese slices. Close the sandwich with the other slice of bread, buttered side up.

5. Grill two panini at a time, with the lid closed, until the cheese is melted and the bread is toasted, 4 to 5 minutes.

Garlic Chicken Panini

Yield: 4 panini

When I was a little kid growing up in the Silicon Valley, my family always managed to unwittingly choose the weekend of the annual garlic festival to drive south through the city of Gilroy—the "Garlic Capital of the World." The not-so-subtle signals would reach our nostrils miles before we reached the city limits. I didn't really know what garlic was, but I was a little afraid of it!

These days garlic and I have a much friendlier relationship—it's one of my favorite big-flavor ingredients, and I cook with it nearly every day. But rest assured, the garlic flavor in these panini comes from the basil-garlic mayonnaise, and it isn't overwhelming. You can still kiss your loved ones after eating these sandwiches . . . which is a good thing, because someone will definitely want to kiss you if you make one for them.

CHICKEN
4 cups water
¼ cup coarse salt
2 tablespoons honey
1 bay leaf
1 garlic clove, crushed
6 whole black peppercorns
A pinch of dried thyme
A pinch of dried parsley
1 tablespoon freshly squeezed
   lemon juice

2 boneless, skinless chicken breasts,
   halved horizontally to create 4 cutlets
   (about 1 pound total)

PANINI
1 French baguette, cut into 4 portions, or
   4 mini baguettes
1 recipe Basil-Garlic Mayonnaise (recipe
   follows)
½ cup sliced marinated artichoke hearts
½ cup sliced roasted red bell peppers
4 ounces Swiss cheese, sliced

1. *Chicken:* In a large bowl, stir together the water, salt, honey, bay leaf, garlic, peppercorns, thyme, parsley, and lemon juice until the salt and honey are dissolved. Add the chicken, cover the bowl with plastic wrap, and let the chicken soak in the brine for 30 to 40 minutes in the refrigerator.

2. *Panini:* Heat the panini press to medium-high heat. If your panini press comes with a removable drip tray, make sure it is in place (see page 2).

3. Remove the chicken from the brine and discard the brine. Pat the chicken cutlets dry and transfer them to the grill. Close the lid and grill the chicken until it's cooked to an internal temperature of 165°F, 3 to 4 minutes. Set the chicken aside. Unplug the grill, carefully wipe it clean, and heat it again to medium-high heat.

4. *For each sandwich:* Slice off the domed top of a baguette portion to create a flat grilling surface. Split the baguette to create top and bottom halves. Spread 1 tablespoon of basil-garlic

mayonnaise inside each baguette half. Place a chicken cutlet on the bottom baguette half and top it with artichoke hearts, roasted red bell peppers, and cheese. Close the sandwich with the top baguette half.

5. Grill two panini at a time, with the lid closed, until the cheese is melted and the baguettes are toasted, 5 to 7 minutes.

Basil-Garlic Mayonnaise
Yield: About ½ cup

This big-flavor condiment not only dresses up any chicken or turkey sandwich, it's also fabulous on burgers or as a dip for veggies or French fries.

½ cup coarsely chopped fresh basil
1 garlic clove, smashed
⅛ teaspoon coarse salt

A dash of cayenne pepper
½ cup mayonnaise

Blend the basil, garlic, salt, and cayenne in a food processor until well combined. Add the mayonnaise and continue to blend until smooth. Transfer the mayonnaise to a small bowl, cover, and refrigerate for 30 minutes to allow the flavors to meld.

Chicken Caesar Panini

Yield: 4 panini

Extra-flavorful grilled chicken breast, melty Asiago cheese, crisp romaine lettuce, tomatoes, red onions, and Caesar dressing on a toasty, crouton-like baguette—it's chicken Caesar salad's sandwich cousin. I nearly overdid chicken Caesar salad in my corporate days back in my twenties. There was a café across the street from my office building in San Francisco that made an excellent version, so I'd order it two or three times a week. These panini bring back some fond—if a little excessive—food memories for me.

CHICKEN
4 cups water
¼ cup coarse salt
2 tablespoons honey
1 bay leaf
1 garlic clove, crushed
6 whole black peppercorns
A pinch of dried thyme
A pinch of dried parsley
1 tablespoon freshly squeezed lemon juice
2 boneless, skinless chicken breasts, halved horizontally to create 4 cutlets (about 1 pound total)

PANINI
1 French baguette, cut into 4 portions, or 4 mini baguettes
½ cup Caesar dressing
2 plum tomatoes (such as Roma), thinly sliced and seeded, or 8 Slow-Roasted Tomato halves (page 135)
¼ medium-size red onion, sliced
4 ounces Asiago pressato or aged Asiago cheese, sliced (see Note)
4 romaine lettuce leaves

1. *Chicken:* In a large bowl, stir together the water, salt, honey, bay leaf, garlic, peppercorns thyme, parsley, and lemon juice until the salt and honey are dissolved. Add the chicken, cover the bowl with plastic wrap, and let the chicken soak in the brine for 30 to 40 minutes in the refrigerator.

2. *Panini:* Heat the panini press to medium-high heat. If your panini press comes with a removable drip tray, make sure it is in place (see page 2).

3. Remove the chicken from the brine and discard the brine. Pat the chicken cutlets dry and transfer them to the grill. Close the lid and grill the chicken until it's cooked to an internal temperature of 165°F, 3 to 4 minutes. Set the chicken aside. Unplug the grill, carefully wipe it clean, and heat it again to medium-high heat.

4. *For each sandwich:* Slice off the domed top of a baguette portion to create a flat grilling surface. Split the baguette to create top and bottom halves. Spread 1 tablespoon Caesar dressing inside each baguette half. Place a chicken cutlet on the bottom baguette half and top it with tomatoes, red onions, and cheese. Close the sandwich with the top baguette half.

5. Grill two panini at a time, with the lid closed, until the cheese is melted and the baguettes are toasted, 5 to 7 minutes. Open the bottom of each sandwich, fold a romaine leaf in half, and tuck it in beneath the chicken (we add the lettuce at the end so it stays fresh and crisp).

NOTE: Asiago pressato, the fresh form of Asiago cheese, melts especially well, but you can also use aged Asiago. I can find both types in the specialty cheese department at my regular grocery store.

Lemon-Thyme Chicken Panini

Yield: 4 panini

I f you love bright, tangy Mediterranean flavors, these panini are for you. The chicken breasts are infused with lemon zest and thyme in a quick brine, then grilled in just a few minutes on the panini press. Then they're made into panini with feta–goat cheese spread, sweet sun-dried tomatoes, and arugula. These are great panini to pack in an insulated bag to take to work or on a picnic.

CHICKEN
4 cups water
¼ cup coarse salt
2 tablespoons honey
1 bay leaf
6 whole black peppercorns
1 teaspoon dried thyme
2 teaspoons grated lemon zest
1 tablespoon freshly squeezed lemon juice
2 boneless, skinless chicken breasts, halved horizontally to create 4 cutlets (about 1 pound total)

PANINI
4 tablespoons (½ stick) butter, at room temperature
8 slices rustic white bread, sliced from a dense bakery loaf
1 recipe Feta–Goat Cheese Spread (recipe follows)
1 cup baby arugula
½ cup sliced oil-packed sun-dried tomatoes

1. *Chicken:* In a large bowl, stir together the water, salt, honey, bay leaf, peppercorns, thyme, lemon zest, and lemon juice until the salt and honey are dissolved. Add the chicken, cover the bowl with plastic wrap, and let the chicken soak in the brine for 30 to 40 minutes in the refrigerator.

2. *Panini:* Heat the panini press to medium-high heat. If your panini press comes with a removable drip tray, make sure it is in place (see page 2).

3. Remove the chicken from the brine and discard the brine. Pat the chicken cutlets dry and place them on the grill. Close the lid and grill the chicken until it's cooked to an internal temperature of 165°F, 3 to 4 minutes.

4. *For each sandwich:* Spread butter on two slices of bread to flavor the outside of the sandwich. Flip over both slices of bread and spread a generous layer of feta–goat cheese spread on the other side of each. Top one slice with a grilled chicken cutlet, followed by a layer of arugula and sun-dried tomatoes. Close the sandwich with the other slice of bread, buttered side up.

5. Grill two panini at a time, with the lid closed, until the sandwich is heated through and the bread is toasted, 2 to 3 minutes.

Feta–Goat Cheese Spread

Yield: About ½ cup

This tangy, soft cheese spread reminds me of the ones my mom would sometimes treat my sisters and me to after school. We'd feel very grown up as we assembled simple little canapés for ourselves on crackers. Tasty spreads like this also make quick panini ingredients, with no melting necessary.

- 1 (5½-ounce) log goat cheese, at room temperature
- 1 ounce (about ¼ cup) crumbled feta cheese
- 1 tablespoon heavy cream or half-and-half
- ⅛ teaspoon freshly ground black pepper

In a mini food processor or in a medium-size bowl with a hand mixer, beat together the goat cheese, feta, cream, and black pepper until whipped and fluffy.

Chicken Sausage, Apple Butter, and Fontina Panini

Yield: 4 panini

For these panini I match the intense, concentrated flavor of apple butter with equally bold smoky, nutty, and sweet flavors for a true sweet and savory mouthful.

4 fully cooked chicken-apple sausage links
(such as Aidells)
1 ciabatta loaf, cut into 4 portions, or
4 ciabatta rolls

4 ounces fontina cheese, sliced
½ cup apple butter
1 cup Caramelized Onions (page 19)

1. Heat the panini press to medium-high heat. If your panini press comes with a removable drip tray, make sure it is in place (see page 2).

2. Slice each chicken-apple sausage link in half lengthwise without slicing all the way through, then fold open the sausage. Place the sausages, cut sides down, on the grill. Close the lid and grill the sausages until they are heated through and grill marks appear, 4 to 5 minutes.

3. *For each sandwich:* Split a ciabatta portion to create top and bottom halves. Lay cheese over the bottom half of the bread, followed by the grilled sausage and caramelized onions. Spread 2 tablespoons apple butter inside the top half of the bread and place it on top of the sandwich to close it.

4. Grill two panini at a time, with the lid closed, until the cheese is melted and the ciabatta is toasted, 5 to 7 minutes.

Red, White, and Blue Cheese Panini

Yield: 4 panini

When I'm at the hair salon, the conversation with my super-hip British stylist quite often turns to food. Sometime around the blow-dry and flat-iron stage I usually extract one or two excellent recommendations for places to eat in downtown San Diego. He introduced me to a lovely bakery café called Con Pane and one of their signature sandwiches, the Turkey Cobb. Roasted turkey, bacon, avocado, sweet roasted Roma tomatoes, just a sprinkling of Gorgonzola cheese, and romaine lettuce on their airy, house-baked rosemary olive-oil bread—Con Pane has created an absolute masterpiece with this one. For my grilled version, I wait until the sandwich comes off the grill to add the romaine. That way I can have the toasted bread and soft Gorgonzola while still keeping the greens fresh and crisp.

On my blog I called these my Red, White, and Blue Cheese Panini in honor of the Fourth of July, but I'll eagerly devour this sandwich any day of the year.

1 tablespoon extra-virgin olive oil
8 slices rosemary olive-oil bread or sourdough bread, sliced from a dense bakery loaf
4 tablespoons mayonnaise
8 ounces carved or deli-sliced roast turkey
8 strips cooked bacon

1 medium-size ripe avocado, pitted, peeled, and thinly sliced
8 oil-packed sun-dried tomatoes, thinly sliced, or 8 Slow-Roasted Tomato halves (page 135)
4 ounces crumbled Gorgonzola cheese
8 romaine lettuce leaves

1. Heat the panini press to medium-high heat.

2. *For each sandwich:* Brush a little olive oil on two slices of bread to flavor the outside of the sandwich. Flip over one slice and spread 1 tablespoon mayonnaise on the other side. Top the mayonnaise with turkey, bacon, avocado, tomatoes, and Gorgonzola cheese. Close the sandwich with the other slice of bread, oiled side up.

3. Grill two panini at a time, with the lid closed, until the cheese has softened and the bread is toasted, 3 to 4 minutes.

4. Remove each sandwich from the grill, flip it over, and carefully remove the bottom slice of bread. Add 2 lettuce leaves and replace the bottom slice of bread.

Turkey Panini, Marbella-Style

Yield: 4 panini

Whenever someone asks me for my all-time favorite chicken dish, without hesitation I mention chicken Marbella. I credit my friend Cyndy for introducing me to this sweet, salty, and tangy classic from *The Silver Palate Cookbook*. After she prepared it for a gourmet club event, I asked her for the recipe and made the dish again at home that same week. The combination of Spanish olives, prunes, capers, garlic, and brown sugar is simply irresistible.

Olive tapenade and plump prunes bring the briny and sweet notes I love so much in chicken Marbella to these panini. I switched the protein to sliced turkey breast because it's what I'm more likely to have on hand, but by all means make these with grilled chicken breasts if you prefer.

1 French baguette, cut into 4 portions, or 4 mini baguettes
4 tablespoons olive tapenade
8 pitted prunes, halved lengthwise

8 ounces carved or deli-sliced roast turkey
½ cup sliced roasted red bell peppers
4 ounces Manchego cheese, thinly sliced

1. Heat the panini press to medium-high heat.

2. *For each sandwich:* Slice off the domed top of a baguette portion to create a flat grilling surface. Split the baguette to create top and bottom halves. Spread 1 tablespoon olive tapenade inside the bottom baguette half. Arrange four prune halves on top of the tapenade. Layer on a few turkey slices, roasted red bell peppers, and cheese. Close the sandwich with the top baguette half.

3. Grill two panini at a time, with the lid closed, until the cheese is melted and the baguettes are toasted, 5 to 6 minutes.

Turkey, Cranberry, and Brie Panini

Yield: 4 panini

Those who truly love the combination of roast turkey and cranberry sauce eat it all year long, not just at Thanksgiving. But the great thing about Thanksgiving is that it brings you an ample supply of carved turkey and, quite often, lots of leftover cranberry sauce as well. Just pick up some Brie and a baguette or two while you're shopping for the big feast and you'll be able to parlay your leftovers into these delectable panini for days.

1 multigrain baguette, cut into 4 portions, or 4 mini baguettes

4 ounces Brie cheese (with or without the rind), sliced

8 ounces carved or deli-sliced roast turkey

4 tablespoons whole-berry cranberry sauce

1. Heat the panini press to medium-high heat.

2. *For each sandwich:* Slice off the domed top of a baguette portion to create a flat grilling surface. Split the baguette to create top and bottom halves. Layer Brie and turkey on the bottom half of the baguette. Spread 1 tablespoon cranberry sauce inside the top baguette half and place it on top of the sandwich to close it.

3. Grill two panini at a time, with the lid closed, until the cheese is melted and the baguettes are toasted, 5 to 7 minutes.

Turkey Jalapeño Melt Panini

Yield: 4 panini

A bright spot in many otherwise nondescript office parks is the hidden deli. It's the little hole-in-the-wall place no one else knows about unless they work in the building. Quite frankly, it's often not really a place an outsider would seek out. You find the usual sandwiches, sodas, coffee, and maybe a jar of day-old cookies. But it's incredibly convenient and offers an easy break from the office grind upstairs.

These panini were inspired by my husband's favorite sandwich from the hidden deli near his office. The hot peppers bring a load of flavor while the Monterey Jack cools things off a bit. We love to make this sandwich with leftover Thanksgiving turkey, but it's just as good with regular deli-sliced turkey any time of the year.

4 tablespoons (½ stick) butter, at room temperature

8 slices sourdough bread, sliced from a dense bakery loaf

4 ounces Monterey Jack cheese, sliced

¼ cup sliced pickled jalapeño peppers (see Note)

8 ounces carved or deli-sliced roast turkey

2 plum tomatoes (such as Roma), thinly sliced and seeded

4 tablespoons mayonnaise

1. Heat the panini press to medium-high heat.

2. *For each sandwich:* Spread butter on two slices of bread to flavor the outside of the sandwich. Flip over one slice and top it with cheese, jalapeños, turkey, and tomatoes. Flip over the other slice and spread 1 tablespoon mayonnaise on the other side. Place it, buttered side up, on top of the sandwich to close it.

3. Grill two panini at a time, with the lid closed, until the cheese is melted and the bread is toasted, 4 to 5 minutes.

NOTE: If, like me, you find most pickled jalapeños to be a little too hot for your taste, look for jars marked "tamed." These peppers are a hybrid that provide big jalapeño flavor with a bit less heat.

Turkey and Wild Mushroom Panini

Yield: 4 panini

My husband was away at a conference in Las Vegas when I emailed him about these panini. I couldn't wait to tell him that I'd come up with a turkey and *mushroom* sandwich that I loved. Me, the one who is more commonly known to *remove* mushrooms from dishes. This combination is fabulous!

1 ciabatta loaf, cut into 4 portions, or
  4 ciabatta rolls
1 recipe Sautéed Wild Mushrooms (recipe
  follows)

4 ounces watercress
8 ounces carved or deli-sliced roast turkey
4 ounces Swiss cheese, sliced
3 tablespoons Dijon mustard

1. Heat the panini press to medium-high heat.

2. *For each sandwich:* Split a ciabatta portion to create top and bottom halves. Spoon a generous layer of mushrooms inside the bottom half, followed by a handful of watercress and a few slices of turkey and cheese. Spread Dijon mustard inside the top half and place it on top of the sandwich to close it.

3. Grill two panini at a time, with the lid closed, until the cheese is melted and the ciabatta is toasted, 4 to 5 minutes.

Sautéed Wild Mushrooms
Yield: About 1¼ cups

In my experience, there aren't many foods that can't be remarkably enhanced by sautéing them in olive oil and butter with garlic and shallots and finishing them with some balsamic vinegar. Mushrooms, it turns out, are no exception.

1 tablespoon extra-virgin olive oil
1 tablespoon unsalted butter
¼ cup thinly sliced shallots
2 garlic cloves, minced
2½ cups sliced wild mushrooms, such as
  shiitake (stemmed), chanterelle, or porcini

2 teaspoons balsamic vinegar
1 tablespoon chopped fresh parsley
Coarse salt and freshly ground black
  pepper

Heat the olive oil and butter in a large skillet over medium heat until the butter is melted. Add the shallots and garlic and cook, stirring frequently, until they're fragrant, 1 to 2 minutes. Add the mushrooms and cook, stirring occasionally, until the mushrooms are tender, 5 to 7 minutes. Stir in the balsamic vinegar and parsley and season with salt and pepper to taste.

Turkey, Fig, Gorgonzola, and Arugula Panini

Yield: 4 panini

'm firmly in the "love it" camp when it comes to Gorgonzola, especially when it's balanced with something sweet, like fig preserves. The whole-grain bread for these panini brings a nuttiness that also pairs perfectly with a strong-flavored cheese like Gorgonzola. Add some turkey and peppery arugula, and you've got a winning sandwich.

4 tablespoons (½ stick) butter, at room temperature
8 slices whole-grain bread, sliced from a dense bakery loaf
½ cup fig preserves

8 ounces carved or deli-sliced roast turkey
1 cup baby arugula
2 ounces crumbled Gorgonzola or other blue cheese

1. Heat the panini press to medium-high heat.

2. *For each sandwich:* Spread butter on two slices of bread to flavor the outside of the sandwich. Flip over both slices and spread a generous layer of fig preserves on the other side of each. On one slice of bread layer turkey, a small handful of arugula, and a sprinkling of Gorgonzola. Close the sandwich with the other slice of bread, buttered side up.

3. Grill two panini at a time, with the lid closed, until the cheese is softened and the bread is toasted, 4 to 5 minutes.

Turkey Monte Cristo Panini

Yield: 4 panini

Every year at Thanksgiving I update my blog with two or three new turkey panini recipes that use leftovers. One year I turned to classic non-turkey sandwiches for inspiration and came up with these Turkey Monte Cristo Panini and Turkey Rachel Panini (page 48).

For the Monte Cristos, I swapped in turkey for the traditional ham and mixed in some cranberry sauce along with the mustard for a tart and tangy kick. And since Monte Cristos are often served with jam, I added a little extra cranberry sauce on the side as well. I didn't include any prosciutto in my sandwich, but if you want to tuck a little in there, I surely wouldn't mind.

3 tablespoons whole-berry cranberry sauce, plus additional for serving
2 tablespoons whole-grain Dijon mustard
8 slices rustic white bread, sliced from a dense bakery loaf
4 ounces Swiss cheese, sliced
8 ounces carved or deli-sliced roast turkey

4 large eggs
½ cup milk
1 teaspoon coarse salt
½ teaspoon freshly ground black pepper
¼ teaspoon nutmeg
Confectioners' sugar, for dusting

1. Heat the panini press to medium-high heat.

2. In a small bowl, whisk together the cranberry sauce and Dijon mustard.

3. *For each sandwich:* Spread cranberry mustard on one slice of bread. Add a layer of Swiss cheese, a layer of turkey, and a second layer of cheese. Top with a second slice of bread to close the sandwich.

4. In a shallow bowl, whisk together the eggs, milk, salt, pepper, and nutmeg. Dip each sandwich in the egg mixture, turning to coat well.

5. Carefully place the panini, two at a time, on the panini grill. Close the lid and grill until the cheese is melted and the egg coating is cooked and lightly browned, 4 to 5 minutes.

6. Dust the tops of the panini with powdered sugar and serve with additional cranberry sauce for dipping.

Turkey Rachel Panini

Yield: 4 panini

I f you know the traditional Reuben (page 140), you're familiar with a robust sandwich piled with corned beef or pastrami, sauerkraut, Swiss cheese, and Russian dressing, served on rye bread. A turkey Reuben, also known as a Rachel or a California Reuben, substitutes turkey and coleslaw for the beef and sauerkraut. To bring in extra Thanksgiving flavor—because I seem to make most of my turkey sandwiches around Thanksgiving—I make a cranberry Russian dressing and toss it with cabbage for a very zesty—and pink—coleslaw.

4 tablespoons (½ stick) butter, at room temperature
8 slices rye bread, sliced from a dense bakery loaf

4 ounces Swiss cheese, sliced
8 ounces carved or deli-sliced roast turkey
¾ cup Cranberry Coleslaw (recipe follows)

1. Heat the panini press to medium-high heat.

2. *For each sandwich:* Spread butter on two slices of bread to flavor the outside of the sandwich. Flip over one slice and top the other side with cheese, turkey, a few spoonfuls of coleslaw, then more turkey and more cheese. Close the sandwich with the other slice of bread, buttered side up.

3. Grill two panini at a time, with the lid closed, until the cheese is melted and the bread is toasted, 4 to 5 minutes.

Cranberry Coleslaw

Yield: About 2 cups

This tangy-sweet slaw, with a kick of horseradish, is just as tasty as a stand-alone side dish as it is layered on your leftover Thanksgiving turkey panini.

⅓ cup mayonnaise
2 tablespoons whole-berry cranberry sauce
2 teaspoons freshly grated horseradish
1 teaspoon Worcestershire sauce

Coarse salt and freshly ground black pepper, to taste
2 cups shredded green cabbage or packaged coleslaw mix

1. Whisk together the mayonnaise, cranberry sauce, horseradish, and Worcestershire sauce in a small bowl. Season the dressing with salt and pepper to taste.

2. In a medium-size bowl, toss the cabbage with the dressing.

Turkey-Apple Panini with Camembert and Arugula Pesto

Yield: 4 panini

A rugula gives these turkey panini a wonderful peppery kick. Add crisp, tart Granny Smith apples and buttery Camembert, and you've got a flavor combination standout.

4 tablespoons (½ stick) butter, at room temperature
8 slices rustic white bread, sliced from a dense bakery loaf
½ cup Arugula Pesto (page 101)

8 ounces carved or deli-sliced roast turkey
1 Granny Smith apple, cored and thinly sliced
4 ounces Camembert or Brie cheese (with or without the rind), sliced

1. Heat the panini press to medium-high heat.

2. *For each sandwich:* Spread butter on two slices of bread to flavor the outside of the sandwich. Flip over both slices and spread 1 tablespoon arugula pesto on the other side of each. Top one slice with turkey breast, apples, and Camembert. Close the sandwich with the other slice of bread, buttered side up.

3. Grill two panini at a time, with the lid closed, until the cheese is melted and the bread is toasted, 4 to 5 minutes.

Turkey-Apple Panini with Fig and Gruyère

Yield: 4 panini

Sandwiches like these taste like autumn to me. It's when figs and apples are at their peak and thoughts of golden roast turkey begin to float through my mind in anticipation of Thanksgiving. They're a sweet and savory hallmark of one of the coziest times of the year.

4 tablespoons (½ stick) butter, at room temperature
8 slices rustic whole-grain bread, sliced from a dense bakery loaf
½ cup fig preserves

8 ounces carved or deli-sliced roast turkey
1 Granny Smith apple, cored and thinly sliced
8 ounces Gruyère cheese, thinly sliced

1. Heat the panini press to medium-high heat.

2. *For each sandwich:* Spread butter on two slices of bread to flavor the outside of the sandwich. Flip over both slices and spread 1 tablespoon fig preserves on the other side of each. Top one slice with turkey, apples, and cheese. Close the sandwich with the other slice of bread, buttered side up.

3. Grill two panini at a time, with the lid closed, until the cheese is melted and the bread is toasted, 4 to 5 minutes.

Smoked Turkey Croque Monsieur Panini

Yield: 4 panini

The name "croque monsieur" is based on the French verb croquer, which means "to crunch." While a traditional croque monsieur is blanketed with a rich, cheesy Mornay sauce, with my grilled version of this classic sandwich you get to bite through a tangy Parmesan crust, a nod to its crunchy origins.

4 tablespoons (½ stick) butter, at room temperature

1 ounce (about ¼ cup) shredded Parmesan cheese

8 slices rustic white bread, sliced from a dense bakery loaf

4 tablespoons Dijon mustard

8 ounces Gruyère cheese, sliced

8 ounces sliced smoked turkey breast

1. In a small bowl, mix the butter and Parmesan cheese until they are well combined.

2. Heat the panini press to medium-high heat.

3. *For each sandwich:* Spread Parmesan butter on two slices of bread. Flip over both slices and spread Dijon mustard on the other side of each. Top one slice with Gruyère cheese, turkey, and more cheese. Close the sandwich with the other slice of bread, buttered side up.

4. Grill two panini at a time, with the lid closed, until the cheese is melted and the bread is toasted with a crispy crust, 4 to 5 minutes.

Smoked Turkey Panini with Manchego, Arugula, and Sun-Dried-Tomato Mayonnaise

Yield: 4 panini

Something wonderful happens to tomatoes when they've had the chance to bask in the sun for days. As they shrink down and dry out, their sweetness concentrates to the point where they are nearly candy-like. Sun-dried tomatoes rank with caramelized onions as one of my favorite sandwich ingredients for the punch of sweet flavor they bring. Here, they are a simple yet robust condiment for smoked turkey.

1 ciabatta loaf, cut into 4 portions, or 4 ciabatta rolls
1 recipe Sun-Dried-Tomato Mayonnaise (recipe follows)

4 ounces Manchego, Asiago, or Swiss cheese, thinly sliced
1 cup baby arugula
8 ounces sliced smoked turkey breast

1. Heat the panini press to medium-high heat.

2. *For each sandwich:* Split a ciabatta portion to create top and bottom halves. Spread 1 tablespoon sun-dried-tomato mayonnaise inside each half. On the bottom half, layer cheese, a small handful of arugula, and a few slices of smoked turkey breast. Close the sandwich with the top ciabatta half.

3. Grill two panini at a time, with the lid closed, until the cheese is melted and the ciabatta is toasted, 4 to 5 minutes.

Sun-Dried-Tomato Mayonnaise

Yield: About ½ cup

Spread this sweet and zesty mayonnaise on everything from sandwiches to burgers to crab cakes.

½ cup Olive Oil Mayonnaise (page 199) or purchased mayonnaise
2 tablespoons minced oil-packed sun-dried tomatoes

2 teaspoons minced fresh basil
½ teaspoon minced garlic
A dash of freshly ground black pepper

In a small bowl, whisk together the mayonnaise, tomatoes, basil, garlic, and pepper. Let the mayonnaise rest in the refrigerator for 30 minutes so the flavors can meld.

Duck Breast Club Panini

Yield: 4 panini

My husband came up with the concept for duck club panini—slices of succulent duck breast layered with strips of smoky bacon, fresh tomatoes and arugula, and creamy Brie. It's a decadent combination for sure, but I doubt you'll have any trouble finding someone willing to split one of these with you.

If you're making the panini right after grilling the duck breasts, it's up to you whether to scrape down the grill. I like the extra-crispy crunch the residual duck fat adds to the panini, so in this case I hold off on cleaning until the end.

4 tablespoons (½ stick) butter, at room temperature (optional)
8 slices sourdough bread, sliced from a dense bakery loaf
2 tablespoons mayonnaise
8 strips cooked bacon
2 Grilled Duck Breasts (page 71), sliced across the grain

½ cup baby arugula
2 plum tomatoes (such as Roma), thinly sliced and seeded, or 8 Slow-Roasted Tomato halves (page 135)
4 ounces Brie cheese (with or without the rind), sliced

1. Heat the panini press to medium-high heat.

2. *For each sandwich:* Spread butter on two slices of bread to flavor the outside of the sandwich (you may want to skip this step if you are taking advantage of the residual duck fat on the grill). Flip over one slice of bread and spread a little mayonnaise on the other side. Top the mayonnaise with 2 bacon strips, some duck slices, a small handful of arugula, tomato slices, and Brie. Close the sandwich with the other slice of bread, buttered side up (if you're using butter).

3. Grill two panini at a time, with the lid closed, until the cheese is melted and the bread is toasted, 4 to 5 minutes.

No-Fuss, No-Flip Chicken Quesadillas

Yield: 4 quesadillas

'll tell you one thing that really impresses me: when chefs can easily and expertly flip food in a skillet with just a quick flick of the wrist. I watch in complete awe—this is not a skill I currently possess. I can usually flip pancakes if the batter is thick enough, but a quesadilla full of shredded cheese and other loose toppings? Forget it.

Enter the panini press, with its ability to cook from both the top and bottom at the same time. It's by far the easiest way that I know of to cook quesadillas and other dishes that you'd otherwise have to flip.

1 tablespoon vegetable oil
8 (8-inch) flour tortillas
8 ounces (about 2 cups) shredded cheese, such as cheddar, Monterey Jack, or Colby, or a mixture

1 (4-ounce) can diced green chiles, drained
1 cup shredded cooked chicken
Salsa, for serving

1. Heat the panini press to medium-high heat.

2. *For each quesadilla:* Brush a little oil on two tortillas. Flip over one tortilla and scatter on a few tablespoons of cheese, leaving a 1-inch margin around the edge to avoid too much ooze during melting. Top the cheese with a few tablespoons of green chiles, some shredded chicken, and more cheese. Place the other tortilla, oiled side up, on top.

3. Carefully transfer one quesadilla to the grill and close the lid. Grill the quesadilla until the cheese is melted and the tortilla is crisped, 3 to 4 minutes. Repeat with the rest of the tortillas.

4. Cut the quesadillas into wedges and serve with salsa.

Southwestern Grilled Chicken

Yield: 2 servings

I knew the first time I tried it that I'd found my go-to spice rub for chicken. It's got the flavors of the Southwest—a little smoky, a little spicy. My friend Jenny Flake, who writes the boundlessly creative cooking blog Picky-Palate.com, put together the combination of spices that first got me hooked. I've since added cumin to the mix, since I love that earthy smokiness.

These grilled chicken legs take less than 30 minutes to prepare, which is why they've become a weeknight favorite in my house.

½ teaspoon coarse salt
½ teaspoon freshly ground black pepper
½ teaspoon smoked paprika
½ teaspoon ancho chile powder
½ teaspoon ground cumin

½ teaspoon garlic powder
2 whole bone-in, skin-on chicken legs (drumstick and thigh), or 4 bone-in, skin-on chicken thighs (about 1½ pounds)
1 tablespoon extra-virgin olive oil

1. Heat the panini press to high heat. If your panini press comes with a removable drip tray, make sure it is in place (see page 2).

2. Combine all of the seasonings in a small bowl. Pat the chicken dry and rub the mixture all over the chicken, including under the skin.

3. Place the chicken on the grill, positioning it toward the center of the grill to ensure that the heat reaches all sides. Drizzle olive oil over the top of the chicken and close the lid. Grill the chicken until it's cooked to an internal temperature of 165°F, 18 to 20 minutes.

BBQ Chicken Thighs

Yield: 2 to 4 servings

For those evenings when it's too cold or too inconvenient or just too chaotic to fire up the outdoor grill, here's how you can enjoy barbecue-style chicken with your panini press. The chicken comes out just as juicy and the skin just as crispy as on the big grill. Of course, there are no flames to produce those smoky notes we love in real barbecue. But there's also no laborious grill scrape-down and no unwieldy grill cover to contend with, and you can grill chicken on your panini press any time of the year. I'd say it all evens out in the end.

½ teaspoon coarse salt
½ teaspoon dried thyme
½ teaspoon sweet paprika
½ teaspoon garlic powder
¼ teaspoon freshly ground black pepper

4 bone-in, skin-on chicken thighs (about 1½ pounds)
2 teaspoons extra-virgin olive oil
½ cup barbecue sauce

1. Heat the panini press to medium high heat. If your panini press comes with a removable drip tray, make sure it is in place (see page 2).

2. Combine the salt, thyme, paprika, garlic powder, and black pepper in a small bowl. Pat the chicken dry and rub the seasonings all over the chicken, including under the skin.

3. Transfer the chicken to the grill, skin side up. Rub the olive oil over the skin side of each piece and close the lid. Grill the chicken until it's cooked to an internal temperature of 165°F and the skin is crispy, about 18 minutes. Let the chicken rest for about 5 minutes.

4. While the chicken is grilling, heat the barbecue sauce in a small saucepan over medium-low heat until it's warmed through.

5. Brush the barbecue sauce over the chicken before serving.

Chicken Teriyaki

Yield: 2 to 4 servings

I knew from the outset that chicken teriyaki would be well suited for a minimal effort–high reward meal on the panini press. Boneless chicken cooks incredibly quickly on the grill, and you can set it in its sweet and salty marinade ahead of time. All I needed was to research the right ingredients to make an authentically Japanese version of this familiar favorite. I found such an approach on Marc Matsumoto's popular food blog, NoRecipes.com. Here, I've adapted Marc's beautifully simple recipe for grilling on the panini press.

CHICKEN
2 tablespoons sake
2 tablespoons reduced-sodium soy sauce
2 tablespoons packed dark brown sugar
2 tablespoons mirin
4 boneless, skin-on chicken thighs (about 1 pound)

TERIYAKI SAUCE
2 tablespoons honey
2 tablespoons reduced-sodium soy sauce
2 tablespoons mirin
2 tablespoons sake

Toasted sesame seeds and chopped scallions, for garnish
Steamed rice, for serving

1. *Chicken:* Mix the sake, soy sauce, brown sugar, and mirin in a small bowl until the sugar dissolves. Place the chicken in a zipper-top plastic bag and pour the marinade over the chicken. Seal the bag and roll the chicken around in the marinade to coat it. Let the chicken marinate in the refrigerator for 1 hour.

2. *Teriyaki Sauce:* While the chicken marinates, combine the honey, soy sauce, mirin, and sake in a small saucepan and bring to a boil over medium heat. Allow the sauce to simmer and reduce for a few minutes until it thickens slightly (it will not become especially thick). Remove it from the heat.

3. Heat the panini press to medium-high heat. If your panini press comes with a removable drip tray, make sure it is in place (see page 2).

4. Remove the chicken from the marinade (discard the remaining marinade) and pat it dry with paper towels. Grill the chicken, with the lid closed, until it's cooked to an internal temperature of 165°F and the skin is crispy, 6 to 8 minutes. Transfer the chicken to a serving platter and spoon some teriyaki sauce over the top. Garnish with toasted sesame seeds and chopped scallions and serve with steamed rice.

Citrus-Marinated Grilled Chicken

Yield: 2 servings

I f you've ever wondered what makes the *pollo asado*, or grilled chicken, at Mexican restaurants so succulent and mouthwatering, the secret is often a citrus marinade. Lemons, limes, oranges—a good soak in their acidic juices makes chicken incredibly tender and flavorful. Serve it with warm tortillas, tomatoes, red onions, and cilantro. Consider grilling up a second batch—there should be enough remaining marinade—and then shred the chicken for No-Fuss, No-Flip Chicken Quesadillas (page 58).

¼ cup extra-virgin olive oil
Juice of 1 orange (about ¼ cup)
Juice of 1 lime (about 2 tablespoons)
Juice of 1 lemon (about 2 tablespoons)
¼ cup chopped fresh cilantro
2 garlic cloves, minced
1 serrano chile, seeded and minced
¼ teaspoon ground cumin

2 whole bone-in, skin-on chicken legs
 (drumstick and thigh), or 4 bone-in, skin-
 on chicken thighs (about 1½ pounds)
½ teaspoon coarse salt
¼ teaspoon freshly ground black pepper
Corn or flour tortillas, for serving
Chopped tomatoes, for serving
Chopped red onion, for serving
Fresh cilantro leaves, for serving

1. Combine the oil, citrus juices, cilantro, garlic, chile, and cumin in a large zipper-top plastic bag. Add the chicken, seal the bag, and roll the chicken around a bit in the marinade to coat it well. Marinate the chicken in the refrigerator for 2 to 4 hours.

2. Heat the panini press to medium-high heat. If your panini press comes with a removable drip tray, make sure it is in place (see page 2).

3. Remove the chicken from the marinade, discarding the leftover marinade. Blot the excess liquid from the meat with paper towels and season both sides of the chicken with salt and pepper. Place the chicken on the grill, positioning it toward the center of the grill to ensure that the heat reaches all sides. Grill the chicken, with the lid closed, until it's cooked to an internal temperature of 165°F, 18 to 20 minutes.

4. Serve with warm tortillas and bowls of chopped tomatoes, chopped onions, and cilantro for tacos.

Grilled Jerk Chicken

Yield: 4 servings

I f you've ever had jerk chicken, then you know what a powerful, spicy kick it has. If you haven't, you're in for a treat. Jerk spice originated in Jamaica and is rubbed onto everything from chicken to fish to tofu. Chicken, though, is probably the most popular jerk dish. What gives jerk its heat is the Scotch bonnet pepper, which is many times hotter than even a jalapeño (which is already pretty hot).

2 scallions, chopped
½ cup chopped red onion
3 garlic cloves, chopped
1 Scotch bonnet or habanero pepper, seeded and chopped (see Note)
2 tablespoons freshly squeezed lime juice
2 tablespoons reduced-sodium soy sauce
1 tablespoon extra-virgin olive oil

1 tablespoon packed brown sugar
2 teaspoons ground allspice
1 teaspoon chopped fresh thyme
½ teaspoon ground cinnamon
¼ teaspoon ground nutmeg
4 boneless, skinless chicken breasts (about 2 pounds)
Coarse salt and freshly ground black pepper

1. Blend the scallions, red onion, garlic, Scotch bonnet pepper, lime juice, soy sauce, olive oil, brown sugar, allspice, thyme, cinnamon, and nutmeg in a blender or mini food processor until it forms a relatively smooth paste.

2. Season the chicken breasts with salt and pepper to taste and place them in a large zipper-top plastic bag. Pour the jerk paste over the chicken, seal the bag, and roll the chicken around in the paste to coat it. Let the chicken marinate in the refrigerator overnight.

3. Heat the panini press to medium-high heat. If your panini press comes with a removable drip tray, make sure it is in place (see page 2).

4. Using tongs, remove the chicken from the marinade (remember, there are hot peppers in there!) and transfer two chicken breasts to the grill.

5. Close the lid and grill the chicken breasts until they are cooked to an internal temperature of 165°F, 9 to 11 minutes. Transfer the chicken to a cutting board and let it rest for 5 to 10 minutes before serving. Meanwhile, cook the remaining two chicken breasts (and discard the remaining jerk paste). While the second batch of chicken is resting, unplug the grill and, while it's still hot, carefully scrape down the grates to remove any cooked-on jerk paste.

NOTE: Wear gloves and be extra careful when handling this super-hot pepper. It's extremely painful if it makes contact with your eyes. But don't skip it either—hot peppers are a signature ingredient in jerk spice!

Brined Turkey Thigh

Yield: 2 servings

L ast Thanksgiving at my in-laws' house, I saw a pan emerge from the oven, and I smiled with relief. They'd roasted an extra batch of turkey drumsticks and thighs. Hooray! No more having to scramble to the front of the line of family members to secure the ever-popular dark meat.

Unlike breasts and drumsticks, bone-in turkey thighs are well suited for grilling on a panini press due to their relatively flat shape. I love to first marinate the thighs overnight in an herb brine for lots of flavor. Don't wait till Thanksgiving to try this—it's great for dinner (with mashed potatoes and cranberry sauce and dressing) any time of the year. I often grill a second thigh while the first one is resting—there is enough brine to flavor two thighs—and slice it up for panini.

4 cups water
2 tablespoons coarse salt
1 tablespoons honey
1 teaspoon dried thyme
1 teaspoon dried sage

½ teaspoon dried rosemary
½ teaspoon freshly ground black pepper
1 (1-pound) bone-in, skin-on turkey thigh
1 tablespoon extra-virgin olive oil

1. In a large bowl, stir together the water, salt, sugar, thyme, sage, rosemary, and black pepper until the salt and honey are dissolved. Submerge the turkey thigh in the brine (weight it with a small plate if necessary), cover the bowl with plastic wrap, and refrigerate for 2 to 3 hours.

2. Heat the panini press to medium-high heat. If your panini press comes with a removable drip tray, make sure it is in place (see page 2).

3. Remove the turkey thigh from the brine, pat it dry with paper towels, rub the skin side with the olive oil, and transfer it to the grill. Close the lid and grill the thigh until it is cooked to an internal temperature of 165°F, about 35 minutes.

4. Let the turkey rest for 10 minutes before serving.

Spatchcocked Game Hen

Yield: 2 servings

S patchcock" is a funny word, but it basically just means to butterfly. Removing the backbone of a chicken—or, in this case, a small game hen to fit on the panini press—and opening it up flat allows the bird to cook quickly and evenly. On a panini press, with heat from both sides, you can grill a game hen in under 20 minutes—about half the time it would take to roast it.

Game hens are often sold frozen, so be sure to allow plenty of time for yours to defrost in the refrigerator (it may take more than a day). This recipe is a very simple preparation, but you should always feel free to experiment with your favorite seasonings and spice rubs.

1 Cornish game hen (1½ to 2 pounds)	½ teaspoon coarse salt
1 tablespoon extra-virgin olive oil	¼ teaspoon freshly ground black pepper

1. Heat the panini press to medium-high heat. If your panini press comes with a removable drip tray, make sure it is in place (see page 2).

2. Lay the game hen, breast side down, on a cutting board. With sturdy kitchen shears, cut through the ribs along both sides of the backbone, from tail to neck, to remove it (discard the backbone or save it to make chicken stock).

3. Open the hen out flat, still breast side down. Using a small paring knife, make a slice down the middle of the keel bone (the diamond-shaped white bone between the two breasts). Next, carefully cut around the thin, oblong strip of cartilage that runs down the middle of the hen. Once you've separated the cartilage from the flesh, reach in with your hands and lift it out and discard it. Don't worry if you're not able to do this as cleanly as you'd like—no one will notice.

4. Pat the hen dry and rub olive oil all over the bird. Season the hen on all sides with salt and pepper.

5. Carefully transfer the hen to the grill, skin side up, and close the lid. Grill the hen until it is cooked to an internal temperature of 165°F, 18 to 20 minutes.

Grilled Duck Breasts

Yield: 4 servings

I grilled duck breast after duck breast on my panini press, trying to figure out how to achieve that irresistible crispy skin everyone loves. Over and over again I got the same result—quickly cooked meat with a rubbery fat cap on top. Almost defeated, I was ready to put aside this idea and move on. But I had one duck breast left, and I went for a Hail Mary pass—cooking the duck, skin side down, *with the grill open*, hoping that this approach would give the duck a chance to render its fat without cooking the meat too fast. After about 9 minutes I peered under the duck to find what had been eluding me thus far: browned, crispy skin! I flipped the duck breast and closed the lid, and the other side finished cooking several minutes later. This, friends, was a triumphant moment in panini grilling.

Note: If your panini press doesn't allow you to adjust the temperature, I wouldn't recommend using it to grill duck breasts. To render the duck's fat slowly, it's important to be able to cook it over lower heat—the default heat setting on a panini press without temperature adjustment may be too high to achieve this.

2 boneless, skin-on duck breasts (about 12 ounces)

Coarse salt and freshly ground black pepper

1. Heat the panini press to medium-low heat. If your panini press comes with a removable drip tray, make sure it is in place (see page 2).

2. Pat the duck breasts dry with a paper towel. With a sharp knife, score the fat layer on the duck breasts by carefully slicing through the skin just until you hit the meat (don't slice through the meat). Make several slices, about an inch apart, in a crosshatch pattern.

3. Season the duck generously on both sides with salt and pepper.

4. Open the panini press lid and lay one or both duck breasts on the grill (work in batches if only one will fit), skin side down. *Leaving the lid open*, grill the duck until much of the fat has rendered and the skin is brown and crispy, 9 to 11 minutes. Since grill temperatures vary, it may take more or less time for the duck to render its fat, crisp up, and brown on your grill. Using tongs, flip the breast(s) over and close the lid. Grill until the meat is cooked to an internal temperature of 150°F, another 3 to 4 minutes. Transfer the duck to a cutting board and allow it to rest for 10 minutes before slicing it across the grain.

Grilled Duck Breast Salad with Fried Goat Cheese and Strawberries

Yield: 4 servings

This is one of my favorite springtime salads—panini-grilled duck breast, crunchy fried goat cheese medallions, and fresh strawberries over arugula, dressed in white balsamic vinaigrette. Don't you just love a salad with goodies all over the place? If you're not able to find duck, grilled chicken will work great here as well.

FRIED GOAT CHEESE
¼ cup panko bread crumbs
¼ cup plain bread crumbs
½ teaspoon coarse salt
¼ teaspoon freshly ground black pepper
¼ cup all-purpose flour
1 large egg, beaten
1 (5½-ounce) log goat cheese, sliced into
⅛-inch medallions (see Note)
3 tablespoons extra-virgin olive oil

SALAD
5 ounces baby arugula
1 cup sliced or quartered strawberries
1 recipe White Balsamic Vinaigrette (recipe follows)
2 Grilled Duck Breasts (page 71), sliced across the grain

1. *Fried Goat Cheese:* Combine the panko, plain breadcrumbs, salt, and pepper in a shallow bowl. Place the flour and beaten egg each in their own separate shallow bowls. Dredge each goat cheese medallion first in flour, then in egg, and lastly in the breadcrumbs.

2. In a medium-size skillet, heat the olive oil over medium heat. Carefully lower the cheese into the hot oil (be sure not to overcrowd the skillet—work in batches if necessary). Brown the cheese, 1 to 2 minutes per side, and drain the medallions on a paper towel.

3. *Salad:* Place the arugula and strawberries in a large salad bowl. Pour vinaigrette over the salad—as much or as little as you'd like—and toss the salad with tongs.

4. To serve, divide the salad among four plates and top each with some fried goat cheese medallions and sliced duck breast.

NOTE: An easy way to make nice, neat goat cheese slices is to cut them with a strand of unflavored dental floss; I keep a roll of floss in my utensil drawer just for this purpose! If you find that your goat cheese is too crumbly to slice, just let it sit out at room temperature for a few minutes.

White Balsamic Vinaigrette

Yield: About ¾ cup

I make a classic vinaigrette with white balsamic vinegar when I want to bring out the sweetness and acidity in ingredients like strawberries and tomatoes without adding the dark color of regular balsamic. Look for white balsamic at the grocery store next to the other vinegars.

3 tablespoons white balsamic vinegar
  (you can substitute regular balsamic)
2 teaspoons chopped shallots
½ teaspoon Dijon mustard

½ teaspoon coarse salt
½ teaspoon freshly ground black pepper
½ cup extra-virgin olive oil

1. In a small bowl, whisk together the vinegar, shallots, Dijon mustard, salt, and pepper. While still whisking, slowly drizzle in the olive oil.

2. You can keep any extra white balsamic vinaigrette in the refrigerator for up to a week. Allow the dressing to come to room temperature and give it a good stir before using it next.

HIGH ON THE HOG

Pork on the Panini Press

MORE FROM THE PANINI PRESS

Ham, Apple, and Smoked Cheddar Panini with a Brown Sugar Crust

Yield: 4 panini

P retty please, with sugar on top? The plea is just as convincing to me now as an adult as it was when I was seven years old, begging my mom to let me ride my banana-seat bike around the cul-de-sac. And let me tell you, brown sugar sprinkled on a ham and cheese sandwich tastes really amazing. The bread gets a sweet crust on the outside just like on a baked ham. Matched with the smoked cheddar cheese and the salty ham, the combination is positively palate-pleasing.

I first got the sugar-crusting idea from the brown sugar–crusted raspberry and mozzarella panini that Giada De Laurentiis makes. While I can't in good health conscience recommend that you put sugar crusts on your panini all the time, definitely keep this sweet little secret in your back pocket for an occasional treat.

4 tablespoons (½ stick) butter, at room temperature
8 slices rustic multigrain bread, sliced from a dense bakery loaf
4 ounces smoked cheddar cheese, sliced

8 ounces sliced ham
1 sweet apple, such as Gala or Jonagold, cored and thinly sliced
2 tablespoons packed brown sugar

1. Heat the panini press to medium-high heat.

2. *For each sandwich:* Spread butter on two slices of bread to flavor the outside of the sandwich. Flip over one slice and layer on cheese, ham, apple slices, and more cheese. Close the sandwich with the other slice of bread, buttered side up. Sprinkle some brown sugar on top.

3. Grill two panini at a time, with the lid closed, until the cheese is melted and the bread is toasted, with a brown sugar crust, 4 to 5 minutes.

Ham, Pineapple, and Mozzarella Panini

Yield: 4 panini

Once I discovered the flatbread trick (see Pepperoni Pizza Panini, page 103), I was eager to try out more flavor combinations. For these panini, I went the sweet and salty Hawaiian pizza route with the classic ham and pineapple. Barbecue sauce—you can use any kind you like—adds a spicy kick that's just perfect with the pineapple.

4 flatbreads, such as naan or pita
½ cup barbecue sauce
8 ounces fresh mozzarella cheese, sliced
8 thin slices red onion

4 ounces sliced ham
8 pineapple rings, canned or fresh, patted dry with paper towels
¼ cup chopped fresh cilantro

1. Heat the panini press to medium-high heat.

2. *For each sandwich:* Cut the flatbread in half across the diameter, creating two semi-circles—these will become your top and bottom halves. Spread a layer of barbecue sauce on both flatbread halves. Top one half with a thin layer of cheese, onion, ham, 2 pineapple slices, a sprinkling of cilantro, and more cheese. Close the sandwich with the other flatbread half, barbecue sauce side down.

3. Grill two panini at a time, with the lid closed, until the cheese is melted and the bread is toasted, 5 to 6 minutes.

Ham, Brie, and Apple Butter–Mustard Panini

Yield: 4 panini

A few slices of salty ham, creamy melted Brie, and some spicy Dijon mustard on a baguette—it doesn't get much better than this simple, classic French sandwich combination. Well, unless maybe you add a little apple butter to the mix.

Apple butter may not be the first condiment you think of when it comes to panini, but perhaps it should be. Apples pair supremely well with cheese. In spread form, you can use it on its own or mix it with another spread—such as Dijon mustard—to add sweet, fruity notes to a sandwich. Especially in autumn, when apples are at their peak, a seasonal touch like this will make your sandwiches extra special.

3 tablespoons apple butter
1 tablespoon Dijon mustard
1 seeded baguette, cut into 4 portions, or 4 mini baguettes

8 ounces sliced ham
4 ounces Brie cheese (with or without the rind), sliced

1. Heat the panini press to medium-high heat.

2. In a small bowl, whisk together the apple butter and Dijon mustard.

3. *For each sandwich:* Slice off the domed top of a baguette portion to create a flat grilling surface. Split the baguette to create top and bottom halves. Spread apple butter–mustard mixture inside each baguette half. Layer ham and Brie on the bottom half. Close the sandwich with the top half.

4. Grill two panini at a time, with the lid closed, until the cheese is melted and the baguettes are toasted, 4 to 5 minutes.

Spicy Elvis Panini

Yield: 4 panini

Peanut butter, bananas, and bacon—really? I avoided trying the famous Elvis sandwich for the longest time. It may have been a favorite of the King of Rock 'n' Roll, but that combination just didn't scream "Love Me Tender" to me. That is, until the day my friend Amanda introduced me to a new twist on peanut butter: spicy. She had mixed sriracha—a Thai hot pepper sauce—into peanut butter and slathered it on bread and could not contain her excitement over her culinary discovery. Suddenly I began to look at peanut butter with new eyes and new possibilities . . . possibilities that could allow the inclusion of bananas and bacon.

Oh all right, I loved it. And I think you will, too, especially if you go for ripe, sweet bananas—perfectly yellow with a little bite to them, not mushy. It's completely up to you just how spicy to make things, but that little kick of heat in combination with the sweet, salty, and smoky flavors in this sandwich is definitely enough to get your taste buds "All Shook Up."

½ cup creamy or chunky peanut butter
½ to 1 teaspoon sriracha or other hot pepper sauce
4 tablespoons (½ stick) butter, at room temperature

8 slices rustic white bread, sliced from a dense bakery loaf
2 ripe bananas, thinly sliced
8 strips cooked bacon

1. Heat the panini press to medium-high heat.

2. Mix the peanut butter and sriracha in a small bowl until well combined.

3. *For each sandwich:* Spread butter on two slices of bread to flavor the outside of the sandwich. Flip over both slices and spread 1 tablespoon spicy peanut butter on each. Top one slice of bread with sliced bananas and 2 bacon strips. Close the sandwich with the other slice of bread, buttered side up.

4. Grill two panini at a time, with the lid closed, until the ingredients are warmed through and the bread is toasted, 2 to 3 minutes.

Bacon, Cheddar, and Tomato Panini

Yield: 4 panini

A close-up of a grilled sandwich with a corner of cheese melting over a ripe slice of red tomato and a curl of crispy bacon has adorned my business cards for years as a visual symbol of PaniniHappy.com. People love that photo—it makes them want to eat that sandwich. When I first posted this recipe on the blog, I called it "one of the most comforting, happy-inducing grilled sandwiches I know how to make," and I still believe that.

4 tablespoons (½ stick) butter, at room temperature
1 garlic clove, minced
2 teaspoons minced fresh basil
8 slices sourdough or other rustic white bread, sliced from a dense bakery loaf

8 ounces sharp cheddar cheese, sliced
8 strips cooked bacon
2 plum tomatoes (such as Roma), thinly sliced and seeded, or 8 Slow-Roasted Tomato halves (page 135)

1. Heat the panini press to medium-high heat.

2. Mix the butter, garlic, and basil in a small bowl.

3. *For each sandwich:* Spread basil-garlic butter on two slices of bread to flavor the outside of the sandwich. Flip over one slice of bread and top it with cheese, bacon, tomatoes, and more cheese. Close the sandwich with the other slice of bread, buttered side up.

4. Grill two panini at a time, with the lid closed, until the cheese is melted and the bread is toasted, 4 to 5 minutes.

Speck, Taleggio, and Grill-Roasted Garlic Panini

Yield: 4 panini

I f you love prosciutto as much as I do, you need to get your hands on some speck, or smoked prosciutto. The Italians sure know how to cure meat to its maximum flavor! Speck is the pride of the Alto Adige region of Italy; it's found everywhere there, but in the United States it's still a specialty item found only at some Italian delis and gourmet shops. Here, I match the smoky, salty speck with fruity, aromatic Taleggio cheese and a few cloves of garlic that I grill right on the panini press. By all means, you can substitute regular prosciutto—or even regular ham—but do keep your eye out for speck. It's a must-try!

4 tablespoons (½ stick) butter, at room temperature
8 slices rustic white bread, sliced from a dense bakery loaf
1 recipe Grill-Roasted Garlic (page 213)

1 cup baby arugula
8 ounces thinly sliced speck or prosciutto
4 ounces Taleggio (rind removed) or fontina cheese, sliced

1. Heat the panini press to medium-high heat.

2. *For each sandwich:* Spread butter on two slices of bread to flavor the outside of the sandwich. Flip over one slice of bread and spread about a tablespoon of roasted garlic on the other side. Top the garlic with a handful of arugula, some speck, and some cheese. Close the sandwich with the other slice of bread, buttered side up.

3. Grill two panini at a time, with the lid closed, until the cheese is melted and the bread is toasted, 4 to 5 minutes.

Soppressata Panini with Mozzarella and Pesto

Yield: 4 panini

When I wrote about these panini on the blog, I described them as "The Best Sandwiches I Never Had." That's because the first time I encountered them, at Armandino Batali's renowned Salumi restaurant in Seattle, I was five months pregnant and cured meats were off the table for me, so to speak. While I made do with a rice salad (comforted by the fact that Mr. Batali was having the same at a small table across from us), I longingly observed my husband savor his garlicky, house-made soppressata sandwich.

My grilled version of that fabulous sandwich can best be described as "pizza-like." The flavor of the soppressata reminds me a lot of pepperoni. There are only a few simple ingredients in this sandwich, but they combine to create something extraordinarily tasty.

1 ciabatta loaf, cut into 4 portions, or
  4 ciabatta rolls
½ cup basil pesto, purchased or homemade
  (page 101)

8 ounces fresh mozzarella cheese, sliced
4 ounces sliced sweet soppressata or Genoa
  salami

1. Heat the panini press to medium-high heat.

2. *For each sandwich:* Split a ciabatta portion to create top and bottom halves. Spread some pesto inside each bread half. On the bottom half layer on cheese and soppressata. Close the sandwich with the top ciabatta half.

3. Grill two panini at a time, with the lid closed, until the cheese is melted and the ciabatta is toasted, 5 to 7 minutes.

Manchego, Honey, and Hot Soppressata Panini

Yield: 4 panini

One spring afternoon on a visit to San Francisco, my husband, Mike, our friend Alissa, and I perched ourselves on the high stools at Blue Barn Gourmet in the city's Marina district and eagerly unwrapped several of their grilled cheese sandwich offerings. Mike's selection, known as the Sheep, was our hands-down favorite—Manchego (my favorite cheese), spicy salami, and fig jam on *levain*. The sweet heat of the salami combined with the buttery Manchego was just out of this world. I couldn't wait to get home and make some of my own. I replaced the fig jam with some floral honey, which I just love with salami.

4 tablespoons (½ stick) butter, at room temperature

8 slices rustic white bread, sliced from a dense bakery loaf

4 teaspoons honey

8 ounces Manchego cheese, thinly sliced

8 ounces sliced hot soppressata

1. Heat the panini press to medium-high heat.

2. *For each sandwich:* Spread butter on two slices of bread to flavor the outside of the sandwich. Flip over both slices and drizzle honey on the other side of each. On one slice layer cheese, soppressata, and more cheese. Close the sandwich with the other slice of bread, buttered side up.

3. Grill two panini at a time, with the lid closed, until the cheese is melted and the bread is toasted, 4 to 5 minutes.

Serrano Ham, Manchego, and Membrillo Panini

Yield: 4 panini

These panini require a few special Spanish ingredients, but I promise it's worth the effort to seek them out. Serrano ham (*jamón serrano*) is similar to prosciutto, but it's cured for a longer time to produce even deeper flavor and a firmer texture. I nearly swore off all other hams the first time I tasted it. Membrillo is a sweet, firm quince paste that's most commonly paired with Manchego, my favorite sheep's milk cheese. Grill them all together on a crusty baguette and you've got wonderfully flavorful, if a bit pricey, Spanish-style panini.

1 French baguette, cut into 4 portions, or 4 mini baguettes

4 tablespoons membrillo (quince paste; see Note)

4 ounces Manchego cheese, sliced

8 ounces sliced Serrano ham

1. Heat the panini press to medium-high heat.

2. *For each sandwich:* Slice off the domed top of a baguette portion to create a flat grilling surface. Split the baguette to create top and bottom halves. Spread 1 tablespoon membrillo inside the bottom half of the baguette. Top the membrillo with cheese, ham, and more cheese. Close the sandwich with the top baguette half.

3. Grill two panini at a time, with the lid closed, until the cheese is melted and the baguettes are toasted, 7 to 9 minutes.

NOTE: Look for membrillo, Manchego, and Serrano ham at Whole Foods Market or other specialty grocers, or at Hispanic markets. You can also find membrillo at gourmet retailers such as Dean & DeLuca.

Grilled Asparagus Panini with Prosciutto and Mozzarella

Yield: 4 panini

Since asparagus and prosciutto make such a wonderful flavor duo, I created this panini recipe, adding some fresh mozzarella for that stretchy cheese effect—and to keep the asparagus in place. Keep this recipe in mind for springtime, when fresh asparagus is at its peak.

8 ounces asparagus, trimmed to the length of a focaccia portion
2 teaspoons extra-virgin olive oil
Coarse salt and freshly ground black pepper

1 focaccia, cut into 4 portions
4 ounces sliced prosciutto
8 ounces fresh mozzarella cheese, sliced

1. Heat the panini press to medium-high heat.

2. In a large bowl, toss the asparagus in the olive oil and season it with salt and pepper to taste. Grill the asparagus, with the lid closed, until they're cooked through and grill marks appear, 3 to 4 minutes. Set them aside.

3. Unplug the grill and carefully clean the grates. Reheat the grill to medium-high heat.

4. *For each sandwich:* Split a focaccia portion to create top and bottom halves. Place some prosciutto inside the bottom half. Top it with cheese and as many grilled asparagus spears as will fit securely. Close the sandwich with the other focaccia half.

5. Grill two panini at a time, with the lid closed, until the cheese is melted and the focaccia is toasted, 4 to 5 minutes.

Prosciutto, Mozzarella, and Arugula Salad Panini

Yield: 4 panini

The first time I ever tasted a sandwich with a salad inside I thought it was a genius idea. Dressing greens in vinaigrette adds acidity and moisture without getting the bread overly soggy. If you think about it, it's pretty much the same as piling cole-slaw on a pulled pork sandwich. It's all about finding creative ways to add flavor. You'll find that, with the arugula tossed in vinaigrette, these panini won't need any other condiments or spreads.

2 cups baby arugula
1 tablespoon White Balsamic Vinaigrette (page 73), or to taste
1 French baguette, cut into 4 portions, or 4 mini baguettes

4 ounces fresh mozzarella cheese, sliced
8 ounces thinly sliced prosciutto

1. Heat the panini press to medium-high heat.

2. Place the arugula in a medium-size bowl and toss it with about a tablespoon of vinai-grette—more or less, depending on your taste.

3. *For each sandwich:* Slice off the domed top of a baguette portion to create a flat grilling surface. Split the baguette to create top and bottom halves. On the bottom baguette half, layer some arugula salad, a little bit of cheese, prosciutto, and some more cheese. Close the sand-wich with the top baguette half.

4. Grill two panini at a time, with the lid closed, until the cheese is melted and the baguettes are toasted, 4 to 5 minutes.

Manchego, Marmalade, and Prosciutto Panini

Yield: 4 panini

I f you enjoy my Manchego, Honey, and Hot Soppressata Panini (page 87), then you should give this one a try as well to compare and contrast. It's got a similar flavor profile—a little sweet, a little porky. But in this one, I replace the heat of the soppressata with gentle prosciutto and add sweet citrus notes with orange marmalade. I can't decide which of the two sandwiches I enjoy more.

4 tablespoons (½ stick) butter, at room temperature

8 slices rustic white bread, sliced from a dense bakery loaf

4 tablespoons sweet orange marmalade

3 ounces thinly sliced prosciutto

8 ounces Manchego cheese, sliced

1. Heat the panini press to medium-high heat.

2. *For each sandwich:* Spread butter on two slices of bread to flavor the outside of the sandwich. Flip over one slice of bread and top it with 1 tablespoon marmalade, some prosciutto, and some cheese. Close the sandwich with the other slice of bread, buttered side up.

3. Grill two panini at a time, with the lid closed, until the cheese is melted and the bread is toasted, 4 to 5 minutes.

Fig, Smoked Gouda, and Prosciutto Panini Stackers

Yield: 12 stackers

The burger world has "sliders"; I like to think of mini panini as "stackers." You can stack up these little sandwiches alongside a cup of piping-hot soup for lunch or pass them on a tray as appetizers. I first came up with this sweet and smoky fig, Gouda, and prosciutto combo to accompany velvety butternut squash soup, but it would be a wonderful complement to all sorts of savory chowders or bisques as well.

24 (¼-inch-thick) French baguette slices
6 slices (about 3 ounces) prosciutto

6 slices (about 6 ounces) smoked Gouda cheese
¼ cup fig preserves

1. Heat the panini press to medium-high heat.

2. Cut the prosciutto and smoked Gouda in half to fit onto the baguette slices.

3. Top half of the baguette slices with a thin layer of fig preserves, a piece of prosciutto, and a piece of smoked Gouda. Close all of the sandwiches with the remaining baguette slices.

4. In batches, grill the panini, with the lid closed, until the cheese is melted and the baguettes are toasted, 4 to 5 minutes.

Antipasto Panini

Yield: 4 panini

If I'm making sandwiches for friends and I'm not sure what kinds of flavors they'll like, I'll either go for a really basic grilled cheese or all the way to the other end of the spectrum with a big-flavored bonanza, such as these panini. They're some of my favorites—basically an antipasto platter on a sandwich, with Italian cured meats, mozzarella, roasted peppers, marinated artichokes, and olive tapenade. Not only are they fabulous on the grill, but these panini also make great cold sandwiches—just assemble them, wrap them up, and bring them to your next picnic!

1 ciabatta loaf, cut into 4 portions, or 4 ciabatta rolls
4 tablespoons olive tapenade
8 ounces fresh mozzarella cheese, sliced
4 ounces thinly sliced prosciutto
8 ounces sliced hot soppressata or other salami
¼ cup sliced roasted red bell peppers
½ cup sliced marinated artichoke hearts

1. Heat the panini press to medium high heat.

2. *For each sandwich:* Split a ciabatta portion to create top and bottom halves. Spread a little olive tapenade inside both halves. On the bottom half, layer a few slices of mozzarella, prosciutto, hot soppressata, roasted red bell peppers, and artichoke hearts. Close the sandwich with the top ciabatta half.

3. Grill two panini at a time, with the lid closed, until the cheese is melted and the ciabatta is toasted, 4 to 5 minutes.

Salami, Prosciutto, and Provolone Panini

Yield: 4 panini

This is my grilled version of a fantastic Italian Combo cold sandwich I ordered at a shop called (appropriately) Panino in the tony little town of Montecito, California, just next door to Santa Barbara. I contemplated naming this sandwich the "Don Johnson," because I spotted the *Miami Vice* actor while I was there! What makes these panini stand out is the Italian-style salsa that coats the inside of the ciabatta, adding tons of fresh, zesty flavor.

SALSA
½ cup chopped seeded plum tomatoes
¼ cup chopped seeded cucumber
¼ cup chopped green bell pepper
¼ cup chopped red onion
2 tablespoons chopped fresh basil
1 tablespoon capers, rinsed and chopped
2 tablespoons extra-virgin olive oil
2 tablespoons red wine vinegar

Coarse salt and freshly ground black pepper

PANINI
1 ciabatta loaf, cut into 4 portions, or
   4 ciabatta rolls
4 ounces provolone cheese, sliced
4 ounces Genoa salami, sliced
4 ounces thinly sliced prosciutto

1. *Salsa:* Combine the tomatoes, cucumbers, bell peppers, red onion, basil, capers, olive oil, and vinegar in a small glass bowl. Season the salsa with salt and pepper to taste. Cover the bowl and let it sit for 1 hour at room temperature to let the flavors meld.

2. *Panini:* Heat the panini press to medium-high heat.

3. *For each sandwich:* Split a ciabatta portion to create top and bottom halves. Spoon some salsa inside the bottom half. Add cheese, salami, prosciutto, more cheese, and more salsa. Close the sandwich with the top ciabatta half.

4. Grill two panini at a time, with the lid closed, until the cheese is melted and the ciabatta is toasted, 5 to 7 minutes.

Salami, Taleggio, and Peach Panini

Yield: 4 panini

I f there's a specialty cheese shop near you—or even a specialty cheese section of your regular grocery store—start chatting up the folks behind the counter for their recommendations. Tasting different cheeses is undoubtedly the best way to learn about cheese. It's how I first learned about Taleggio. Someone behind the counter gave me a sample of the Italian cow's milk cheese along with a slice of salami. It was love at first bite. Taleggio's aroma is on the strong side, but its flavor is comparatively mild—with a hint of fruitiness that pairs well with sweet peaches. Fontina, another easy-melting cow's milk cheese with a nutty and somewhat fruity flavor, is a good substitute and tends to be easier to find in stores.

1 tablespoon extra-virgin olive oil
8 slices whole-grain bread, sliced from a dense bakery loaf
½ cup pesto, purchased or homemade (page 101)

4 ounces Taleggio cheese, rind removed, sliced
4 ounces Genoa salami, sliced
1 medium-size peach, pitted and sliced

1. Heat the panini press to medium-high heat.

2. *For each sandwich:* Brush olive oil on two slices of bread to flavor the outside of the sandwich. Flip over both slices of bread and spread pesto on the other side of each. On one slice layer cheese, salami, peach slices, and more cheese. Close the sandwich with the other slice of bread, oiled side up.

3. Grill two panini at a time, with the lid closed, until the cheese is melted and the bread is toasted, 4 to 5 minutes.

Pesto

Yield: About 1¼ cups

Pesto is one of the most flavorful condiments I can think of. It instantly adds a fresh, zesty, garlicky punch to panini, as well as pasta, pizzas, and many other dishes. You can find jars of pesto at the grocery store, but it's easy enough to make at home. Plus, if you make it yourself you're able to increase or decrease ingredient quantities according to your preferences.

Pesto can be made with a variety of different herbs. Basil pesto is probably the most common form, but I've also included instructions for a lemony arugula pesto.

2 large garlic cloves
⅓ cup pine nuts
2 cups fresh basil leaves
⅔ cup extra-virgin olive oil

⅔ cup grated Parmesan or Pecorino Romano cheese
Coarse salt and freshly ground black pepper

1. Using a blender or food processor, blend the garlic and pine nuts for a few seconds until they're the texture of coarse meal. Add the basil leaves. Continue to blend, drizzling in the olive oil through the feed tube, until the pesto is completely pureed. Add the cheese and blend until it's fully mixed in.

2. Transfer the pesto to a small bowl, taste it, and season with salt and pepper as needed.

3. Store the pesto for up to 5 days in the refrigerator or up to 2 months in the freezer. Cover the pesto with a thin layer of olive oil to help preserve its bright green color.

For arugula pesto: Substitute ⅓ cup chopped walnuts for the pine nuts and 2 cups baby arugula for the basil. Blend in 1 tablespoon grated lemon zest and 1 tablespoon freshly squeezed lemon juice along with the cheese.

Pepperoni Pizza Panini

Yield: 4 panini

Of all the panini ideas that people have suggested to me — it tends to be a popular topic of conversation—Pepperoni Pizza Panini is probably the most common. I'm not quite sure why that is. I'm guessing it's because it was a rather obvious omission from my blog for the longest time. Honestly, I didn't think it was worth posting a recipe for something that everyone in America knows how to make—pepperoni, cheese, sauce, and bread is very standard fare.

But it turns out that these aren't quite as straightforward as I thought. You see, if you spread marinara sauce directly on sliced bread or a roll, as I typically do with most panini condiments, the bread turns soggy. And that's not good. After some trial and error I discovered a solution: flatbread. Sauce doesn't seep into flatbreads like naan or pita as easily as it does with cut sides of other breads. Plus, with its crust-like texture, it feels like you're eating a folded pizza. Come to think of it, I would have viewed folding a slice of cold leftover pizza and popping it into the panini press as a very viable reheating method back in my college days.

4 flatbreads, such as naan or pita
½ cup marinara sauce
8 ounces fresh mozzarella cheese, sliced

4 ounces sliced pepperoni
8 fresh basil leaves, torn

1. Heat the panini press to medium-high heat.

2. *For each sandwich:* Cut the flatbread in half across the diameter, creating two semicircles—these will become your top and bottom halves. Spread a layer of marinara on both flatbread halves. Top one half with a thin layer of cheese and arrange pepperoni slices to cover the cheese. Scatter some basil pieces over the pepperoni and top with more cheese. Close the sandwich with the other flatbread half, marinara side down.

3. Grill two panini at a time, with the lid closed, until the cheese is melted and the bread is toasted, 5 to 6 minutes.

BBQ Rib Melt Panini

Yield: 4 panini

The next time you find yourself with leftover ribs after a barbecue, don't just reheat them—or eat them cold out of the fridge (come on, admit it!). Instead, turn them into these amazing panini. Rib meat is usually so fall-off-the-bone succulent that it really doesn't need anything more than a simple roll to make a great sandwich. That said, I'm pretty sure that if you take me up on the suggestion of including a pile of grilled onions and creamy smoked Gouda into the mix, you won't be the least bit disappointed.

1 tablespoon vegetable oil
1 medium-size onion, sliced crosswise into ½-inch-thick rounds (rings intact)
4 tablespoons (½ stick) butter, at room temperature

8 slices sourdough or other rustic white bread, sliced from a dense bakery loaf
8 ounces barbecued pork rib meat, removed from the bone
4 ounces smoked Gouda cheese, sliced

1. Heat the panini press to medium-high heat.

2. Brush vegetable oil over both sides of the onion rounds. Set the onions on the grill, close the lid, and grill them until they're tender and grill marks appear, 4 to 6 minutes.

3. *For each sandwich:* Spread butter on two slices of bread to flavor the outside of the sandwich. Flip over one slice of bread and layer on grilled onions, rib meat, and smoked Gouda. Close the sandwich with the other slice of bread, buttered side up.

4. Grill two panini at a time, with the lid closed, until the cheese is melted and the bread is toasted, 4 to 5 minutes.

Sausage, Peppers, and Smoked Mozzarella Panini

Yield: 4 panini

nspired by classic Italian sausage and peppers, these panini are perfect to enjoy while watching a big game. I layer sausage links with sautéed bell peppers and onions, smoked mozzarella, and mustard and grill it all on crusty Italian rolls. You can heat fully cooked sausages right on the panini press and, better yet, you don't even have to turn them! Try Italian-style chicken sausages if you're looking to cut down on fat without sacrificing much flavor.

4 fully cooked Italian sausage lInks (hot or sweet)
1 tablespoon extra-virgin olive oil
1 red bell pepper, cored, seeded, and sliced
1 green bell pepper, cored, seeded, and sliced
1 medium-size onion, halved and sliced

2 teaspoons balsamic vinegar
Coarse salt and freshly ground black pepper
1 ciabatta loaf, cut into 4 portions, or 4 ciabatta rolls or other crusty rolls
4 tablespoons Dijon mustard
4 ounces smoked mozzarella cheese, sliced

1. Heat the panini press to medium-high heat. If your panini press comes with a removable drip tray, make sure it is in place (see page 2).

2. Slice each sausage link in half lengthwise without slicing all the way through, then fold open the sausage. Place the sausages, cut sides down, on the grill. Close the lid and grill the sausages until they are heated through and grill marks appear, 4 to 5 minutes.

3. In the meantime, heat the olive oil in a large skillet over medium-high heat. Add the peppers, onions, and balsamic vinegar and season them with salt and pepper. Cook the vegetables, stirring occasionally, until they're browned and tender, about 10 minutes.

4. *For each sandwich:* Split a ciabatta portion to create top and bottom halves. Spread a thin layer of mustard inside each half. Add a generous amount of peppers and onions to the bottom half. Set a butterflied sausage on top of the peppers and onions. Add a few slices of cheese and close the sandwich with the top half of the roll.

5. Grill two panini at a time, with the lid closed, until the cheese is melted and the ciabatta is toasted, 5 to 7 minutes.

Chorizo Tortas

Yield: 4 tortas

My taste buds immediately perk up when I see that Mexican chorizo is an ingredient in a dish. I just love that combination of chile and vinegar flavors. In these tortas (Mexican sandwiches) I layer ground chorizo with refried beans and top them with avocado, red onions, and queso fresco on traditional *telera* rolls.

You'll need uncooked Mexican chorizo for these sandwiches. It's soft, minced, and deep red in color from a good amount of chiles. It's not the same as Spanish chorizo, which is hard and dry-cured—another delicious sausage for another day.

10 ounces uncooked Mexican chorizo (not dry-cured)

½ cup refried beans (see Note)

4 *bolillo* or *telera* rolls (kaiser rolls will work well, too)

1 medium-size ripe avocado, pitted, peeled, and sliced

½ small red onion, sliced

2 ounces crumbled *queso fresco* (or mild feta cheese)

1. Place the chorizo in a large skillet over medium heat. Cook the chorizo, breaking it up with a wooden spoon, until it's cooked through, about 10 minutes. Use a slotted spoon to transfer the cooked chorizo to a plate lined with paper towels to drain the excess fat.

2. While the chorizo is cooking, heat the refried beans in a small saucepan over medium heat, stirring occasionally.

3. Heat the panini press to medium-high heat.

4. *For each sandwich:* Split a roll to create top and bottom halves. Spread 2 tablespoons refried beans inside the bottom half of the roll. Top the beans with chorizo, avocado, red onions, and queso fresco. Close the sandwich with the top half of the roll.

5. Grill two tortas at a time, with the lid closed, until the rolls are toasted, 4 to 5 minutes.

NOTE: Refried beans typically come canned in a larger quantity than you'll need for this recipe. What to do with the remaining beans? You could use them in Grilled Steak Tortas (page 129) or swap them for the mashed black beans in Grilled Shrimp Tostadas (page 177). If you store the beans in a covered glass or plastic container, they'll keep in the refrigerator for 3 to 4 days.

Cubano Panini

Yield: 4 panini

Once upon a time I used to work up the street from Porto's, a bustling, family-owned Cuban restaurant in Glendale, California, and what I enjoyed more than anything was their traditional Cuban sandwich. Slow-roasted pork, sliced ham, Swiss cheese, pickles, and mustard pressed on baguette-like Cuban bread—Cubanos rank among my absolute favorites.

If I happen to have roast pork on hand, it's the best for making Cubano-style panini. But for a quicker option, I simply marinate thin-sliced boneless pork chops in the same zesty citrus marinade that I use for Citrus-Marinated Grilled Chicken (page 64) and grill them on the panini press in just a minute or two.

MARINATED PORK
¼ cup extra-virgin olive oil
Juice of 1 orange (about ¼ cup)
Juice of 1 lime (about 2 tablespoons)
Juice of 1 lemon (about 2 tablespoons)
¼ cup chopped fresh cilantro
2 garlic cloves, minced
1 serrano chile, seeded and minced
¼ teaspoon ground cumin
4 (½-inch-thick) boneless pork chops
   (about 8 ounces; see Note)

½ teaspoon coarse salt
¼ teaspoon freshly ground black pepper

PANINI
1 French baguette, cut into 4 portions,
   or 4 mini baguettes
4 tablespoons yellow mustard
8 ounces sliced ham
¼ cup dill pickle slices
8 ounces Swiss cheese, sliced

1. *Marinated Pork:* Combine the oil, citrus juices, cilantro, garlic, chile, and cumin in a large zipper-top plastic bag. Add the pork, seal the bag, and roll the pork around a bit in the marinade to coat it well. Marinate the pork in the refrigerator for 2 to 4 hours.

2. Heat the panini press to medium-high heat. If your panini press comes with a removable drip tray, make sure it is in place (see page 2).

3. Remove the pork from the marinade (discard the remaining marinade) and blot the excess liquid from the meat with paper towels. Season both sides of the meat with salt and pepper.

4. Transfer the seasoned meat to the grill and close the lid. Grill the pork until it's cooked to an internal temperature of 145°F, 1 to 2 minutes.

5. *Panini:* Unplug the grill, carefully clean the grates, and then reheat the panini press to medium-high heat.

6. *For each sandwich:* Slice off the domed top of a baguette portion to create a flat grilling surface. Split the baguette to create top and bottom halves. Spread 1 tablespoon mustard inside both baguette halves. Top the bottom half with a piece of grilled pork, followed by some ham, pickles, and cheese. Close the sandwich with the top baguette half.

7. Grill two panini at a time, with the lid closed, until the cheese is melted and the baguettes are toasted, 4 to 5 minutes.

NOTE: I can often find thin-sliced pork chops in the grocery store, but when I can't, I just ask the butcher to cut them for me.

Pork Tenderloin, Caramelized Pear, and Cheddar Panini

Yield: 4 panini

Apples and pears have got to be the most versatile panini ingredients that I grill with. Their flavors naturally complement pork, chicken, turkey, and even beef. They also pair well with a huge variety of cheeses, including cheddar, Brie, goat cheese, and—my favorite—Manchego. Mix and match all of those together and—boom!—apples and pears turn out to be real workhorses.

Caramelized pears with pork tenderloin and sharp aged cheddar is a winning sweet-and-savory combination. Grill it on raisin bread and just watch all of those flavors go to work.

CARAMELIZED PEAR
½ tablespoon butter
1 medium-size ripe, firm pear (such as Bosc), peeled, cored, and sliced (see Note)
½ teaspoon sugar

PANINI
4 tablespoons (½ stick) butter, at room temperature
8 slices raisin bread, sliced from a dense bakery loaf
4 ounces sharp cheddar cheese, sliced
8 ounces Sweet and Smoky Grilled Pork Tenderloin Medallions (page 117) or other leftover cooked pork, sliced

1. *Caramelized Pear:* Melt the butter in a large skillet over high heat. Add the pear and sugar and cook, stirring occasionally, until the slices are tender, with a browned caramelized crust on the outside, 4 to 6 minutes. Transfer the pears to a plate.

2. *Panini:* Heat the panini press to medium-high heat.

3. *For each sandwich:* Spread butter on two slices of bread to flavor the outside of the sandwich. Flip over one slice of bread and top it with cheese, caramelized pears, sliced pork tenderloin, and more cheese. Close the sandwich with the other slice of bread, buttered side up.

4. Grill two panini at a time, with the lid closed, until the cheese is melted and the bread is toasted, 4 to 6 minutes.

NOTE: Don't make your pear slices too thin or they will turn mushy when you cook them—aim for somewhere between ¼ inch and ½ inch thick.

Pork Tenderloin, Apple Butter, and Provolone Panini

Yield: 4 panini

Pork and apples—it's a classic sweet-and-savory combination that I just can't get enough of. As you've probably noticed, I use sliced apples quite often in panini, but I also appreciate the more concentrated (and spreadable) flavor that comes from apple butter. You'll find that my Sweet and Smoky Grilled Pork Tenderloin Medallions—with brown sugar and smoked paprika in the spice paste—work especially well with the apple butter and smoky provolone in these panini.

4 tablespoons (½ stick) butter, at room temperature
8 slices rustic white bread, sliced from a dense bakery loaf
4 ounces provolone cheese, sliced

8 ounces Sweet and Smoky Grilled Pork Tenderloin Medallions (page 117) or other leftover cooked pork, sliced
4 tablespoons apple butter

1. Heat the panini press to medium-high heat.

2. *For each sandwich:* Spread butter on two slices of bread to flavor the outside of the sandwich. Flip over one slice of bread and top it with cheese, pork, apple butter, and more cheese. Close the sandwich with the other slice of bread, buttered side up.

3. Grill two panini at a time, with the lid closed, until the cheese is melted and the bread is toasted, 4 to 6 minutes.

Grilled Pork Bánh Mì

Yield: 4 sandwiches

When Vietnamese *bánh mì* sandwiches first began hitting the mainstream foodie consciousness, my husband must have sought out every *bánh mì* shop (and there are a lot of them) within a 20-mile radius, to taste what all the hype over a $3 sandwich was about. Each time, he'd text me something like, "Found a *bánh mì* place in San Marcos. Got the pork. SO GOOD." Once I finally had the opportunity to do some *bánh mì* scouting of my own I, too, was reeled in by the tender marinated meat and all of the mouthwatering condiments that filled the soft, warm baguette.

I adapted the succulent pork marinade for the *bánh mì* from a recipe on Food52.com.

MARINATED GRILLED PORK
3 tablespoons fish sauce
2 tablespoons honey
1 tablespoon vegetable oil
½ teaspoon sesame oil
1 tablespoon packed dark brown sugar
2 tablespoons reduced-sodium soy sauce
2 garlic cloves, minced
½ teaspoon grated fresh ginger
½ teaspoon freshly ground black pepper
1 pound pork tenderloin, sliced into
  ½-inch-thick medallions

BÁNH MÌ
1 soft French baguette, cut into 4 portions,
  or 4 mini baguettes
4 tablespoons mayonnaise
1 recipe Pickled Daikon and Carrot (recipe
  follows)
2 jalapeño peppers, seeded and thinly
  sliced lengthwise
A handful of fresh cilantro

1. *Marinated Grilled Pork:* Whisk together the fish sauce, honey, vegetable and sesame oils, dark brown sugar, soy sauce, garlic, ginger, and black pepper in a small bowl, dissolving the honey and dark brown sugar.

2. Place a few pork tenderloin medallions between two sheets of plastic wrap and use a meat pounder or rolling pin to flatten them to a ¼-inch thickness. Repeat with the remaining pork medallions. Place the flattened pork medallions in a zipper-top plastic bag and pour in the marinade. Seal the bag and shake it around a bit to fully coat the pork. Marinate the pork in the refrigerator for 30 minutes.

3. Heat the panini press to medium-high heat.

4. Working in batches, grill the pork, with the lid closed, until it's cooked through, about 2 minutes. Use tongs to transfer the meat to a plate and tent the plate with foil to keep it warm.

5. *For each bánh mì:* Split a baguette portion without cutting all the way through (leave a hinge intact). Spread 1 tablespoon mayonnaise on the bottom half of each baguette. Fill each sandwich with pork, pickled daikon and carrot, jalapeños, and cilantro.

Pickled Daikon and Carrot

Yield: About 1 cup

It wouldn't be *bánh mì* without the crisp sweet-and-sour bite of pickled vegetables in the mix. Double the recipe to keep some on hand for snacking!

¼ cup distilled white vinegar
¼ cup sugar
¼ cup water
½ teaspoon coarse salt

1 medium-size carrot, peeled and cut into matchstick strips
½ medium-size daikon radish, peeled and cut into matchstick strips

Whisk together the vinegar, sugar, water, and salt in a medium-size bowl. Add the carrots and daikon. Cover the bowl and refrigerate it for at least 4 hours. The pickles will keep, covered in the refrigerator, for several weeks.

Grilled Bacon

Yield: 6 strips

You won't believe how easy it is to grill bacon on a panini press. It takes less time than frying or baking, and it's the perfect option on hot summer days when you don't want to stand over a stove or turn on the oven.

6 strips uncooked bacon

1. Heat the panini press to medium-high heat. If your panini press comes with a removable drip tray, make sure it is in place (see page 2).

2. Arrange as many bacon slices as will fit neatly on your grill, without overlapping. Depending on the size of your grill, you may need to trim the bacon to fit.

3. If you have a grill that allows you to adjust the height of the upper plate, set it to just barely graze the surface of bacon and not fully press the strips. Close the lid and grill the bacon until it's cooked through and crispy, 10 to 13 minutes, depending on the thickness of your bacon.

Beer-Grilled Bratwursts

Yield: 4 servings

Don't let rain put a damper on your sports watching (and eating) plans. Grill your brats inside on the panini press. Actually, you'll only be finishing the sausages on the grill—the main cooking will happen in a pot full of beer and onions on the stove. While the bratwursts simmer and soak in all that great flavor, grill some onions on the panini press. Then crisp up the brats on the grill—you won't even need to turn them.

Beyond bratwurst, you can grill pretty much any precooked sausage on the panini press—hot dogs, chicken sausages, breakfast links, you name it. The key is to keep the heat on the lower side to avoid bursting the casings. If your panini press doesn't allow you to adjust the heat, you may want to test it out on just one sausage at first.

2 tablespoons butter
2 medium-size onions
4 uncooked bratwursts (about 1 pound)
2 to 3 (12-ounce) bottles or cans beer (see Note)

1 teaspoon vegetable oil
4 bratwurst buns or hot dog buns, toasted if desired
1 cup sauerkraut
German-style or Dijon mustard, to taste

1. Melt the butter in a Dutch oven or large pot over medium-high heat. Halve and slice one of the onions, add the slices to the pot, and cook, stirring occasionally, until they're softened, 4 to 5 minutes. Add the bratwursts and enough beer to cover them. Bring the beer to a boil, then immediately reduce the heat to a simmer. Continue cooking the bratwursts for another 10 minutes (if the total weight of your bratwursts is more than a pound, cook them for an extra few minutes—but not too much longer, as you don't want to overcook these). They will feel denser to the touch when they're done—don't slice into them or all of the juices will escape!

2. While the bratwursts are simmering, heat the panini press to medium-high heat. Slice the remaining onion crosswise into ½-inch-thick rounds, keeping the rings intact. Brush vegetable oil over both sides of the onion rounds and grill them, with the lid closed, until they're tender and grill marks appear, 4 to 6 minutes. Transfer the onions to a plate.

3. Reduce the heat on the panini press to medium-low (if the heat is too high it may cause the bratwurst skin to burst). With a pair of tongs, remove the bratwursts from the beer, set them on the panini press, and close the lid. Grill the bratwursts until dark grill marks appear, 4 to 5 minutes.

4. Serve the bratwursts on buns with grilled onions, sauerkraut, and mustard.

NOTE: Many people suggest using dark beer for braising bratwurst, but at the end of the day you're best off choosing whichever kind you like to drink—or, more accurately, smell, because the aromas of simmering beer are about to fill your kitchen!

Sweet and Smoky Grilled Pork Tenderloin Medallions

Yield: 4 servings

True to its name, this recipe is sweet and smoky—and extremely easy to prepare on a weeknight. I make a quick spice paste, starring brown sugar and smoked paprika, and let it soak into the pork while I prepare a simple side dish. Then, after just 2 minutes on the panini press, the meat is juicy, flavorful . . . and done!

Turn your leftovers from this dish into Pork Tenderloin, Caramelized Pear, and Cheddar Panini (page 110) or Pork Tenderloin, Apple Butter, and Provolone Panini (page 111).

1 tablespoon packed brown sugar
1 teaspoon coarse salt
1 teaspoon smoked paprika
¼ teaspoon dry mustard
¼ teaspoon garlic powder

¼ teaspoon freshly ground black pepper
A dash of cayenne pepper
2 teaspoons vegetable oil
1 (1-pound) pork tenderloin

1. In a small bowl, mix the brown sugar, salt, smoked paprika, dry mustard, garlic powder, black pepper, and cayenne until they're well combined. Stir in the vegetable oil to form a paste.

2. Cut the pork tenderloin crosswise into 8 pieces, each about 1 inch thick. Use the heel of your hand to press each piece into a ½-inch-thick medallion.

3. Rub ¼ to ½ teaspoon of the spice paste over the top and bottom of each pork medallion. Let the pork sit at room temperature for 30 minutes to allow the flavors to seep in.

4. Heat the panini press to high heat. If your panini press comes with a removable drip tray, make sure it is in place (see page 2).

5. Working in batches if necessary, place the pork medallions on the grill and close the lid. Grill the pork until it's cooked to an internal temperature of 145°F, about 2 minutes. Allow the pork to rest for 5 minutes before slicing.

THE BUTCHER'S BEST

Beef and Lamb on the Panini Press

PANINI

MORE FROM THE PANINI PRESS

Roast Beef, Asiago, Tomato, and Watercress Panini

Yield: 4 panini

When I tasted watercress for the first time, I was shocked by just how peppery these greens are. Whoa, almost spicy! It made sense once I learned that watercress is related to radishes and mustard. On its own the flavor of watercress is a bit too strong for me, but paired with roast beef it brings just the right amount of peppery perkiness, much like horseradish does. Not to mention its delicate leaves look really pretty on panini.

½ cup mayonnaise

2 tablespoons pesto, purchased or home-made (page 101; see Note)

1 ciabatta loaf, cut into 4 portions, or 4 ciabatta rolls

8 ounces thinly sliced roast beef

1 (8-ounce) bunch watercress

2 plum tomatoes (such as Roma), thinly sliced and seeded, or 8 Slow-Roasted Tomato halves (page 135)

4 ounces Asiago or Swiss cheese, thinly sliced

1. Heat the panini press to medium-high heat.

2. In a small bowl, whisk together the mayonnaise and pesto until well combined.

3. *For each sandwich:* Split a ciabatta portion to create top and bottom halves. Spread some pesto mayonnaise inside both halves. On the bottom half, layer some roast beef, a small handful of watercress, tomatoes, and cheese. Close the sandwich with the top ciabatta half.

4. Grill two panini at a time, with the lid closed, until the cheese is melted and the ciabatta is toasted, 5 to 7 minutes.

NOTE: Alternatively, if you don't have pesto on hand, you can mix up a quick batch of Basil-Garlic Mayonnaise (page 31).

Roast Beef, Cheddar, and Arugula Salad Panini

Yield: 4 panini

toss together an arugula salad both here and in my Prosciutto, Mozzarella, and Arugula Salad Panini (page 92) for a punch of peppery flavor and acidity. Along with spicy whole-grain mustard, it's the perfect match for the richness of the roast beef and cheddar cheese.

2 cups baby arugula
1 tablespoon White Balsamic Vinaigrette (page 73), or to taste
4 tablespoons (½ stick) butter, at room temperature

8 slices rustic white bread, sliced from a dense bakery loaf
4 ounces sharp cheddar cheese, sliced
8 ounces thinly sliced roast beef
2 tablespoons whole-grain mustard

1. Heat the panini press to medium-high heat.

2. Place the arugula in a medium-size bowl and toss it with about a tablespoon of vinai-grette—more or less, depending on your taste.

3. *For each sandwich:* Spread butter on two slices of bread to flavor the outside of the sandwich. Flip over one slice of bread and top it with cheese, some arugula salad, roast beef, and more cheese. Flip over the other slice of bread and spread a thin layer of mustard on the other side. Close the sandwich with the other slice of bread, buttered side up.

4. Grill two panini at a time, with the lid closed, until the cheese is melted and the bread is toasted, 4 to 5 minutes.

Hawaiian Flank Steak Teriyaki Panini

Yield: 4 panini

Believe it or not, I built these panini around the sweet Maui onions rather than the steak. Just the thought of Maui onions takes me right back to my honeymoon and Kula Lodge, the dark wood restaurant perched on a hillside in the island's upcountry, where they served my husband and me Maui onion soup—with a side of sweeping views of the Pacific. To bring these nostalgia-inducing onions into my sandwiches, I fry them nice and crispy and, in keeping with the Hawaiian mood, match them with teriyaki-marinated flank steak, grilled pineapple, cilantro, and teriyaki mayonnaise. Since there's no cheese to melt on these panini, I simply toast the bread on the panini press rather than grill the sandwiches.

MARINATED FLANK STEAK
3 tablespoons mirin
3 tablespoons reduced-sodium soy sauce
3 tablespoons sake
1 tablespoon packed dark brown sugar
2 teaspoons grated fresh ginger
1 (1- to 1½-pound) flank steak

TERIYAKI MAYONNAISE
½ cup mayonnaise
1 tablespoon reduced-sodium soy sauce
1 tablespoon mirin
1 teaspoon grated fresh ginger

PANINI
1 ciabatta loaf, cut into 4 portions,
   or 4 ciabatta rolls
8 pineapple rings, canned or fresh,
   patted dry with paper towels
¼ cup chopped fresh cilantro
1 recipe Crispy Fried Onions
   (page 124)

1. *Marinated Flank Steak:* Whisk together the mirin, soy sauce, sake, dark brown sugar, and ginger in a small bowl until the sugar has dissolved. Place the flank steak in a large zipper-top plastic bag and pour in the marinade. Seal the bag and rotate the steak around a bit to make sure the marinade fully coats it. Marinate the steak in the refrigerator for at least 4 hours and up to 24 hours.

2. *Teriyaki Mayonnaise:* In a small bowl, whisk together the mayonnaise, soy sauce, mirin, and ginger until well combined and smooth. Refrigerate the mayonnaise until you're ready to use it.

3. *Panini:* Heat the panini press to medium-high heat.

4. Grill two ciabatta portions at a time, cut sides down, until they're toasted and grill marks appear, about 2 minutes. Set aside.

(continued on next page)

5. Grill the pineapple slices, in batches if necessary, until they're caramelized and dark grill marks appear, 3 to 4 minutes. Carefully scrape the excess pineapple juices from the grates with a grill scraper.

6. Raise the heat on the panini press to high. If your panini press comes with a removable drip tray, make sure it is in place (see page 2).

7. Remove the flank steak from the plastic bag, discarding the marinade. Place the steak on the grill, close the lid, and grill the steak to your desired doneness, 8 to 10 minutes for medium (137°F). Allow the steak to rest on a cutting board for 10 minutes before slicing it thinly across the grain. Meanwhile, unplug the grill and, while it's still hot, carefully scrape down the grates with your grill scraper to remove any stuck-on bits of meat.

8. *For each sandwich:* Spread 1 tablespoon teriyaki mayonnaise on the cut sides of a toasted ciabatta portion. On the bottom half, lay 2 pineapple rings, some steak, a sprinkling of chopped cilantro, and some fried onions. Close the panini with the top ciabatta half.

Crispy Fried Onions
Yield: About I cup

I wish I didn't love these onions so much. By the time the last batch is done, I've often already polished off the first batch! Snacking aside, these crispy onions are perfect for adding a savory crunch to beef and vegetable panini or as a garnish for dishes like Grilled Rib-Eye Steak (page 151) or Grilled Salmon with Old Bay Aioli (page 180).

½ cup vegetable oil
½ cup all-purpose flour
½ teaspoon coarse salt

1 sweet onion (such as Maui, Walla Walla, or Vidalia), halved and thinly sliced

I. Heat the vegetable oil in a medium-size skillet over medium-high heat until a pinch of flour sizzles on contact.

2. Combine the flour and salt in a shallow bowl and toss the onions around in the mixture until they're well coated. Carefully add the onions to the hot oil—in batches if necessary to avoid overcrowding the pan—and cook them, stirring occasionally, until they are golden brown and crisp, 4 to 5 minutes. Use a slotted spoon to transfer the onions to a plate lined with paper towels to drain.

Chimichurri Skirt Steak Panini with Provolone and Sun-Dried Tomatoes

Yield: 4 panini

Once you've tried steak with chimichurri sauce, it's a natural inclination to want to make a sandwich out of it. Not only do the tender slices of steak combine beautifully with sharp melted cheese, but the zesty, garlicky Argentine sauce is a real treat when it soaks into bread. Here, I've chosen to use a sturdy French baguette that can absorb all of that sauce without sacrificing its firm texture. A few sun-dried tomatoes scattered over the top bring a sweet burst to each bite.

Use Leftovers: You can make these panini with any leftover steak you have on hand, and substitute pesto (purchased or homemade, page 101) for the chimichurri sauce.

1 French baguette, cut into 4 portions, or 4 mini baguettes
½ cup Chimichurri Sauce (page 147)
1 recipe Chimichurri Skirt Steak (page 146)

¼ cup thinly sliced oil-packed sun-dried tomatoes
4 ounces provolone cheese, sliced

1. Heat the panini press to medium-high heat.

2. *For each sandwich:* Slice off the domed top of a baguette portion to create a flat grilling surface. Split the baguette to create top and bottom halves. Spoon 1 tablespoon chimichurri sauce inside each half. On the bottom half layer steak, sun-dried tomatoes, and cheese. Close the sandwich with the top baguette half.

3. Grill two panini at a time, with the lid closed, until the cheese is melted and the baguettes are toasted, 5 to 7 minutes.

Tri-Tip French Dip Panini au Jus

Yield: 4 panini

Back in 1918, when Philippe Mathieu accidentally dropped a French sandwich roll into a roasting pan filled with hot juices at his Los Angeles restaurant, Philippe the Original, little did he know that he'd invented a sandwich people would love all the way into the next century. It's the rich *jus* (the meat roasting juices) that sets the classic French Dip apart from the rest—the sandwich literally drips with flavor.

I love to grill a nicely marbled tri-tip steak on the panini press and pile it on a baguette with horseradish cheddar and sweet caramelized onions. Since grilling doesn't yield quite the same amount of juices as oven-roasting the beef, I simply simmer my own broth-based *jus* on the stove.

Short on Time? You can use regular deli-sliced roast beef in place of the grilled tri-tip.

TRI-TIP
1 (1½-pound) tri-tip steak
1 teaspoon coarse salt
½ teaspoon freshly ground black pepper

PANINI
1 French baguette, cut into 4 portions, or
   4 mini baguettes
4 ounces horseradish cheddar cheese,
   thinly sliced
1 cup Caramelized Onions (page 19)

JUS
1 tablespoon unsalted butter
1 shallot, thinly sliced
2 garlic cloves, minced
3 cups low-sodium beef broth
1 bay leaf
1 teaspoon dried thyme
½ teaspoon ground coriander
½ teaspoon celery seeds
A pinch of ground cloves
Coarse salt and freshly ground black pepper

1. *Tri-tip:* Heat the panini press to medium-high heat. If your panini press comes with a removable drip tray, make sure it is in place (see page 2).

2. Season the steak with salt and pepper. Set the steak on the grill, close the lid, and grill it to your desired doneness, 20 to 22 minutes for medium (137°F).

3. Transfer the steak to a cutting board. Allow it to rest for at least 10 minutes before slicing it thinly across the grain. You can either clean off your grill at this point or take advantage of the extra flavor those leftover juices will add to your panini when it comes time to grill them.

4. *Jus:* While the steak is grilling, prepare your *jus.* In a medium-size saucepan, melt the butter over medium heat. Add the shallot and cook, stirring occasionally, until softened, about 2 minutes. Add the garlic and cook until the garlic is fragrant and just beginning to brown, another 30 to 60 seconds. Pour in the beef broth and add the bay leaf, thyme, coriander, celery seeds, and cloves. Bring the broth to a simmer and continue simmering for 15 minutes to allow the flavors to blend. Remove the *jus* from the heat and season with salt and pepper to taste. Discard the bay leaf and cover the pan to keep the broth warm.

5. *Panini:* Reheat the panini press to medium-high heat.

6. *For each sandwich:* Slice off the domed top of a baguette portion to create a flat grilling surface. Split the baguette to create top and bottom halves. Inside the bottom half, layer on cheese, caramelized onions, tri-tip, and more cheese. Close the sandwich with the top baguette half.

7. Grill two panini at a time, with the lid closed, until the cheese is melted and the baguettes are toasted, 5 to 7 minutes. Serve each sandwich with a little bowl of warm *jus* for dipping.

Grilled Steak Tortas

Yield: 4 tortas

This recipe calls for cumin-grilled flatiron steak and *rajas* (grilled red bell peppers, poblanos, and onions) for you to turn into Mexican steak tortas, but in reality these hearty grilled sandwiches are an excellent way to use up any leftover meat or chicken you might have on hand. You just split a sandwich roll, spread on some refried beans, and then top them with meat, cheese, *rajas*, and any other toppings you like.

STEAK
1 (1-pound) flatiron or top blade steak
1 teaspoon coarse salt
1 teaspoon garlic powder
½ teaspoon ground cumin
½ teaspoon freshly ground black pepper

TORTAS
½ cup refried beans
4 *bolillo* or *telera* rolls (kaiser rolls will also work well)
1 recipe *Rajas* (page 292)
1 medium-size ripe avocado, pitted, peeled, and sliced
4 ounces pepper Jack cheese, sliced

1. *Steak:* Heat the panini press to high heat. If your panini press comes with a removable drip tray, make sure it is in place (see page 2).

2. Season both sides of the steak with salt, garlic powder, cumin, and pepper. Grill the steak, with the lid closed, to your desired doneness, 5 to 7 minutes for medium (137°F).

3. Transfer the steak to a cutting board and let it rest for 10 minutes before slicing it very thinly across the grain. Meanwhile, unplug the grill and, while it's still hot, carefully scrape down the grates with a grill scraper to remove any stuck-on bits of meat.

4. *Tortas:* Reheat the panini press to medium-high heat. Heat the refried beans in a small saucepan over medium heat, stirring occasionally.

5. *For each sandwich:* Split a roll to create top and bottom halves. Spread 2 tablespoons refried beans on the bottom half of the roll. Top it with steak, *rajas*, avocado, and cheese. Close the sandwich with the top half of the roll.

6. Grill two tortas at a time, with the lid closed, until the cheese is melted and the rolls are toasted, 4 to 5 minutes.

Green Chile Steak Melt Panini

Yield: 4 panini

At the end of a long day of kite flying and butterfly chasing on a family vacation in Santa Barbara, I ordered a fantastic spicy steak sandwich at a restaurant that evening. It was a Southwestern take on the classic cheese steak, made with thinly sliced steak, chiles, onions, pepper Jack cheese, and chipotle *crema* on a baguette. The concept went straight into the Notes app on my iPhone to remind me to re-create it when I got back home. For my version, I caramelized the onions to bring in more sweetness and dialed down the spice level a touch by using Monterey Jack rather than pepper Jack. Lastly, I converted the chipotle *crema* to a chipotle mayonnaise (which still has a touch of cooling sour cream in it).

Use Leftovers: If you've got leftover steak on hand, go ahead and use it here instead of grilling a new steak.

1 (1-pound) New York strip steak
Coarse salt and freshly ground black pepper
1 ciabatta loaf, cut into 4 portions, or
   4 ciabatta rolls
1 recipe Chipotle Mayonnaise (recipe follows)

4 ounces Monterey Jack cheese, sliced
1 cup Caramelized Onions (page 19)
1 (7-ounce) can roasted whole green chiles,
   drained and chopped

1. Heat the panini press to high heat. If your panini press comes with a removable drip tray, make sure it is in place (see page 2).

2. Season the steak generously with salt and pepper.

3. Grill the steak, with the lid closed, to your desired doneness, 10 to 15 minutes for medium (137°F). Transfer the steak to a cutting board and let it rest for 10 minutes before slicing it very thinly across the grain. Meanwhile, unplug the grill and, while it's still hot, scrape down the grates with a grill scraper. Let the grill cool, and clean the grates.

4. Reheat the panini press to medium-high heat.

5. *For each sandwich:* Split the ciabatta to create top and bottom halves. Spread 1 tablespoon chipotle mayonnaise inside each half. On the bottom half layer cheese, steak, onions, chiles, and more cheese. Close the sandwich with the top half.

6. Grill two panini at a time, with the lid closed, until the cheese is melted and the rolls are toasted, 5 to 7 minutes.

Chipotle Mayonnaise

Yield: About ½ cup

Get ready for a Southwestern kick! Smoky chipotle peppers (which are ripe jalapeños that have been smoke-dried) bring fiery flavor to this spread, which I adore on everything from steak to turkey to salmon. The sour cream cools things off, keeping the spice level in check. If you find it too hot for your taste, just add more sour cream.

½ cup mayonnaise
1 tablespoon sour cream
1 tablespoon finely chopped chives

1 canned chipotle in adobo sauce, plus
   1½ teaspoons of the adobo sauce
1 teaspoon freshly squeezed lemon juice
Coarse salt and freshly ground black pepper

Combine the mayonnaise, sour cream, chives, chipotle, adobo sauce, and lemon juice in a food processor or blender. Process or blend until smooth. Season the mayonnaise with salt and pepper to taste. Cover the bowl and refrigerate the mayonnaise until you are ready to serve it.

Cheese Steak Panini

Yield: 4 panini

A lot of folks swear that for a truly authentic Philly cheese steak, you've got to go to Philadelphia—and I'm inclined to believe them. But I still like to make my own Philly-style cheese steaks at home, grilling a juicy flatiron steak, slicing it thin, and piling it on a roll with grilled onions, sharp provolone, and hot peppers.

GRILLED STEAK
1 (1-pound) flatiron or top blade steak
1 teaspoon coarse salt
1 teaspoon garlic powder
½ teaspoon freshly ground black pepper

PANINI
1 tablespoon vegetable oil

1 medium-size onion, cut crosswise into ½-inch-thick slices (rings intact)
Coarse salt and freshly ground black pepper
1 ciabatta loaf, cut into 4 portions, or 4 ciabatta rolls
4 to 6 jarred hot Italian peppers, such as banana peppers or fried "longhot" cayenne peppers, sliced
4 ounces sharp provolone, sliced

1. *Grilled Steak:* Heat the panini press to high. If your panini press comes with a removable drip tray, make sure it is in place (see page 2).

2. Season both sides of the steak with salt, garlic powder, and pepper. Grill the steak, with the lid closed, to your desired doneness, 5 to 7 minutes for medium (137°F).

3. Transfer the steak to a cutting board and let it rest for 10 minutes before slicing it very thinly across the grain. Meanwhile, unplug the panini press and, while it's still hot, carefully scrape down the grates with a grill scraper to remove any stuck-on bits of meat. Allow the grill to cool and clean the grates.

4. *Panini:* Reheat the panini press to medium-high heat.

5. Brush oil on both sides of the onion slices and season them with salt and pepper. Grill the onions until they're tender and dark grill marks appear, 6 to 8 minutes. Transfer the onions to a bowl and toss them to break up the rings.

6. *For each sandwich:* Split a ciabatta portion to create top and bottom halves. Pile some of the onion rings inside the bottom half and add sliced steak, peppers, and cheese. Close the sandwich with the top half.

7. Grill two panini at a time, with the lid closed, until the cheese is melted and the ciabatta is toasted, 5 to 6 minutes.

Meatloaf Melt Panini

Yield: 4 panini

Out of all the panini that I make from leftovers, these set themselves apart in an important way: a built-in condiment. It's the ketchup—or barbecue sauce or marinara, or whatever sauce you might have chosen to top your meatloaf. Each slice comes with its own strip of sauce, so all you need to add is cheese, onions, and bread, and you've got a perfect sandwich.

As an aside, can you think about meatloaf without hearing Will Ferrell hollering "MA! THE MEATLOAF!!" as Chazz in the movie *Wedding Crashers*? Neither can I.

4 tablespoons (½ stick) butter, at room temperature

8 slices rye or other rustic bread, sliced from a dense bakery loaf

1 cup Caramelized Onions (page 19)

4 thick slices leftover meatloaf, preferably with a topping like ketchup

4 ounces Swiss or sharp cheddar cheese, sliced

1. Heat the panini press to medium-high heat.

2. *For each sandwich:* Spread butter on two slices of bread to flavor the outside of the sandwich. Flip over one slice of bread and top it with caramelized onions, a slice of meatloaf, and cheese. Close the sandwich with the other slice of bread, buttered side up.

3. Grill two panini at a time, with the lid closed, until the cheese is melted and the bread is toasted, 4 to 5 minutes.

California Steak Panini

Yield: 4 panini

There is a San Diego food specialty that the tourist guidebooks probably won't tell you about. You can get it at one place only, and you actually have to cook it yourself. It's the burgundy pepper tri-tip—affectionately dubbed "Cardiff Crack" by those in the know—at Seaside Market in Cardiff-by-the-Sea. Bathing an already flavorful cut of beef in a bold marinade is bound to get you some notice. It's no surprise that they don't publicize the recipe, or I'd tell you what was in it. The best way I can describe it is that it tastes just like a really great steak, only better.

I call these California Steak Panini because each of the ingredients is particularly beloved in my home state. I usually make them with leftover marinated tri-tip from Seaside Market, but this simple salt-and-pepper steak works great, too.

TRI-TIP
1 (1½-pound) tri-tip steak
1 teaspoon coarse salt
½ teaspoon freshly ground black pepper

PANINI
4 tablespoons Chipotle Mayonnaise (page 131) or purchased plain mayonnaise

4 sourdough rolls
1 medium-size ripe avocado, pitted, peeled, and sliced
8 Slow-Roasted Tomato halves (recipe follows) or oil-packed sun-dried tomatoes
4 ounces Monterey Jack or pepper Jack cheese, sliced

1. *Tri-tip:* Heat the panini press to medium-high heat. If your panini press comes with a removable drip tray, make sure it is in place (see page 2).

2. Season the steak with salt and pepper. Set the steak on the grill, close the lid, and grill to your desired doneness, 20 to 22 minutes for medium (137°F).

3. Transfer the steak to a cutting board and allow it to rest for at least 10 minutes before slicing it thinly across the grain. You can either clean off your grill at this point or take advantage of the extra flavor those leftover juices will add to your panini when it comes time to grill them.

4. Reheat the panini press to medium-high heat.

5. *For each sandwich:* Split a roll to create top and bottom halves. Spread 1 tablespoon chipotle mayonnaise inside the bottom half. Layer on avocado slices, steak, 2 tomato halves, and cheese. Close the sandwich with the top half of the roll.

6. Grill two panini at a time, with the lid closed, until the cheese is melted and the rolls are toasted, 5 to 7 minutes.

Slow-Roasted Tomatoes

Yield: 24 halves

Even sweeter than fresh tomatoes and plumper than sun-dried ones, roasted tomatoes bring big, juicy bursts of flavor to everything from panini to pasta to pizzas. Just let them bake away in a low oven for several hours, all the while filling your kitchen with marinara-like aromas. I adapted this simple method from the Smitten Kitchen blog.

12 plum tomatoes (such as Roma), halved lengthwise
Extra-virgin olive oil

Coarse salt and freshly ground black pepper

1. Heat the oven to 225°F. Arrange the tomato halves, cut sides up, on a parchment-lined baking sheet. Drizzle the tomatoes lightly with olive oil and season them with salt and pepper. Use a light hand with the seasoning, as the tomatoes will be naturally very flavorful once they are roasted.

2. Roast the tomatoes in the oven until they are shriveled and mostly dry, 3 to 4 hours.

3. Use the tomatoes immediately or allow them to cool, cover them with more olive oil, and store them in the refrigerator for sandwiches, pasta, pizzas, or just snacking over the next several days.

Cheeseburger Patty Melt Panini

Yield: 4 panini

I might go so far as to say that a patty melt is even better than a regular burger. Grilled on rye bread and enveloped in cheese, a patty melt tends to hold its ingredients intact better than its burger counterpart. Condiments like grilled onions and Thousand Island dressing are an insurance policy, so that on the off chance you overcook the patty, you'll still end up with a flavorful sandwich. And then there's the rye bread—bread that actually *tastes like something*—cradling your burger patty. Yup, give me a good patty melt over a regular burger any day.

1 tablespoon vegetable oil

1 medium-size onion, sliced into ½-inch-thick rounds (rings intact)

1 pound 85% lean ground beef

1 teaspoon coarse salt

½ teaspoon freshly ground black pepper

4 tablespoons (½ stick) butter, at room temperature

8 slices rye bread or rustic white bread, sliced from a dense bakery loaf

4 ounces sharp cheddar or Swiss cheese, sliced

1 recipe Thousand Island Dressing (page 141)

1. Heat the panini press to medium-high heat. If your panini press comes with a removable drip tray, make sure it is in place (see page 2).

2. Brush vegetable oil on both sides of the onions. Grill the onions until they're tender and dark grill marks appear, 6 to 8 minutes. Transfer the grilled onions to a plate.

3. While the onions are grilling, divide the ground beef into four equal patties. Season the patties on both sides with salt and pepper. After the onions are cooked, grill the burgers to your desired doneness, 4 to 5 minutes for medium (137°F). Carefully scrape the grates with a grill scraper to remove most of the excess grease and cooked-on bits (they don't need to be completely clean).

4. *For each sandwich:* Spread butter on two slices of bread to flavor the outside of the sandwich. Flip over one slice and top the other side with cheese, grilled onions, a burger patty, a dollop of Thousand Island dressing, and more cheese. Close the sandwich with the other slice of bread, buttered side up.

5. Grill two panini at a time, with the lid closed, until the cheese is melted and the bread is toasted, 4 to 5 minutes.

Southwestern Chili Panini

Yield: 4 panini

As you might imagine, being married to someone who writes a panini blog is pretty rewarding when it comes to having good lunch options to bring to work—just ask my husband. When I grill sandwiches I'll often eat half, wrap the rest in aluminum foil, and stick it in the fridge. Mike grabs a few of these foil packets on his way out the door to work every morning and is greeted with a (hopefully nice) surprise when he unwraps them at lunchtime.

When the mystery foil revealed my Southwestern Chili Panini one day, Mike was a little unsure of what he was eating. He knew that he loved the blend of flavors—often these things taste even better the next day—and there curiously seemed to be beans in the sandwich. "What was that?" he asked later that evening. Apparently, my transformation of the previous night's leftover chili into a deluxe sloppy joe had stood up as a dish on its own. Success!

4 ciabatta or sourdough rolls
½ small red onion, sliced
1 cup leftover chili

¼ cup sour cream
4 ounces sharp cheddar cheese, sliced

1. Heat the panini press to medium-high heat.

2. *For each sandwich:* Split a roll, but don't cut all the way through—leave a hinge intact to help keep the chili from falling out of the sandwich. Pull some of the crumbs out of the interior of the roll to make extra room for the fillings. Lay a few red onion slices inside the bottom half of the roll. Top them with a few spoonfuls of chili, a dollop of sour cream, and some cheddar cheese.

3. Grill two panini at a time, with the lid closed, until the cheese is melted and the rolls are toasted, 6 to 7 minutes.

Pastrami and Aged Cheddar Panini

Yield: 4 panini

I thought I knew pastrami until I tasted the famous pastrami sandwich at Katz's Delicatessen on Manhattan's Lower East Side. Just thinking about it now makes my mouth water. Thick, juicy (let's be honest, there's fat involved here) slices of some of the most flavorful 30-day cured beef imaginable. Seriously, put it on your dining bucket list—I had no idea pastrami could be that good. In the meantime, enjoy my favorite smoky and tangy pastrami panini at home, with sharp aged cheddar, pepperoncini, and horseradish sauce.

8 slices pumpernickel bread, sliced from a
  dense bakery loaf
1 recipe Horseradish Sauce (recipe follows)
4 ounces thinly sliced pastrami

2 tablespoons sliced pepperoncini (see
  Note)
4 ounces sharp aged cheddar cheese, thinly
  sliced

1. Heat the panini press to medium-high heat.

2. *For each sandwich:* Spread horseradish sauce on one slice of bread. Top it with pastrami, pepperoncini, and cheese. Close the sandwich with a second slice of bread.

3. Grill two panini at a time, with the lid closed, until the cheese is melted and the bread is toasted, 4 to 5 minutes.

NOTE: You can find jarred pepperoncini—pickled sweet or hot Italian peppers— in the condiments aisle at the grocery store, near the olives.

Horseradish Sauce

Yield: About ½ cup

This horseradish sauce, which won't clear out your nostrils like straight prepared horseradish, is the perfect accompaniment to any beef dish.

¼ cup sour cream
2 tablespoons mayonnaise
1 tablespoon prepared horseradish
1 teaspoon finely grated onion

½ teaspoon Worcestershire sauce
Coarse salt and freshly ground black
  pepper

Whisk together the sour cream, mayonnaise, horseradish, onion, and Worcestershire sauce in a small bowl, and season with salt and pepper to taste. Cover the bowl and refrigerate the sauce until you're ready to use it.

Reuben Panini

Yield: 4 panini

Once upon a time I asked Panini Happy readers to name their favorite sandwich. The overwhelming choice turned out to be the Reuben. It wasn't hard for me to understand why. Just the sight of all of that bright pink, salty corned beef piled on top of mouthwatering sauerkraut, with Thousand Island dressing and melted Swiss cheese on rye . . . well, you know you're in for a flavor explosion.

There are lots of Reuben variations out there—some use turkey or pastrami instead of corned beef, some opt for Russian dressing rather than Thousand Island. This version happens to be the one I like best, especially after St. Patrick's Day, when there is leftover corned beef in the fridge.

4 tablespoons (½ stick) butter, at room
   temperature
8 slices rye bread, sliced from a dense
   bakery loaf
4 ounces Swiss cheese, sliced

8 ounces sliced corned beef
1 recipe Thousand Island Dressing (recipe
   follows)
½ cup sauerkraut

1. Heat the panini press to medium-high heat.

2. *For each sandwich:* Spread butter on two slices of bread to flavor the outside of the sandwich. Flip over one slice and top the other side with cheese, corned beef, a dollop of Thousand Island dressing, sauerkraut, and more cheese. Close the sandwich with the other slice of bread, buttered side up.

3. Grill two panini at a time, with the lid closed, until the cheese is melted and the bread is toasted, 4 to 5 minutes.

Thousand Island Dressing

Yield: About ½ cup

Classic Thousand Island dressing is good for more than just an iceberg lettuce salad. Use this creamy, tangy condiment for everything from a spread for burgers and turkey sandwiches to a dip for shrimp.

½ cup mayonnaise
2 tablespoons ketchup
2 teaspoons sweet pickle relish
2 teaspoons Worcestershire sauce

2 teaspoons minced onion
Coarse salt and freshly ground black
   pepper

Whisk together the mayonnaise, ketchup, pickle relish, Worcestershire sauce, and onion in a small bowl, and season with salt and pepper to taste. Cover the bowl and refrigerate the dressing until you're ready to use it.

Lamb, Asiago, and Tomato Panini

Yield: 4 panini

Have leftover lamb in the fridge? Then chances are you've already got all of the ingredients you need to make these flavorful lamb panini. The secret to this recipe is the basil-garlic mayonnaise. You'll see it pop up throughout this cookbook because it's such a fabulous, easy way to punch up the flavor in so many types of sandwiches. Here, the basil and garlic are a perfect match for lamb.

Make It Fresh: By all means, don't wait until you've got leftovers to make these panini. Grill the Marinated Lamb Chops on page 152 to make these sandwiches anytime you get the urge.

4 tablespoons (½ stick) butter, at room temperature

8 slices rustic white bread, sliced from a dense bakery loaf

1 recipe Basil-Garlic Mayonnaise (page 31)

8 ounces leftover cooked lamb, thinly sliced

2 plum tomatoes (such as Roma), thinly sliced and seeded, or 8 Slow-Roasted Tomato halves (page 135)

4 ounces Asiago or provolone cheese, sliced

1. Heat the panini press to medium-high heat.

2. *For each sandwich:* Spread butter on two slices of bread to flavor the outside of the sandwich. Flip over both slices of bread and spread on a thin layer of basil-garlic mayonnaise. On one slice of bread layer lamb, tomatoes, and cheese. Close the sandwich with the other slice of bread, buttered side up.

3. Grill two panini at a time, with the lid closed, until the cheese is melted and the bread is toasted, 4 to 5 minutes.

Lamb, Fig, and Goat Cheese Panini with Fennel Slaw

Yield: 4 panini

ne of the best ways I know to add crunch and acidity to a sandwich is with a slaw. Here, a simple slaw with shaved fennel tossed in lemon juice and olive oil is the perfect complement to the marinated lamb, sweet fig preserves, and creamy goat cheese.

1 French baguette, cut into 4 portions, or
   4 mini baguettes
4 tablespoons fig preserves
4 ounces goat cheese, at room temperature,
   sliced into thin medallions

1 recipe Fennel Slaw (recipe follows)
8 ounces Marinated Lamb Chops (page
   152) or leftover cooked lamb or beef,
   thinly sliced

1. Heat the panini press to medium-high heat.

2. *For each sandwich:* Slice off the domed top of a baguette portion to create a flat grilling surface. Split the baguette to create top and bottom halves. Spread 1 tablespoon fig preserves inside the bottom half and a layer of goat cheese inside the top half. Top the preserves with fennel slaw and lamb. Close the sandwich with the top baguette half.

3. Grill two panini at a time, with the lid closed, until the goat cheese is softened and the baguettes are toasted, 3 to 4 minutes.

Fennel Slaw

Yield: About 1½ cups

This slaw is a fresh, crisp, flavorful side dish in its own right, but the raw fennel and lemony dressing also bring wonderful crunch and acidity to panini.

1 tablespoon extra-virgin olive oil
1 tablespoon freshly squeezed lemon juice
A pinch of sugar

Coarse salt and freshly ground black
   pepper
1 medium-size fennel bulb

In a medium-size bowl, whisk together the olive oil, lemon juice, and sugar. Season the dressing with a few pinches of salt and pepper to taste. Cut off the stalks and fronds from the fennel bulb and save them for another use. With a sharp knife or, ideally, a mandoline, carefully shave the fennel into very thin slices. Toss the shaved fennel with the dressing.

Greek Lamb Panini with Feta, Tapenade, and Sun-Dried Tomatoes

Yield: 4 panini

can add feta, olive tapenade, and sun-dried tomatoes to almost anything and be happy. These zesty Mediterranean flavors go particularly well with lamb.

4 pita breads
4 tablespoons olive tapenade
½ small red onion, thinly sliced
8 ounces Marinated Lamb Chops (page 152) or leftover cooked lamb or beef, thinly sliced

8 oil-packed sun-dried tomatoes, thinly sliced, or 8 Slow-Roasted Tomato halves (page 135)
8 fresh basil leaves, roughly torn
4 ounces crumbled feta cheese

1. Heat the panini press to medium-high heat.

2. *For each sandwich:* Cut a pita in half across the diameter, creating two semicircles—these will become your top and bottom halves. Spread 1 tablespoon tapenade on one pita half. Top the tapenade with red onions, lamb, sun-dried tomatoes, basil, and feta. Close the sandwich with the other pita half.

3. Grill two panini at a time, with the lid closed, until they're heated through and the pitas are toasted, 3 to 4 minutes.

Chimichurri Skirt Steak

Yield: 2 to 4 servings

've chosen to dress this simple grilled skirt steak in chimichurri sauce, but you can always take the same steak, add your own favorite seasonings, and use it in tacos, salads, or, of course, sandwiches. You may want to double the recipe to make Chimichurri Skirt Steak Panini with Provolone and Sun-Dried Tomatoes (page 125) later in the week.

1 (1-pound) skirt steak (see Note)
Coarse salt and freshly ground black pepper

1 recipe Chimichurri Sauce (recipe follows)

1. About 30 minutes before you're ready to grill, set the steak out at room temperature. If necessary, trim the length of the steak strips to fit your grill.

2. Heat the panini press to high heat. If your panini press comes with a removable drip tray, make sure it is in place (see page 2).

3. Pat the steak dry with paper towels, season it generously with salt and pepper, and place it on the grill. Close the lid so that the upper plate is resting on the meat.

4. Grill the steak until it's cooked to your desired doneness, 4 to 5 minutes for medium (137°F).

5. Let the steak rest for 5 minutes before slicing it thinly across the grain, with your knife set at a 45° angle (this will give you really tender slices). Serve the steak with the chimichurri sauce.

NOTE: You might be able to find skirt steak in the butcher department of your regular grocery store; if not, look for it at a specialty grocer or butcher shop. Alternatively, you can substitute flank steak for this recipe.

Chimichurri Sauce

Yield: About ¾ cup

The first time I ever tried chimichurri sauce I was blown away by how much fresh, herby, garlicky flavor was packed inside it. The sauce, which originated in Argentina, reminds me a bit of pesto, minus the creaminess. It's the kind of stuff that makes you start looking around your fridge and pantry for all kinds of ways to use it—bread to drizzle it on, potatoes to toss it in for a salad, vegetables to marinate in it. You don't want a single drop of this to go to waste.

1 cup packed finely chopped fresh Italian parsley
4 garlic cloves, minced
½ cup extra-virgin olive oil
1 tablespoon red wine vinegar
1 tablespoon freshly squeezed lemon juice
1 tablespoon dried oregano
1 teaspoon coarse salt
¼ teaspoon freshly ground black pepper
¼ teaspoon red pepper flakes

Combine all of the ingredients in a medium nonreactive bowl and set the sauce aside at room temperature until ready to use. You can store any leftover chimichurri sauce in an airtight container in the refrigerator for a day or two—just bring it back to room temperature before you serve it.

Grilled Flank Steak Fajitas

Yield: 4 servings

Fajitas are high on my list of go-to weeknight meals. Everyone in my house customizes what goes into their tortillas, so we're all happy. The hardest part is remembering to marinate the meat ahead of time so all of those fabulous Southwestern flavors have a chance to sink in. The 20 minutes that it takes for the steak to grill and rest gives me ample time to sauté some bell peppers and onions and assemble all of our fixings. Yay, fajita night!

3 tablespoons extra-virgin olive oil
½ cup reduced-sodium soy sauce
2 tablespoons freshly squeezed lime juice
2 tablespoons packed brown sugar
1 tablespoon ancho chile powder
2 teaspoons ground cumin
1 teaspoon ground coriander
¼ teaspoon cayenne pepper
2 garlic cloves, minced
1 (1¼-pound) flank steak (see Note)
1 medium-size onion, halved and sliced
1 red bell pepper, cored, seeded, and sliced
1 green bell pepper, cored, seeded, and sliced

ACCOMPANIMENTS
Warm flour tortillas
Sliced avocados
Chopped tomatoes
Sour cream
Shredded cheddar and/or Monterey Jack cheese
Salsa

1. In a small bowl, whisk together 2 tablespoons of the olive oil, the soy sauce, lime juice, brown sugar, ancho chile powder, cumin, coriander, cayenne, and garlic.

2. Place the flank steak in a large zipper-top bag. Pour in the marinade and seal the bag. Gently squeeze the steak around in the bag a bit to ensure the marinade coats it well. Transfer the bag to the refrigerator and marinate the steak for 8 hours.

3. Heat the panini press to high heat. If your panini press comes with a removable drip tray, make sure it is in place (see page 2).

4. Remove the steak from the marinade (discard the remaining marinade) and pat it dry with paper towels. Lay the steak on the grill, close the lid, and cook the steak to your desired doneness, 8 to 10 minutes for medium (137°F). Let the steak rest on a cutting board for 10 minutes before slicing it thinly across the grain.

5. Meanwhile, heat a large skillet over medium high heat. Swirl in the remaining 1 tablespoon olive oil and add the onion and bell peppers. Cook the vegetables, stirring occasionally, until they're tender, about 10 minutes.

6. Serve the steak, onions, and peppers in warm flour tortillas. Dress up the fajitas however you like, with accompaniments such as sliced avocado, chopped tomatoes, sour cream, shredded cheese, and salsa.

NOTE: Depending on the size of your grill, you may need to trim the steak in order for it to fit.

Ten Summertime Dinners to Make on the Panini Press

It's six o'clock, and it's too hot in the kitchen to turn on the stove or oven for longer than 5 minutes. Here is your summertime answer to getting dinner on the table: ten tasty meals you can prepare right on your panini press.

1. **Chicken Teriyaki** (page 63)
2. **Spatchcocked Game Hen** (page 68)
3. **Grilled Rib-Eye Steak** (page 151)
4. **Marinated Lamb Shawarma** (page 153)
5. **Grilled Shrimp Tostadas with Mashed Black Beans and Avocado Salsa Fresca** (page 177)
6. **Grilled Salmon Packets with Pesto and Tomatoes** (page 179)
7. **Grilled Salmon with Old Bay Aioli** (page 180)
8. **Grilled Fish Tacos** (page 186)
9. **Grilled Tofu and Bok Choy Bowl** (page 233)
10. **Spinach-Feta Quinoa Cakes with Lemon-Dill Yogurt Sauce** (page 234)

Of course, panini with a side salad makes a great dinner option, too!

Grilled Rib-Eye Steak

Yield: 2 servings

Most often I grill with big-flavor marinades, but once in a while I yearn for the simplicity of the salt-and-pepper-only route. Especially when I've got a thick, wonderfully marbled cut of meat like a rib-eye, I want the natural richness of the meat to really shine through.

1 (1¼-pound) rib-eye steak, about
  1½ inches thick
1 tablespoon extra-virgin olive oil

Freshly ground black pepper
Coarse salt

1. Pat the steak dry with paper towels, rub olive oil all over it, and season it generously with black pepper. Set it out at room temperature for about 30 minutes.

2. Heat the panini press to high heat. If your panini press comes with a removable drip tray, make sure it is in place (see page 2).

3. Season the steak generously with coarse salt and set it on the grill. Close the lid so that it's resting right on top of the meat. Don't bother adjusting the height of the upper plate (if your grill has that feature). The steak will shrink a little as it cooks, and if your grill height is in a fixed position it will likely lose contact with the meat.

4. Grill the steak to your desired doneness, 12 to 15 minutes for medium (137°F). If your steak happens to weigh more or less than 1¼ pounds, just adjust your grilling time. I can't underscore enough how helpful an instant-read thermometer is for grilling to the right temperature.

5. Let the steak rest for 10 minutes on a cutting board before slicing it thinly across the grain.

Marinated Lamb Chops

Yield: 4 servings

W hat do you mean *he don't eat no meat?!*" Aunt Voula reacts in disbelief to Toula's vegetarian fiancé in *My Big Fat Greek Wedding*. Everyone around them stops their conversations and stares. "That's okay. That's okay. I make lamb!" Thanks to that hilarious movie I can't help but think to myself "I make lamb" whenever I'm getting ready to grill these chops. Not only are they an incredibly easy weeknight main dish—after marinating in the refrigerator overnight they grill in less than 20 minutes—but the juicy, flavorful meat (sorry, Aunt Voula!) is perfect for sandwiches. Use any leftovers for Marinated Lamb Shawarma (page 153), Greek Lamb Panini with Feta, Tapenade, and Sun-Dried Tomatoes (page 144), or Lamb, Asiago, and Tomato Panini (page 142).

¼ cup extra-virgin olive oil
¼ cup balsamic vinegar
2 teaspoons dried rosemary
2 garlic cloves, minced
1 teaspoon Dijon mustard

½ teaspoon freshly ground black pepper
2 pounds boneless lamb shoulder chops, about 1 inch thick (see Note)
½ teaspoon coarse salt

1. In a small bowl, whisk together the olive oil, balsamic vinegar, rosemary, garlic, mustard, and black pepper. Pour the marinade into a large zipper-top plastic bag. Add the lamb chops and gently massage the marinade into the meat. Seal the bag and marinate the lamb in the refrigerator for at least 4 hours, and preferably overnight.

2. Heat the panini press to high heat. If your panini press comes with a removable drip tray, make sure it is in place (see page 2).

3. Remove the lamb from the marinade (discard the remaining marinade) and pat it dry with paper towels. Season the lamb chops on both sides with salt. Working in batches, grill the lamb, with the lid closed, until it's cooked to an internal temperature of 145°F, 6 to 8 minutes. Allow the lamb to rest for 10 minutes on a cutting board before slicing it thinly across the grain.

NOTE: Shoulder chops are usually sold boneless, but if you can find only bone-in chops, buy slightly more than 2 pounds. Bone-in chops may take a little longer to cook—be sure to check the temperature with a meat thermometer.

Marinated Lamb Shawarma

Yield: 4 shawarmas

Whenever I see a guy standing in a Middle Eastern food stand or restaurant expertly shaving thin strips of the most flavorful slow-roasted meat imaginable from a vertical spit, I find it nearly impossible to resist placing an order. Shawarma is the name not only of this incredible style of meat preparation, but also of the sandwiches made from this meat. Until I'm able to get one of those rotisseries installed in my house, I will settle for the next best way to make shawarma at home—with marinated lamb chops grilled on my panini press.

4 pita breads
4 red leaf lettuce leaves
2 medium-size ripe tomatoes, thinly sliced
½ cucumber, peeled and thinly sliced

¼ medium-size red onion, thinly sliced
1 recipe Marinated Lamb Chops (page 152)
1 recipe Lemon-Dill Yogurt Sauce (page 235)

For each shawarma: If your pitas are dry, heat them for a few seconds in the microwave so they'll fold more easily without breaking. Lay a lettuce leaf on top of one of the pitas. Top it with tomatoes, cucumbers, onions, and lamb. Add a few spoonfuls of the yogurt sauce on top. Carefully fold the pita in half and enjoy.

GIFTS FROM THE SEA

Seafood on the Panini Press

PANINI

MORE FROM THE PANINI PRESS

Grilled Shrimp, Mango, and Avocado Panini with Pepper Jelly and Monterey Jack Cheese

Yield: 4 panini

always keep frozen shrimp on hand—they defrost and cook quickly for weeknight dinners or for sandwiches like these. Here, I give my panini-grilled shrimp the sweet and spicy treatment with ripe, fresh mangoes and pepper jelly.

8 ounces raw medium-size shrimp, peeled and deveined

2 teaspoons vegetable oil

Coarse salt and freshly ground black pepper

1 ciabatta loaf, cut into 4 portions, or 4 ciabatta rolls

4 tablespoons pepper jelly

1 medium-size ripe mango, pitted, peeled, and sliced

1 medium-size ripe avocado, pitted, peeled, and sliced

4 ounces Monterey Jack cheese, sliced

1. Heat the panini press to medium-high heat.

2. In a medium-size bowl, toss the shrimp in the oil and season them lightly with salt and pepper.

3. Arrange the shrimp in a single layer on the grill (work in batches if necessary) and close the lid. Grill the shrimp until they're cooked through and opaque, about 2 minutes.

4. Unplug the grill and, while it's still hot, carefully scrape off any cooked-on shrimp with a grill scraper. Once the grill is cool, clean the grates.

5. Reheat the panini press to medium-high heat.

6. *For each sandwich:* Split a ciabatta portion to create top and bottom halves. Spread pepper jelly inside both halves of the roll. On the bottom half layer mango slices, grilled shrimp, avocado slices, and Monterey Jack. Close the sandwich with the other ciabatta half.

7. Grill two panini at a time, with the lid closed, until the cheese is melted and the ciabatta is toasted, 5 to 7 minutes.

Greek Shrimp Panini with Pesto, Feta, and Sun-Dried Tomatoes

Yield: 4 panini

The trouble with making sandwiches with shrimp is that the little guys have a tendency to slip and slide around a bit. I've played around with a lot of different shrimp panini concepts and I finally figured out the key to making them work: a wide berth of bread. Give shrimp a little wiggle room—either on a dense sliced bread or a wider ciabatta—and they play nicely with your other ingredients. Which is a very good thing, because these flavorful panini deserve to be grilled as often as possible.

8 ounces raw medium-size shrimp, peeled and deveined
2 teaspoons vegetable oil
Coarse salt and freshly ground black pepper
1 ciabatta loaf, cut into 4 portions, or 4 ciabatta rolls

4 tablespoons pesto, purchased or home-made (page 101)
4 ounces crumbled feta cheese
8 oil-packed sun-dried tomatoes, thinly sliced
4 fresh basil leaves, roughly torn

1. Heat the panini press to medium-high heat.

2. In a medium-size bowl, toss the shrimp in the oil to coat them. Season the shrimp lightly with salt and pepper.

3. Arrange the shrimp in a single layer on the grill (work in batches if necessary) and close the lid. Grill the shrimp until they're cooked through and opaque, about 2 minutes. Unplug the grill and, while it's still hot, carefully scrape off any cooked-on shrimp with a grill scraper. Once the grill is cool, clean the grates.

4. Reheat the panini press to medium-high heat.

5. *For each sandwich:* Split a ciabatta portion to create top and bottom halves. Spread a thin layer of pesto inside each ciabatta half. On the bottom half layer shrimp, feta, sun-dried tomatoes, and basil. Close the sandwich with the top ciabatta half.

6. Grill two panini at a time, with the lid closed, until the cheese is softened and the ciabatta is toasted, 3 to 4 minutes.

Grilled Salmon Sandwiches with BBQ Rémoulade

Yield: 4 panini

This is a darn good grilled fish sandwich. Sorry, I know that's not overly descriptive, but those are the words that run through my head every time I bite into one. It's what you get when you take a fresh, flavorful fish like salmon, grill it to perfection in minutes on the panini press, dress it in a creamy-tangy, barbecue sauce–spiked rémoulade sauce, and layer it in with tomatoes, onions, and arugula on crunchy grilled bread.

2 tablespoons extra-virgin olive oil
8 slices sourdough bread, sliced from a dense bakery loaf
1 (1-pound) skin-on salmon fillet
Coarse salt and freshly ground black pepper
1 recipe BBQ Rémoulade (recipe follows)

½ cup baby arugula
8 thin slices red onion, separated into rings
2 plum tomatoes (such as Roma), thinly sliced and seeded, or 8 Slow-Roasted Tomato Halves (page 135)

1. Heat the panini press to medium-high heat. If your panini press comes with a removable drip tray, make sure it is in place (see page 2).

2. Brush 1 tablespoon olive oil over one side of all the bread slices to flavor the outside of the sandwiches. In batches, grill the bread until it's toasted, 2 to 3 minutes.

3. Divide the salmon into four equal portions. Rub the remaining 1 tablespoon olive oil over the salmon, season it with salt and pepper, and transfer it, skin side down, to the grill. Close the lid and grill the salmon until it's cooked through, 5 to 7 minutes. Remove the salmon skin.

4. *For each sandwich:* Lay two slices of grilled bread on a cutting board, oiled sides down. Spread some BBQ rémoulade on each. On one slice, pile a small bed of arugula, some red onion rings, a portion of salmon, and a few slices of tomato. Close the sandwich with the other slice of bread.

BBQ Rémoulade

Yield: About ¾ cup

Rémoulade starts out similar to tartar sauce, but cooks often add different spices and ingredients that make it its own distinct sauce. I've given this rémoulade a smoky barbecue spin that not only tastes great with salmon, but also makes a great dip for vegetables or shrimp, or even a steak condiment.

½ cup mayonnaise
¼ cup barbecue sauce
1 scallion, chopped
2 tablespoons chopped fresh parsley

2 tablespoons minced celery
1 garlic clove, minced
Coarse salt and freshly ground black pepper

In a small bowl, whisk together the mayonnaise, barbecue sauce, scallion, parsley, celery, and garlic, and season with salt and pepper to taste. Cover the bowl and refrigerate the rémoulade until you're ready to use it.

Grilled Salmon BLT Panini

Yield: 4 panini

Could the BLT be the best sandwich invention ever? Someone somewhere along the line figured out that three simple key ingredients—bacon, lettuce, and tomato—form a trifecta that is not only perfect as a stand-alone sandwich but also sets the foundation for so many others. You can add almost anything—including salmon—to a BLT and it will still taste amazing!

½ cup mayonnaise

2 tablespoons pesto, purchased or home-made (page 101; see Note)

2 tablespoons extra-virgin olive oil

8 slices sourdough bread, sliced from a dense bakery loaf

1 (1-pound) skin-on salmon fillet

Coarse salt and freshly ground black pepper

½ cup baby arugula

8 strips cooked bacon

2 plum tomatoes (such as Roma), thinly sliced and seeded

1. In a small bowl, whisk together the mayonnaise and pesto until well combined. Cover the bowl and put it in the refrigerator until you're ready to assemble the panini.

2. Heat the panini press to medium-high heat. If your panini press comes with a removable drip tray, make sure it is in place (see page 2).

3. Brush 1 tablespoon olive oil over one side of all the bread slices to flavor the outside of the sandwiches. In batches, grill the bread until it's toasted, 2 to 3 minutes.

4. Divide the salmon into four equal portions. Rub the remaining 1 tablespoon olive oil over the salmon, season it with salt and pepper, and transfer it, skin side down, to the grill. Close the lid and grill the salmon until it's cooked through, 5 to 7 minutes. Remove the salmon skin.

5. *For each sandwich:* Lay two slices of grilled bread on a cutting board, oiled sides down. Spread some pesto on each. On one slice, pile a small bed of arugula, a portion of salmon, 2 bacon strips, and a few slices of tomato. Close the sandwich with the other slice of bread.

NOTE: Alternatively, if you don't have pesto on hand, you can mix up a quick batch of Basil-Garlic Mayonnaise (page 31).

Tuna Melt Panini

Yield: 4 panini

Sandwiches made with a salad of canned tuna, mayonnaise, and celery were "tunafish" to me growing up because that's what my parents, both New Yorkers, called them. But I've rarely, if ever, heard the word in California, where I've lived for most of my life. It's always "tuna salad" or "tuna sandwich"—never "tunafish." I'm thinking it might be a regional term, like "pocketbook," "dungarees," and "AHHranges"—other notables from my early vocabulary that used to perplex my childhood friends on the West Coast.

Whatever you want to call it, few things beat a good old-fashioned, diner-style tuna melt, draped in cheese on toasty bread. I like my tuna/tunafish/tuna salad very simple, with just mayonnaise and celery, but if there are other ingredients you prefer to add in, go right ahead—the more the merrier!

TUNA SALAD
2 (5-ounce) cans solid white albacore tuna packed in water, drained
1 celery rib, minced
2 tablespoons mayonnaise
Coarse salt and freshly ground black pepper
4 tablespoons (½ stick) butter, at room temperature

PANINI
8 slices sourdough, rye, or other rustic bread, sliced from a dense bakery loaf
8 thin slices red onion, separated into rings
2 plum tomatoes (such as Roma), thinly sliced and seeded, or 8 Slow-Roasted Tomato halves (page 135)
4 ounces sharp cheddar or Swiss cheese, sliced

1. In a medium-size bowl, mix the tuna, celery, and mayonnaise until well combined. Season the tuna salad with salt and pepper to taste.

2. Heat the panini press to medium-high heat.

3. *For each sandwich:* Spread butter on two slices of bread to flavor the outside of the sandwich. Flip over one slice of bread and top it with tuna salad, onions, tomatoes, and cheese. Close the sandwich with the other slice of bread, buttered side up.

4. Grill two panini at a time, with the lid closed, until the cheese is melted and the bread is toasted, 4 to 5 minutes.

Pan Bagnat Panini
(French-Style Tuna Melt)

Yield: 4 panini

The *pan bagnat* (pahn bahn-YAH) sandwich from France gets its name, which translates to "bathed bread," from the boldly flavored fillings that seep into the crusty baguette. I've taken the traditional ingredients—tuna, olives, green bell peppers, red onions, and tomatoes—and added some zesty marinated mozzarella to create a tuna melt–style panini version of this French classic.

MARINATED MOZZARELLA
2 tablespoons extra-virgin olive oil
1 garlic clove, minced
¼ teaspoon dried basil
¼ teaspoon dried oregano
¼ teaspoon dried thyme
A pinch of red pepper flakes
4 ounces fresh mozzarella cheese, sliced

PANINI
1 French baguette, cut into 4 portions, or
    4 mini baguettes
4 tablespoons olive tapenade
½ medium-size green bell pepper, thinly sliced
2 (5-ounce) cans solid white albacore tuna
    packed in oil, drained and flaked
½ small red onion, sliced
2 plum tomatoes (such as Roma), thinly
    sliced and seeded, or 8 Slow-Roasted
    Tomato halves (page 135)

1. *Marinated Mozzarella:* Combine the olive oil, garlic, basil, oregano, thyme, and red pepper flakes in a medium-size bowl. Add the mozzarella and toss the cheese in the marinade to coat it well. Let the cheese marinate for 1 hour at room temperature to allow the flavors to seep in.

2. Heat the panini press to medium-high heat.

3. *For each sandwich:* Slice off the domed top of a baguette portion to create a flat grilling surface. Split the baguette to create top and bottom halves. Spread 1 tablespoon olive tapenade inside the bottom half of the baguette. Top the tapenade with green bell peppers, tuna, red onions, tomatoes, and marinated mozzarella. Close the sandwich with the top baguette half.

4. Grill two panini at a time, with the lid closed, until the cheese is melted and the baguettes are toasted, 5 to 6 minutes.

Italian Tuna Melt Panini

Yield: 4 panini

Here's a flavorful Italian twist on the classic American tuna melt. I first make a zesty tuna salad with olive oil, vinegar, and capers (yes, capers—they taste fabulous with tuna!) and then grill it on olive bread with tomatoes, fresh mozzarella, and peppery arugula. It's nothing like your typical diner tuna melt, but I bet you'll love it just as much.

TUNA SALAD
2 (5-ounce) cans solid white albacore tuna packed in oil
1 tablespoon capers, rinsed
1 tablespoon white wine vinegar
Coarse salt and freshly ground black pepper

PANINI
1 tablespoon extra-virgin olive oil
8 slices rustic olive bread, sliced from a dense bakery loaf
1 cup baby arugula
2 plum tomatoes (such as Roma), thinly sliced and seeded, or 8 Slow Roasted Tomato halves (page 135)
4 ounces fresh mozzarella cheese, sliced

1. *Tuna salad:* Drain the tuna, reserving 2 tablespoons of the oil. Combine the tuna, reserved oil, capers, and white wine vinegar in a medium-size bowl. Season the tuna salad with salt and pepper to taste.

2. *Panini:* Heat the panini press to medium-high heat.

3. *For each sandwich:* Brush olive oil on two slices of bread to flavor the outside of the sandwich. Flip over one slice of bread and top it with a small handful of arugula, tuna salad, tomatoes, and mozzarella. Close the sandwich with the other slice of bread, oiled side up.

4. Grill two panini at a time, with the lid closed, until the cheese is melted and the bread is toasted, 4 to 5 minutes.

Tuna and White Bean–Chive Hummus Tartines

Yield: 4 panini

I think of these tartines (open-faced sandwiches) as lighter versions of a tuna melt. You still have the star ingredient—tuna salad—but it's tossed in red wine vinegar and olive oil rather than mayonnaise. Instead of cheese, the white bean–chive hummus brings a creamy texture to the sandwich as well as lots of fresh flavor. For even more flavor, as well as a bit of crunch, I like to use olive bread for these tartines. You can serve these as open-faced tartines or grill more bread to close the sandwiches.

2 (5-ounce) cans solid white albacore tuna packed in water, drained and flaked
2 tablespoons extra-virgin olive oil
1 tablespoon red wine vinegar
Coarse salt and freshly ground black pepper
4 slices olive bread, sliced from a dense bakery loaf

½ cup White Bean-Chive Hummus (recipe follows)
2 plum tomatoes (such as Roma), thinly sliced and seeded, or 8 Slow-Roasted Tomato halves (page 135)
½ small red onion, sliced
2 tablespoons chopped fresh basil

1. Toss the tuna with 1 tablespoon of the olive oil and the vinegar in a medium-size bowl. Season the tuna with salt and pepper to taste.

2. Heat the panini press to high heat.

3. Brush the remaining 1 tablespoon olive oil on each slice of olive bread. Grill the bread, with the lid closed, until it's toasted and golden grill marks appear, about 2 minutes.

4. Spread 2 tablespoons of hummus on each slice of grilled bread. Top the hummus with tomato slices, tuna, red onions, and chopped basil.

White Bean–Chive Hummus

Yield: About 1½ cups

A favorite pastime of my youngest sister when were growing up was to grab a handful of the chives that my mom grew in our backyard, eat them, and then come running up to my middle sister and me, breathing a loud "HHHHHHiiiiiiii!!" in our direction. Despite that rather fragrant introduction to chives, I'm still a big fan of them—for both their gentle oniony flavor and the fact that they look like green herb sprinkles when you chop them. When I was considering how to bring bright, herbal flavors to plain white bean hummus, chives and parsley both jumped to mind. That pale green hue lets you know right away that you're in for something fresh tasting.

You can use hummus as a healthy substitute for ingredients like cheese or mayonnaise on your panini, or just serve it as a dip for pita chips and raw veggies.

1 (15-ounce) can cannellini beans, rinsed and drained
2 tablespoons tahini
2 tablespoons freshly squeezed lemon juice
1 garlic clove, peeled

2 tablespoons chopped fresh chives
2 tablespoons chopped fresh parsley
¼ teaspoon ground cumin
¼ teaspoon coarse salt
A pinch of cayenne pepper

Combine all of the ingredients in a food processor and process until the mixture is smooth. Serve the hummus immediately or cover and refrigerate until you're ready to use it.

Bacon Crab Melt Panini

Yield: 4 panini

This is the type of sandwich that, to me, falls under the category of "diner food." And I say that as someone who has a high respect for diners and their iconic place in American culture. Let's be honest: Some of the ingredients they use aren't always the healthiest—but, man, the food sure tastes good.

If I ever encountered Bacon Crab Melt Panini on a diner menu—or any menu, really—it's a safe bet that I'd order it. The sandwich starts with crabmeat that's tossed in a dressing with tons of bright, fresh flavors, and then layered onto sourdough bread with sliced tomato, bacon, and sharp cheddar cheese. And then, of course, it gets all toasty and melty on the grill. I'm not ashamed to admit that I like to indulge in such things from time to time. Somehow I have a feeling I'm not the only one!

4 tablespoons mayonnaise
2 tablespoons chopped celery
1 tablespoon freshly squeezed lemon juice
½ teaspoon Old Bay Seasoning
½ teaspoon Dijon mustard
Coarse salt and freshly ground black pepper
12 ounces lump crabmeat, drained well

4 tablespoons (½ stick) butter, at room temperature
8 slices sourdough or other rustic white bread, sliced from a dense bakery loaf
4 ounces sharp cheddar cheese, sliced
8 strips cooked bacon
2 plum tomatoes (such as Roma), thinly sliced and seeded

1. Heat the panini press to medium-high heat.

2. In a medium-size bowl, combine the mayonnaise, celery, lemon juice, Old Bay seasoning, Dijon mustard, and salt and pepper to taste. Stir in the drained crabmeat.

3. *For each sandwich:* Spread butter on two slices of bread to flavor the outside of the sandwich. Flip over one slice and top the other side with cheese, crab salad, bacon, tomatoes, and more cheese. Close the sandwich with the other slice of bread, buttered side up.

4. Grill two panini at a time, with the lid closed, until the cheese is melted and the bread is toasted, 4 to 5 minutes.

Smoked Salmon and Avocado Panini

Yield: 4 panini

If you enjoy smoked salmon with cream cheese, you've got to try it with avocado. Pureed avocado is just as creamy as cream cheese—even smoother, perhaps—and a squeeze of lemon juice gives it a nice tang (and salmon, as we know, tastes great with lemon). For these sandwiches, my idea of deluxe smoked salmon panini, I slather both cream cheese and my avocado spread on the bread and pile on beautiful smoked salmon, dill, tomatoes, and red onions.

4 tablespoons (½ stick) butter, at room temperature

8 slices pumpernickel bread, sliced from a dense bakery loaf

½ cup cream cheese, at room temperature

4 tablespoons Avocado Spread (recipe follows)

4 ounces smoked salmon

2 teaspoons chopped fresh dill

2 plum tomatoes (such as Roma), thinly sliced and seeded

½ small red onion, sliced

1. Heat the panini press to medium-high heat.

2. *For each sandwich:* Spread butter on two slices of bread to flavor the outside of the sandwich. Flip over both slices of bread. Spread 2 tablespoons cream cheese on the other side of one slice and 1 tablespoon avocado spread on the other slice. Top the cream cheese with smoked salmon, dill, tomatoes, and red onion. Close the sandwich with the other slice of bread, buttered side up.

3. Grill two panini at a time, with the lid closed, until the bread is toasted, 3 to 4 minutes.

Avocado Spread

Yield: About ½ cup

Avocado has a creamy texture like mayonnaise, but it's lower in overall fat and calories and high in nutrients like potassium and monounsaturated fats (which can help reduce your bad cholesterol and lower your risk of heart disease and stroke). When I'm looking for a creamy condiment that's lighter than mayonnaise and doesn't sacrifice an ounce of flavor, I puree avocado with lemon juice to make a smooth spread.

Beyond panini, try this spread on top of salmon or other fish, as a dip for vegetables, or to cool a spicy gazpacho.

1 medium-size ripe avocado, pitted and peeled
1 tablespoon freshly squeezed lemon juice

¼ teaspoon coarse salt
⅛ teaspoon cayenne pepper

In a small food processor or blender, puree the avocado, lemon juice, salt, and cayenne until it's smooth and creamy. Give the mixture a taste and season with more salt or lemon juice as needed. This spread is best if used the day it's made.

Smoked Salmon, Goat Cheese, and Fennel Slaw Panini

Yield: 4 panini

S
moked salmon—preferably on a sesame bagel—is my husband's favorite food in the whole world. On those few occasions throughout the year when he treats himself to some, it turns into a bit of a production. He gathers all of the necessary items within easy reach—a small plate, a butter knife, his just-toasted bagels, a tub of whipped cream cheese, and, of course, his sleeve of salmon. Then he takes his place at the kitchen table and digs in. He doesn't say much as he repeatedly assembles "the perfect bite" with just the right ratio of salmon to cream cheese, but when I glance over at him, the look on his face lets me know that he's one contented man.

4 bagels (plain, sesame, poppy seed, or everything are all good choices)
4 ounces goat cheese, at room temperature, sliced into medallions

1 recipe Fennel Slaw (page 143)
4 ounces smoked salmon

1. Heat the panini press to medium-high heat.

2. *For each sandwich:* Cut a sliver off the rounded top surface of a bagel to create a flat grilling surface. Split the bagel to create top and bottom halves. Spread a layer of goat cheese on the bottom half, then top it with fennel slaw and smoked salmon. Close the sandwich with the top bagel half.

3. Grill two panini at a time, with the lid closed, until the goat cheese is softened and the bagels are toasted, 4 to 6 minutes.

Smoked Trout, Boursin, and Cucumber Panini

Yield: 4 panini

Admittedly, smoked salmon and smoked trout look and taste a whole lot alike (the two fish are closely related), but for some reason it feels as though I'm eating something a little more exotic when I go for the trout. Maybe it just seems special because I don't see it quite as often in stores or on menus. Here, I've paired smoked trout with Boursin—a creamy cheese that comes in a variety of flavors—for a slightly different spin on the smoked salmon and cream cheese combination we've all enjoyed forever.

4 tablespoons (½ stick) butter, at room
   temperature
8 slices whole-grain bread, sliced from a
   dense bakery loaf

1 (5.2-ounce) package Boursin cheese
   (see Note)
4 ounces smoked trout fillets, skin removed
½ cucumber, peeled and thinly sliced

1 Heat the panini press to medium-high heat.

2. *For each sandwich:* Spread butter on two slices of bread to flavor the outside of the sandwich. Flip over both slices of bread and spread Boursin on the other side of each slice. Top one slice with smoked trout and cucumbers. Close the sandwich with the other slice of bread, buttered side up.

3. Grill two panini at a time, with the lid closed, until the bread is toasted, about 3 minutes.

NOTE: You can find Boursin near the cream cheese in the refrigerated section of most grocery stores. I particularly like the Garlic and Fine Herbs flavor for this recipe.

Grilled Shrimp Tostadas with Mashed Black Beans and Avocado Salsa Fresca

Yield: 4 tostadas

You can grill half a pound of shrimp on the panini press in about 2 minutes. That is reason enough to have panini-grilled shrimp in your regular weeknight dinner rotation, don't you think?

For these tostadas I first let the shrimp bathe in a chili-lime marinade before they hit the grill. Also grilled on the panini press: the tostada shells. You just brush a little oil on regular tortillas and after a minute or so on the grill they're toasty, crisp, and ready for toppings. Black beans mashed with garlic (a terrific technique I learned from a Rick Bayless recipe) and sprinkled with *queso fresco* make a flavorful base to hold the shrimp on the tostada, and an avocado salsa fresca brings a punch of bright, Southwestern flavor to the dish.

SHRIMP
2 tablespoons vegetable oil
1 teaspoon freshly squeezed lime juice
1 teaspoon chili powder
¼ teaspoon ground cumin
¼ teaspoon coarse salt
1 pound raw large shrimp, peeled and deveined

MASHED BLACK BEANS
2 tablespoons vegetable oil
3 garlic cloves, minced

1 (15-ounce) can black beans, rinsed and drained
1 to 2 tablespoons water
Coarse salt

TOSTADAS
1 tablespoon vegetable oil
4 (8-inch) flour tortillas
Coarse salt
4 ounces (about 1 cup) crumbled queso fresco or shredded Monterey Jack
1 cup Avocado Salsa Fresca (page 178)

1. *Shrimp:* In a medium-size bowl, stir together the vegetable oil, lime juice, chili powder, cumin, and salt. Add the shrimp and toss to coat them in the marinade. Cover the bowl and let the shrimp marinate in the refrigerator while you prepare the rest of the dish. (Note: The citric acid in the lime juice can start to "cook" the shrimp after a while, so I don't recommend marinating the shrimp for longer than 30 minutes.)

2. *Mashed Black Beans:* Heat the vegetable oil in a large skillet over medium heat. Add the garlic and stir it in the oil until it's fragrant and just beginning to brown, about 1 minute. Add the black beans. Give the beans a rough mash with a potato masher (they should still be a bit

(continued on next page)

chunky) and cook them for another minute or two until they're heated through. Take the pan off the heat and stir in 1 to 2 tablespoons of water, until the beans are spreadable. Season the beans with coarse salt to taste and partially cover the pan to keep them warm.

3. *Tostadas:* Heat the panini press to medium-high heat.

4. Lightly brush a tortilla with vegetable oil and transfer it to the grill. Sprinkle the tortilla with a little salt and close the lid. Grill the tortilla until it's crisped and golden grill marks appear, 1 to 2 minutes. Repeat with the rest of the tortillas. Keep the grill heated.

5. Remove the shrimp from the marinade (discard the remaining marinade) and put half of them on the grill. Close the lid and grill the shrimp until they're cooked through and opaque, about 2 minutes. Repeat with the remaining shrimp.

6. Spread some mashed black beans over each grilled tortilla (if the beans have cooled off too much to be spreadable, put them back on the stove over low heat for a few minutes and stir in water, 1 teaspoon at a time). Top them with *queso fresco*, grilled shrimp, and avocado salsa fresca and serve.

Avocado Salsa Fresca
Yield: About 2 ½ cups

Mix up this fresh and easy avocado salsa and set it in the refrigerator; by the time you're done preparing the tostadas, the flavors will have had a chance to blend together just right. Scoop up any leftover salsa with tortilla chips or use it to top tacos, fish, or crostini.

- 1 medium-size ripe avocado, pitted, peeled, and diced
- 2 medium-size ripe tomatoes, diced
- 3 tablespoons chopped red onion
- ½ jalapeño pepper, seeded and finely chopped
- 2 tablespoons chopped fresh cilantro
- 1 tablespoon freshly squeezed lime juice
- ¼ teaspoon coarse salt

Toss all of the ingredients together in a medium-size bowl. Cover the bowl and refrigerate for 30 minutes to allow the flavors to combine. The salsa is best the day it's made, but it will stay fresh in the refrigerator for up to 2 days.

Grilled Salmon Packets with Pesto and Tomatoes

Yield: 2 to 3 servings

Grilling food in a foil or parchment packet is an easy, efficient way to steam a number of items all at once, allow their flavors to meld, and retain the food's moisture. Here, "packet grilling" produces a moist and flavorful salmon with basil pesto and fresh tomatoes. This recipe is adapted from one my friend Kalyn Denny created on her blog, Kalynskitchen.com. The entire dish takes just 20 minutes to prepare and, since you cook it inside the packet, there's nearly no cleanup!

2 teaspoons extra-virgin olive oil
1 (1-pound) skin-on center-cut salmon fillet
2 to 3 tablespoons pesto, purchased or
  homemade (page 101)

1 medium-size tomato, sliced about
  ¼ inch thick

1. Heat the panini press to high heat.

2. Drizzle olive oil in the center of a piece of foil large enough to wrap the salmon with some overlapping. Lay the salmon on top of the oil. Spread pesto all over the top of the salmon. Arrange the sliced tomatoes over the pesto so that they cover the top of the salmon.

3. Wrap the salmon securely in the foil, doubling over the seam and ends several times. Take care to create a flat seam on top so that the grill lid can heat the surface evenly. Place the salmon packet on the grill. Close the lid so that the upper plate makes contact with the packet without pressing it. Grill for 10 minutes.

4. Remove the salmon from the grill and let it sit for 2 to 3 minutes before carefully opening the packet. Serve immediately.

Grilled Salmon with Old Bay Aioli

Yield: 4 servings

My first real taste of Old Bay seasoning, the Baltimore specialty, actually wasn't on crab or any other seafood. It was on French fries I bought on the boardwalk in Bethany Beach, Delaware, a few years ago on a family vacation. Talk about flavor! There is definitely something about the combination of salt, a little heat, and some subtle sweetness that makes you want to shake this stuff on just about everything. The spice blend dates back to the 1940s, but it's as popular as ever today, especially in the Mid-Atlantic.

A spoonful of Old Bay in the aioli that dresses this grilled salmon adds wonderful complexity to its flavor. The salmon itself is as simple as can be—just seasoned with salt and pepper and grilled for 7 minutes—so even on a busy weeknight, you'll have time to whip up this fabulous sauce and enjoy a quick yet sophisticated meal.

2 tablespoons extra-virgin olive oil
Coarse salt and freshly ground black
  pepper

1 (1-pound) skin-on center-cut salmon fillet,
  cut into 4 portions
1 recipe Old Bay Aioli (recipe follows)

1. Heat the panini press to medium-high heat. If your panini press comes with a removable drip tray, make sure it is in place (see page 2).

2. Pour the olive oil into a shallow bowl or glass pie plate. Add the salmon to the dish and turn each piece to coat with olive oil. Season the salmon with salt and pepper.

3. Place the salmon on the grill, skin side down, and close the lid so that the upper plate makes contact with the salmon without pressing it. Grill until the salmon is cooked through and opaque, 6 to 7 minutes, depending on the thickness of the fish.

4. Serve the salmon with the Old Bay Aioli.

Old Bay Aioli

Yield: About 1 cup

I can't promise that you won't start hunting around your fridge and pantry for other items to dunk into this fantastic aioli. Seafood is the most natural pairing for Old Bay–seasoned condiments, but you might also serve this aioli along with crudités or French fries, or even on hamburgers.

1 large egg yolk
1½ teaspoons apple cider vinegar
1½ teaspoons freshly squeezed lemon juice
1 garlic clove, minced

1 anchovy fillet, minced
¾ cup vegetable oil
¼ cup extra-virgin olive oil
1 teaspoon Old Bay seasoning

1. Roll up a kitchen towel and wrap it around the base of a medium-size bowl to keep it stable. Whisk together the egg yolk, vinegar, lemon juice, garlic, and anchovy until well combined.

2. Start adding the vegetable oil a few drops at a time while whisking vigorously. Continue whisking while gradually pouring in the remaining vegetable oil in a thin, thread-like stream. The mixture will slowly turn an opaque golden yellow. As you add more oil, the aioli will become thicker and creamy and take on a paler yellow color.

3. Whisk in the olive oil, also in a thin stream. Whisk in the Old Bay seasoning. Give the aioli a taste and add more lemon juice if it needs it. Cover the bowl and refrigerate the aioli until you're ready to use it, for up to 4 days.

Seared Ahi and Avocado Salad

Yield: 4 servings

One of my best friends doesn't consider herself to be much of a cook, but she knows good, healthy food when she eats it. The queen of our local takeout scene, she is fully prepared for any last-minute ordering, with all of the restaurants programmed into her cell phone. A favorite order of hers is a seared ahi salad that's been tossed in ginger vinaigrette with goodies like avocado, edamame, roasted red bell peppers, and greens. I ventured to make my own version at home—searing the ahi to perfection on the panini press for a mere 90 seconds—and was won over by this fabulous Cal-Asian salad combination as well.

TUNA
1 tablespoon extra-virgin olive oil
1 (1-pound) sashimi-grade ahi tuna steak,
  about 1 inch thick
Coarse salt and freshly ground black pepper

SALAD
1 head butter lettuce, torn into large pieces

¼ red onion, thinly sliced
½ cup sliced roasted red bell peppers
½ cup shelled cooked edamame, thawed
  if frozen
1 recipe Ginger Vinaigrette (recipe follows)
1 medium-size ripe avocado, pitted, peeled,
  and sliced

1. *Tuna:* Heat the panini press to high heat. If your panini press comes with a removable drip tray, make sure it is in place (see page 2).

2. Brush the olive oil over both sides of the tuna and season the tuna with salt and pepper.

3. Grill the tuna, with the lid closed, until it's seared on the outside but still bright red on the inside, about 90 seconds. Transfer the fish to a cutting board and slice it thinly across the grain.

4. *Salad:* Toss the lettuce, onion, peppers, edamame, and 2 tablespoons of the ginger vinaigrette together in a large bowl.

5. Divide the salad among four plates. Arrange slices of tuna and avocado on top of each salad and drizzle more ginger vinaigrette over the top (you probably will have extra dressing for later use).

Ginger Vinaigrette
Yield: About ¾ cup

When it comes to salad dressings, I'm a vinaigrette girl all the way. Once you've got the classic ratio down—3 parts oil, 1 part vinegar or other acid—you can customize vinaigrettes to fit any flavor profile. For Asian-inspired salads, a ginger-based dressing is a perfect complement.

1 tablespoon reduced-sodium soy sauce
1 tablespoon freshly squeezed lemon juice
1 tablespoon plus 2 teaspoons rice wine
  vinegar
2 garlic cloves, minced
2 teaspoons grated fresh ginger

1 teaspoon honey
½ teaspoon Dijon mustard
½ teaspoon sugar
½ cup extra-virgin olive oil
Freshly ground black pepper

In a small bowl, whisk together the soy sauce, lemon juice, vinegar, garlic, ginger, honey, mustard, and sugar. Gradually whisk in the olive oil. Season the vinaigrette with black pepper to taste. Store any leftovers in an airtight container in the refrigerator for up to 4 days.

Ahi Tuna Burgers

Yield: 4 burgers

I love a juicy beef burger as much as the next girl—probably more so—but once in a while I go for a healthier burger option. My only requirement, though, is that it has to taste really good—I'm not willing to give up flavor to save calories. With these ahi tuna burgers, I dare say you actually *gain* flavor over traditional burgers. Between the ginger, shallots, and Dijon mustard in the patties themselves and the kick of wasabi mayonnaise on top, there is plenty to keep your taste buds happy.

½ cup panko bread crumbs (see Note)
¼ cup minced fresh cilantro
1 tablespoon reduced-sodium soy sauce
1 tablespoon minced shallots
1 tablespoon minced fresh ginger
1 tablespoon Dijon mustard
½ teaspoon red pepper flakes

1 large egg, beaten
1½ pounds ahi tuna fillets, finely chopped
4 hamburger buns, toasted if desired
1 recipe Wasabi Mayonnaise (recipe follows)
1 medium-size ripe avocado, pitted, peeled, and sliced
½ small red onion, sliced

1. Heat the panini press to medium-high heat. If your panini press comes with a removable drip tray, make sure it is in place (see page 2).

2. In a large bowl, combine the panko, cilantro, soy sauce, shallots, ginger, Dijon mustard, red pepper flakes, and egg. Add the tuna and mix until everything is combined. Divide the mixture into four portions and shape each into a patty.

3. Transfer the ahi burgers, two at a time, to the grill and close the lid so that the upper plate is resting on the burgers without pressing them (they flatten easily). Grill until they're browned on the outside and still a little rare on the inside, 1 to 2 minutes depending on the thickness.

4. Transfer the burgers to hamburger buns and top them with wasabi mayonnaise, avocado slices, and onion.

NOTE: I can usually find panko bread crumbs alongside the American-style bread crumbs in my grocery store, but some stores stock them with other Asian foods.

Wasabi Mayonnaise

Yield: About ¾ cup

As any sushi lover knows, wasabi and seared tuna are a match made in heaven. The pungency of the wasabi is tempered somewhat by the mayonnaise but—rest assured—this condiment still packs a flavorful punch.

½ cup mayonnaise
2 tablespoons chopped scallions
1 tablespoon powdered wasabi (see Note)

1 tablespoon water
1 teaspoon freshly squeezed lemon juice

Whisk together all of the ingredients in a small bowl. Cover the bowl and refrigerate the mayonnaise to let the flavors blend while you prepare the ahi burgers. It will stay fresh for about 3 days in the refrigerator.

NOTE: Powdered wasabi can be found in tiny cans or jars in the Asian foods section of your grocery store. Be sure to look for packages marked "100 percent powdered wasabi."

Grilled Fish Tacos

Yield: 4 servings

When out-of-town friends come to visit us in San Diego, there's one local delicacy that's always high on their list to try: fish tacos. They first became popular down in Baja California and, thankfully, found their way north of the border. When you're used to having mainly chicken or steak in your tortilla, fish tacos may sound a little odd, but trust me—they're San Diego's most popular dish for good reason.

Grilling the fish on the panini press takes a matter of minutes and it comes out moist, flaky, and flavorful. I add some spicy chipotles to the traditional sour cream sauce to boost the overall flavor even further.

FISH
¼ cup vegetable oil
2 tablespoons freshly squeezed lime juice
2 teaspoons ancho chili powder
¼ teaspoon coarse salt
1 (1-pound) flaky white fish fillet, such as
   mahi mahi or halibut

ACCOMPANIMENTS
8 (8-inch) corn or flour tortillas, warmed
Shredded cabbage
Hot sauce or salsa
Sliced red onions
Sliced scallions
Chipotle Sour Cream (recipe follows)
Chopped fresh cilantro
Lime wedges

I. *Fish:* Whisk together the oil, lime juice, ancho chile powder, and salt in a shallow glass dish. Add the fish and turn to coat it in the marinade. Cover the dish and let the fish marinate in the refrigerator for 20 minutes.

2. Heat the panini press to medium-high heat. If your panini press comes with a removable drip tray, make sure it is in place (see page 2).

3. Transfer the fish to the grill and close the lid so that the upper plate is resting on the fish without pressing it. Grill the fish until it's cooked through, 3 to 4 minutes. With a spatula, carefully transfer the fish to a plate.

4. Divide the fish among the tortillas (it should flake easily) and top each taco with cabbage, salsa, onions, scallions, and a dollop of chipotle sour cream. Garnish with a little chopped cilantro and serve with lime wedges.

Chipotle Sour Cream

Yield: About ¾ cup

Good things come to those who wait . . . but you won't have to wait long at all to enjoy this quick and easy sauce on top of your tacos, quesadillas, or any other dish that could use a spicy-yet-cool boost.

¼ cup sour cream
¼ cup mayonnaise

3 tablespoons freshly squeezed lime juice
1 chipotle in adobo sauce, minced

In a small bowl, whisk together the sour cream, mayonnaise, lime juice, and chipotle. Cover the bowl and refrigerate the mixture until you're ready to use it. It will stay fresh in the refrigerator for about 3 days.

NATURE'S BOUNTY

Fruit, Vegetables, and Beans on the Panini Press

PANINI

MORE FROM THE PANINI PRESS

Roasted Apples, Brie, and Pecan Panini

Yield: 4 panini

The idea for combining roasted apples and Brie in a sandwich came from a PaniniHappy.com reader from Vancouver. At the time that I first posted this recipe on the blog, I had never tried roasted apples before. I immediately fell in love with the caramelized crust that forms on the bottom from the sugars in the apple. In keeping with these homey, autumnal flavors, I added crunchy pecans for some nutty texture and grilled it all on cinnamon raisin bread.

1 medium-size apple, cored and cut into ¼-inch-thick slices

4 tablespoons (½ stick) butter, at room temperature

8 slices cinnamon raisin bread, sliced from a dense bakery loaf

4 ounces Brie cheese (with or without the rind), sliced

¼ cup chopped pecans

1. Heat the oven or toaster oven to 400°F.

2. Spray a baking sheet with nonstick cooking spray and arrange the apples on the sheet. Roast the apples until they are soft and golden brown, with a caramelized crust on the bottom, 15 to 20 minutes.

3. Heat the panini press to medium-high heat.

4. *For each sandwich:* Spread butter on two slices of bread to flavor the outside of the sandwich. Flip over one slice and top the other side with Brie, roasted apple slices, and pecans. Close the sandwich with the other slice of bread, buttered side up.

5. Grill two panini at a time, with the lid closed, until the cheese is melted and the bread is toasted, 4 to 5 minutes.

Sunflower Butter, Banana, and Honey Panini Sliders

Yield: 6 sliders

"Yummmm!!" and "I got sandwich!" were the enthusiastic reviews from my 4-year-old daughter and 2-year-old son when I handed them their fun-shaped mini panini. The crunchy sandwiches fit right in the palms of their little hands, and they were elated. Our preschool is peanut-free, so we often have allergy-friendly sunflower seed butter (also known as SunButter) on hand. It tastes just as good with bananas and honey as peanut butter does. Cutting out the shapes is, of course, purely optional, but kids do love them. Keep this recipe in mind for lunches and snacks, or make a whole bunch for a birthday party.

12 slices rustic white or whole-grain bread, sliced from a dense bakery loaf
4 tablespoons (½ stick) butter, at room temperature

6 tablespoons sunflower butter or any nut butter
1 banana, just ripe (all yellow with no brown spots), thinly sliced
1½ teaspoons honey (see Note)

1. Heat the panini press to medium-high heat.

2. Use large cookie cutters to cut shapes, each about 3 inches in diameter, out of the slices of bread. (Save your bread scraps for other uses, such as bread crumbs or croutons.)

3. Spread butter on one side of each bread shape to flavor the outside of the sandwiches. Flip them all over and spread sunflower butter on the other side. Top half of the bread shapes with a layer of banana slices and drizzle about ¼ teaspoon honey over the bananas. Close all of the sandwiches with the remaining bread shapes, buttered side up.

4. Working in batches if necessary, grill the sliders, with the lid closed, until the bread is toasted, 3 to 4 minutes. Allow the sandwiches to cool for a few minutes before serving them to young children.

NOTE: Honey is not recommended for children younger than 1 year old.

Homemade Peanut Butter and Caramelized Banana Panini

Yield: 4 panini

Here is my idea of the ultimate peanut butter sandwich: heaps of homemade peanut butter—lightly sweetened with honey—and sweet caramelized bananas spread on good-quality white bread (even better if it's freshly baked at home!), grilled nice and toasty on the panini press. Sweet, savory, gooey, and messy—it doesn't get any better, if you ask me.

PEANUT BUTTER
1½ cups roasted unsalted shelled peanuts
1 teaspoon honey
¼ teaspoon coarse salt

PANINI
4 tablespoons (½ stick) butter, at room temperature
8 slices rustic white bread, sliced from a dense bakery loaf
1 recipe Caramelized Bananas (recipe follows)

1. *Peanut Butter:* Grind the peanuts, honey, and salt in a food processor, scraping the sides of the bowl as needed. The nuts will transform into a thick, smooth paste after about 4 minutes.

2. *Panini:* Heat the panini press to medium-high heat.

3. *For each sandwich:* Spread butter on two slices of bread to flavor the outside of the sandwich. Flip over both slices of bread and spread a generous amount of peanut butter on the other side of each. Arrange a single layer of caramelized bananas on one slice of bread and close the sandwich with the other slice, buttered side up.

4. Grill two panini at a time, with the lid closed, until the bread is toasted and golden grill marks appear, 3 to 4 minutes.

Caramelized Bananas

Yield: About 2 cups

These bananas, which take an ordinary peanut butter sandwich to a sweet next level, also make an extra-special topping for ice cream, waffles, and crepes.

2 tablespoons unsalted butter

3 underripe bananas (slightly green), cut into ¼-inch-thick slices

¾ cup packed light brown sugar

A dash of ground cinnamon

Melt 1 tablespoon of the butter in a large nonstick frying pan over medium-high heat. Add the bananas in a single layer and let them brown for about 30 seconds without moving them. With a wooden spoon or spatula, carefully turn the bananas over, then add the brown sugar, cinnamon, and the remaining 1 tablespoon butter. Cook for about a minute longer, shaking the pan to keep the bananas moving, until the sugar is melted and the bananas are caramelized. Remove the pan from the heat.

Grilled Asparagus Tartines with Fresh Ricotta, Pesto, and Scallions

Yield: 4 tartines

first made these tartines in celebration of St. Patrick's Day—not that they're especially Irish, but they sure are green. With grilled asparagus, scallions, and basil pesto, they're packed with fresh, springtime flavor, and they come together in minutes. You can easily scale down these open-faced sandwiches to crostini size, using rounds of baguette, and serve them as appetizers.

1 pound asparagus, trimmed to the length of a ciabatta slice
2 tablespoons extra-virgin olive oil
Coarse salt and freshly ground black pepper
4 slices ciabatta or other crusty rustic bread

4 tablespoons pesto, purchased or home-made (page 101)
½ cup ricotta cheese
1 scallion, chopped

1. Heat the panini press to medium-high heat.

2. In a large bowl, toss the asparagus with 2 teaspoons of the olive oil and season with salt and pepper. Grill the asparagus, with the lid closed, until they're tender and grill marks appear, 3 to 4 minutes.

3. Brush another 2 teaspoons of the olive oil over the ciabatta slices and grill the bread, with the lid closed, until it's toasted and grill marks appear, 2 to 3 minutes.

4. Spread 1 tablespoon pesto on each slice of ciabatta. Spoon on a few tablespoons of ricotta and top it with grilled asparagus (you'll have extra asparagus—you can save it to enjoy on its own, add it to a salad or pasta, or just make more tartines!) and a sprinkling of chopped scallions. Finish the tartines by drizzling the remaining 2 teaspoons olive oil over the top and grinding on a little more black pepper.

Heirloom Tomato Panini

Yield: 4 panini

Just tomatoes? That's it? It took every ounce of restraint I could muster to get myself to try a good old-fashioned tomato sandwich in the way that nature intended—bread, mayonnaise, and thick slices of fresh summer heirloom tomatoes sprinkled with a little salt and pepper. I couldn't have imagined how such simple ingredients—and so few of them—could combine into such blissfully sweet, salty, briny bites. The beauty of this sandwich is in its simplicity. Take a few minutes to whip up your own olive oil mayonnaise—it's well worth it.

4 tablespoons (½ stick) butter, at room temperature

8 slices sourdough bread, sliced from a dense bakery loaf

4 tablespoons Olive Oil Mayonnaise (recipe follows) or purchased mayonnaise

2 medium-size ripe heirloom tomatoes, thickly sliced

Coarse salt and freshly ground black pepper

1. Heat the panini press to high.

2. *For each sandwich:* Spread butter on two slices of bread to flavor the outside of the sandwich. Flip over both slices and spread 1 tablespoon mayonnaise on the other side of each. Layer enough tomato slices onto one slice of bread to cover it. Season the tomatoes with salt and pepper. Close the sandwich with the other slice of bread, buttered side up.

3. Place two panini on the grill and close the lid so that the lid is resting on the top of the sandwiches without pressing them. Grill the panini, two at a time, just until the bread is toasted, 1 to 2 minutes.

Olive Oil Mayonnaise

Yield: About 1 cup

Most mayonnaise recipes give very precise measurements and advice for meticulously assembling the ingredients to create a perfectly fluffy emulsion. The approach below is delightfully inexact, drawn from Amy Finley's food memoir, *How to Eat a Small Country* (Clarkson Potter, 2011). In the book, the author learns an important lesson about cooking and about life: relax and let go. She abandoned her failed, methodical mayonnaise-making process in favor of a confident, freeform approach and voilà—perfect mayonnaise every time.

1 egg yolk
A slosh of white wine vinegar
A sprinkle of salt

A spoonful of Dijon mustard
1 cup extra-light olive oil

1. Roll up a kitchen towel and wrap it around the base of a medium-size bowl to keep it stable. Whisk together the egg yolk, white wine vinegar, salt, and Dijon mustard until well combined. Continue whisking briskly while pouring the olive oil slowly and steadily into the bowl, until the mayonnaise is emulsified, light, and fluffy.

2. Refrigerate any unused mayonnaise in a covered bowl. It's best to use it within 3 days.

Five Ways to Lighten Up Panini

Thick-cut rustic breads, creamy cheeses, flavorful meats, and condiments—who doesn't love to indulge in these fabulous panini ingredients every now and then? If only they were as fabulous for the waistline. Sigh.

Here are my best tips for cutting back on the extra fat, calories, carbs, and sodium in panini without losing any of the flavor.

1. Substitute Avocado for Mayo. Oh mayonnaise . . . why can't I quit you? Mayo brings moisture and flavor to a sandwich, but we all know it's not that good for you. Reduced-fat mayonnaise is an easy substitute, but an even better one is avocado. It's got a creamy texture like mayonnaise, but it's lower in overall fat and calories and high in nutrients like potassium and monounsaturated fats (which can help reduce your bad cholesterol and lower your risk of heart disease and stroke). I puree avocado with lemon juice to make a creamy spread (see page 173), but you could always dress up a sandwich with some of your favorite guacamole or even just simply sliced avocado.

2. Combine Salumi with Leaner Meats. It doesn't get any more mouthwatering than an Italian meat sandwich layered with thin slices of salty soppressata, prosciutto, and ham. But a little goes a long way with these flavorful meats. To get that cured meat flavor while cutting down on the saturated fat, calories, and sodium, layer just a single slice of salumi on your sandwich and swap out the rest for something leaner, like roast turkey breast. Better yet, choose reduced-sodium turkey, as a lot of regular deli turkey contains nearly as much salt as ham.

3. Choose Cheeses That Are Naturally Lower in Fat. I'm not a fan of "reduced fat" versions of cheese, at least where melting is concerned. It has been my experience over many years of trying out different brands that reduced-fat cheese can occasionally measure up to its full-fat counterparts flavor-wise but degrade into rubbery unpleasantness when it's melted. My preferred approach to cutting down on fat, where cheese is concerned, is to choose cheeses that are naturally lower in fat. Goat cheese, feta, Parmesan, and even mozzarella typically have less fat than cheeses like cheddar and Colby. Some of my favorite recipes that incorporate these lower-fat cheeses include Lemon-Thyme Chicken Panini (page 34), Mediterranean Chicken Flatbread Panini (page 20), and Prosciutto, Mozzarella, and Arugula Salad Panini (page 92).

4. Make It a Wrap. If it tastes great between two slices of bread, chances are it'll make a great wrap, too. A flour tortilla contains roughly the same number of calories and carbs as a slice of traditional bread, but you need just one tortilla to fold around your filling ingredients to make a wrap. Go even healthier with a whole-wheat tortilla.

5. Go Bare. I often flavor the outside of the bread with butter or olive oil, but it's definitely an "extra," not a functional necessity. The bread isn't in danger of sticking to the nonstick grill, and it will crisp up just fine without it. Butter and olive oil do help in two areas: added flavor and grill marks. If I'm preparing panini to serve to friends or, say, to take pretty photographs for the blog, I'll go for these flourishes. But if I'm grilling something quick for myself, I usually leave it out.

Caprese Panini

Yield: 4 panini

When people get a new panini press and ask me which sandwich they should grill first, I always suggest the classic combination of tomato, basil, and mozzarella. Based on the Italian *insalata caprese*, it couldn't be simpler, and meat lovers and vegetarians alike love it. For the best results, be sure to use really sweet, ripe summer tomatoes.

1 French baguette, cut into 4 portions, or 4 mini baguettes
½ cup pesto, purchased or homemade (page 101)

4 ounces fresh mozzarella cheese, sliced
2 medium-size ripe tomatoes, sliced
8 fresh basil leaves

1. Heat the panini press to medium-high heat.

2. *For each sandwich:* Slice off the domed top of a baguette portion to create a flat grilling surface. Split the baguette to create top and bottom halves. Spread a layer of pesto inside each baguette half. On the bottom half layer some mozzarella, tomatoes, basil, and more mozzarella. Close the sandwich with the top baguette half.

3. Grill two panini at a time, with the lid closed, until the cheese is melted and the bread is toasted, 5 to 6 minutes.

Burrata Caprese Tartines

Yield: 4 tartines

I fell in love with burrata cheese the very first time I tried it. My knife broke through the outer mozzarella shell of the little white ball of cheese and released the cream and mozzarella on the inside. With a sprinkle of salt and a splash of olive oil on top, it was simply divine. Here, I've added burrata to summery caprese-style open-faced sandwiches with grilled fresh tomatoes, basil pesto, and crunchy roasted pistachios.

It's easier to find burrata on restaurant menus than in stores, but I seek it out in specialty cheese shops. Water-packed fresh mozzarella is a good alternative if burrata isn't available near you.

4 slices Italian, sourdough, or other rustic white bread, sliced from a dense bakery loaf

2 tablespoons extra-virgin olive oil, plus more for garnish

4 plum tomatoes (such as Roma), halved lengthwise

Coarse salt and freshly ground black pepper

4 tablespoons pesto, purchased or homemade (page 101)

1 (4-ounce) ball burrata cheese, cut into 4 portions

¼ cup roasted, salted shelled pistachios

1. Heat the panini press to high heat.

2. Brush 1 tablespoon olive oil on the bread slices and grill them, with the lid closed, until they're toasted, about 2 minutes.

3. Drizzle another tablespoon of olive oil over the cut sides of the tomatoes and season them with salt and pepper. Place the tomatoes, cut sides down, on the grill, close the lid, and grill them until they're tender and wrinkly and caramelized on the bottom, 8 to 10 minutes.

4. Spread a layer of pesto on each slice of grilled bread. Top the pesto with grilled tomatoes, a portion of burrata, and a scattering of pistachios. Drizzle a little olive oil over the top and season the tartines with salt and pepper to taste.

Greek-Style Caprese Panini

Yield: 4 panini

My friend Eleni, born and raised in Greece, once suggested an incredible sandwich combination to me, with feta ("Make sure it's Greek!" she insisted), tomatoes, oregano, and olive oil on olive bread. I made it and loved it—it was right up my alley, with all the bold flavors. In fact, it reminded me of the classic Italian Caprese Panini (page 201), a popular favorite, with feta and oregano in place of the mozzarella and basil. If you can, wait until summer to get a really sweet in-season tomato. By the way, feta softens but doesn't really melt, so we're grilling mainly to get the bread toasted, which takes just a few minutes.

1 tablespoon extra-virgin olive oil, plus more for drizzling
8 slices rustic olive bread, sliced from a dense bakery loaf (see Note)
4 ounces crumbled Greek feta cheese

2 plum tomatoes (such as Roma), thinly sliced and seeded, or 8 Slow-Roasted Tomato halves (page 135)
Coarse salt and freshly ground black pepper
1 tablespoon torn fresh oregano leaves

1. Heat the panini press to medium-high heat.

2. *For each sandwich:* Brush olive oil on two slices of olive bread to flavor the outside of the sandwich. Flip over one slice and scatter some crumbled feta on the other side. Top the feta with tomatoes and season the tomatoes with salt and pepper to taste. Add some oregano and a drizzle of olive oil. Close the sandwich with the other slice of bread, oiled side up.

3. Grill two panini at a time, with the lid closed, until the bread is toasted, 2 to 3 minutes.

NOTE: As an alternative to olive bread, you could spread a little olive tapenade on plain rustic white bread.

Marinated Portobello Mushroom Panini

Yield: 4 panini

Aportobello mushroom is simply a brown cremini mushroom that's matured and grown a large cap. Thick and meaty, these large caps can absorb a tremendous amount of flavor from a marinade. Look to portobello mushrooms as the perfect ingredient to bring a whole lot of substance and flavor to panini, especially when you're hosting vegetarians.

For those who prefer meat, these zesty, Mediterranean-style panini also taste great with sliced steak, chicken, or turkey in place of the mushrooms.

1 French baguette, cut into 4 portions, or 4 mini baguettes
½ cup pesto, purchased or homemade (page 101)
4 ounces Manchego cheese, sliced

4 Marinated Portobello Mushrooms (recipe follows)
8 oil-packed sun-dried tomatoes, thinly sliced
4 fresh basil leaves, roughly torn

1. Heat the panini press to medium-high heat.

2. *For each sandwich:* Slice off the domed top of a baguette portion to create a flat grilling surface. Split the baguette to create top and bottom halves. Spread a thin layer of pesto inside each baguette half. On the lower half, layer cheese, a mushroom cap (cut in half, if necessary, to fit on the baguette), sun-dried tomatoes, basil, and more cheese. Close the sandwich with the top baguette half.

3. Grill two panini at a time, with the lid closed, until the cheese is melted and the baguettes are toasted, 7 to 9 minutes.

Marinated Portobello Mushrooms

Yield: 4 servings

Portobello mushroom caps can soak up marinade like a sponge and grill in just minutes on the panini press. This is great news for vegetarians and omnivores alike. Given their meaty texture, I like to use a big-flavor marinade with balsamic vinegar, garlic, thyme, and mustard that's similar to the ones I use for beef and lamb. These mushrooms are perfect for Portobello Patty Melt Panini (page 209) and Grilled Portobello Cheese Steak Panini (page 210)—or even as a stand-alone main dish with vegetables or pasta.

Make It Ahead: You can marinate and grill your mushrooms ahead of time—they'll keep for 3 to 5 days in a covered container in the refrigerator.

4 portobello mushrooms	1 teaspoon dried thyme
¼ cup extra-virgin olive oil	1 teaspoon Dijon mustard
¼ cup balsamic vinegar	½ teaspoon coarse salt
2 garlic cloves, minced	¼ teaspoon freshly ground black pepper

1. Wipe any dirt from the mushroom caps with a damp paper towel. Pop out the stems and scoop out the gills with a spoon; discard the stems and gills.

2. Combine the olive oil, vinegar, garlic, thyme, mustard, salt, and pepper in a shallow bowl. Add the mushroom caps and roll them around in the marinade a bit to coat them. Let the mushrooms marinate at room temperature, turning them occasionally, for 30 minutes.

3. Heat the panini press to medium-high heat. If your panini press comes with a removable drip tray, make sure it is in place (see page 2).

4. Remove the mushrooms from the marinade (discard the remaining marinade), transfer them to the grill, and close the lid. Grill the mushrooms until they're tender and dark grill marks appear, about 5 minutes.

Portobello Patty Melt Panini

Yield: 4 panini

My sister Julie told me about a dish she makes of portobello mushrooms topped with Asiago cheese and leeks and then slipped under the broiler. That sounded like a great panini idea to me, so I gave it a try. A few little tweaks and—voilà!—these panini were born. In place of leeks, I use my perennial favorite, sweet caramelized onions, and I've added fresh baby arugula. With all of the bright flavors in here, this just might be my very favorite meatless sandwich.

1 ciabatta loaf, cut into 4 portions,
   or 4 ciabatta rolls
8 ounces Asiago cheese, sliced
1 cup Caramelized Onions (page 19)

4 Marinated Portobello Mushrooms
   (page 207)
1 cup baby arugula

1. Heat the panini press to medium-high heat.

2. *For each sandwich:* Split a ciabatta portion to create top and bottom halves. On the bottom half layer cheese, caramelized onions, a mushroom cap (cut in half, if necessary, to fit on the bread), arugula, and more cheese. Close the sandwich with the top ciabatta half.

3. Grill two panini at a time, with the lid closed, until the cheese is melted and the ciabatta is toasted, 8 to 10 minutes.

Grilled Portobello Cheese Steak Panini

Yield: 4 panini

We established in my Cheese Steak Panini recipe (page 132) that while it's probably not possible to grill truly authentic Philly cheese steaks at home, we can still make darn good steak sandwiches that are inspired by the Philadelphia classic. For the non-meat-eaters in your life, try these panini. Meaty marinated portobello mushroom caps replace the traditional steak, but I swear you'll hardly notice.

1 tablespoon vegetable oil
1 medium-size onion, sliced into ½-inch-thick rounds (rings intact)
1 ciabatta loaf, cut into 4 portions, or 4 ciabatta rolls

4 Marinated Portobello Mushrooms (page 207), cut into strips
4 jarred hot Italian peppers, such as banana peppers or fried "longhot" cayenne peppers, sliced
4 ounces sharp provolone cheese, sliced

1. Heat the panini press to medium-high heat.

2. Brush oil on both sides of the onion slices and season them with salt and pepper. Grill the onions until they're tender and dark grill marks appear, 6 to 8 minutes. Separate the onion rounds into rings.

3. *For each sandwich:* Split a ciabatta portion to create top and bottom halves. Pile some of the onion rings inside the bottom half. Top the onions with sliced mushrooms, peppers, and cheese. Close the sandwich with the top ciabatta half.

4. Grill two panini at a time, with the lid closed, until the cheese is melted and the ciabatta is toasted, 5 to 6 minutes.

Wild Mushroom Melt Panini

Yield: 4 panini

I wish we could make this a scratch-and-sniff book so you could experience right now the aroma that will fill your kitchen when you sauté these mushrooms in butter and olive oil with shallots and garlic. It's absolutely heavenly. Layering them with melty Gruyère on rye bread is guaranteed to make your day a whole lot cozier!

4 tablespoons (½ stick) butter, at room temperature
8 slices rye bread, sliced from a dense bakery loaf

8 ounces Gruyère or Swiss cheese, sliced
1 recipe Sautéed Wild Mushrooms (page 45)

1. Heat the panini press to medium-high heat.

2. *For each sandwich:* Spread butter on two slices of bread to flavor the outside of the sandwich. Flip over one slice and top the other side with cheese, sautéed mushrooms, and more cheese. Close the sandwich with the other slice of bread, buttered side up.

3. Grill two panini at a time, with the lid closed, until the cheese is melted and the bread is toasted, 4 to 5 minutes.

Kale, Grill-Roasted Garlic, and Cheddar Panini

Yield: 4 panini

People have gone crazy for kale. It's full of nutrients and health benefits and you can add the flavorful greens to so many dishes—yes, even panini! The slight bitterness of sautéed kale is a wonderful counterpoint to tangy sharp cheddar cheese and sweet grill-roasted garlic.

Save any extra sautéed kale to enjoy as a side dish—it's fantastic on its own. It will keep for up to 5 days in a covered container in the refrigerator.

SAUTÉED KALE
1 tablespoon extra-virgin olive oil
1 shallot, thinly sliced
⅛ teaspoon red pepper flakes
1 pound kale, stems removed and leaves roughly chopped
½ cup water
1 tablespoon apple cider vinegar
Coarse salt

PANINI
4 tablespoons (½ stick) butter, at room temperature
8 slices rustic white bread, sliced from a dense bakery loaf
1 recipe Grill-Roasted Garlic (recipe follows)
4 ounces sharp cheddar cheese, sliced

1. *Sautéed Kale:* Heat the olive oil in a large pot or Dutch oven over medium-high heat. Add the shallot and cook, stirring, until tender and fragrant, about 1 minute. Add the red pepper flakes and the kale and carefully toss the kale to coat it in the oil. Pour in the water. Cover the pot, reduce the heat to medium-low, and cook the kale until it's wilted and tender, another 10 minutes. Remove the pot from the heat, stir in the vinegar, and season the kale with salt to taste.

2. *For each sandwich:* Spread butter on two slices of bread to flavor the outside of the sandwich. Flip over one slice of bread and spread about a tablespoon of soft garlic on the other side. Top the garlic with sautéed kale and cheese. Close the sandwich with the other slice of bread, buttered side up.

3. Grill two panini at a time, with the lid closed, until the cheese is melted and the bread is toasted, 4 to 5 minutes.

Grill-Roasted Garlic

Yield: 1 head garlic

I roast the garlic right on the panini press—it takes less time than the oven and, especially in summer, I'm glad don't have to heat up the house. Besides using grill-roasted garlic as a flavorful spread for panini, you can also puree it for sauces and dips, add it as a pizza or pasta topping, or even just eat the sweet cloves on their own. It's the recipe that keeps on giving!

1 head garlic
2 teaspoons extra-virgin olive oil

A pinch of coarse salt

1. Heat the panini press to medium-high heat.
2. Peel away the papery outer skin from the head of garlic, keeping the head intact. Slice off ¼ inch from the top of the garlic head, exposing the cloves. Lay the garlic head on a piece of aluminum foil large enough to wrap it. Drizzle the cut side with olive oil and season it with salt. Wrap the garlic in the foil and place it, cut side down, on the grill. Close the lid and grill the garlic until the cloves are very soft and tender, about 30 minutes. Once they're cool enough to touch, squeeze the roasted garlic cloves out of their skins. You can freeze any leftover whole cloves on a baking sheet and then transfer them to a zipper-top plastic bag or covered container.

Broccoli Rabe, White Bean–Chive Hummus, and Roasted Red Pepper Panini

Yield: 4 panini

I practically did a little happy dance right there in the produce department when I finally tracked down broccoli rabe (also called rapini) for the first time. Even when it is in season—from fall to early spring—it can be elusive at the markets. But it's definitely worth hunting down this bitter green vegetable, which is closely related to broccoli. Aside from being an easy-to-prepare sautéed side dish, broccoli rabe makes a flavorful and hearty panini ingredient as well. Here, I match it with my white bean–chive hummus, some zesty roasted red bell peppers, and sharp Asiago pressato cheese. Even non-vegetarians won't miss the meat in these sandwiches.

1 pound broccoli rabe, thick stems trimmed
1 tablespoon extra-virgin olive oil
1 garlic clove, thinly sliced
Coarse salt and freshly ground black pepper
1 ciabatta loaf, cut into 4 portions, or
    4 ciabatta rolls

½ cup White Bean–Chive Hummus (page 169) or purchased hummus
¼ cup sliced roasted red bell peppers
4 ounces Asiago pressato or aged Asiago cheese, sliced

1. Set a steamer in a large pot of water over high heat. Bring the water to a boil, add the broccoli rabe, and steam it, covered, for 5 minutes. Transfer the broccoli rabe to a bowl of ice water to cool for a minute or two.

2. While the broccoli rabe is cooling, heat the olive oil in a large skillet over medium heat. Add the garlic and cook until the garlic starts to brown, about 2 minutes. Drain the broccoli rabe well and add it to the skillet. With tongs, toss the broccoli rabe in the oil to coat it and cook, tossing occasionally, until the stems are tender, 2 to 3 minutes. Season the broccoli rabe with salt and pepper to taste and transfer it to a plate.

3. Heat the panini press to medium-high heat.

4. *For each sandwich:* Split a ciabatta portion to create top and bottom halves. Spread 2 tablespoons hummus inside the bottom half. Top with broccoli rabe, roasted red bell peppers, and Asiago pressato. Close the sandwich with the top ciabatta half.

5. Grill two panini at a time, with the lid closed, until the cheese is melted and the ciabatta is toasted, 4 to 5 minutes.

Mediterranean Grilled Vegetable Tartines

Yield: 4 tartines

L ooking back, I've probably been making tartines (open-faced sandwiches with a French name) since I was a kid. I used to pile a bunch of ingredients I liked—salami, American cheese, and ketchup may or may not have been involved—on a slice of bread, heat it all up in the microwave, and enjoy. Ah, youth. . . .

These days marinated grilled vegetables, white bean–chive hummus, and feta are more my style. It's a terrific assortment of Mediterranean flavors all set atop some crunchy grilled bread. Meat lovers: Don't let all the vegetables fool you—this healthy-yet-hearty sandwich definitely gives you something to sink your teeth into.

1 tablespoon extra-virgin olive oil
4 slices rustic white bread, sliced from a
  dense bakery loaf
½ cup White Bean–Chive Hummus
  (page 169)

½ recipe Grilled Herbed Vegetables
  (page 225)
4 ounces crumbled feta cheese
Chopped chives, for garnish

1. Heat the panini press to high heat.

2. Brush a little olive oil on one side of each slice of bread. Working in batches if necessary, transfer the bread slices, oiled sides up, to the grill, close the lid, and grill until they are toasted and grill marks appear, 2 to 3 minutes.

3. Spread 2 tablespoons hummus on each slice of bread. Top the hummus with vegetables and a sprinkling of feta and chives.

Grilled Eggplant Parmigiana Panini

Yield: 4 panini

Using the panini press to grill eggplant makes these panini super easy and relatively quick to make. It's just like eggplant parmigiana in handheld form, inspired by a recipe for eggplant parm hero sandwiches I once came across in the *Gourmet Live* iPad app (how do you like that—digital media inspiring the traditional print world!). I moved the marinara toward the middle of the panini to keep the moisture out of the bread, with the added bonus that it makes for zesty bursts of sauce in each bite.

1 large eggplant, sliced crosswise into ½-inch-thick slices
2 tablespoons extra-virgin olive oil
Coarse salt and freshly ground black pepper
4 ounces (about 1 cup) shredded mozzarella cheese

2 ounces (about ½ cup) shredded Parmigiano-Reggiano cheese
8 slices Italian bread, sliced from a dense bakery loaf
½ cup marinara sauce
8 fresh basil leaves, roughly torn

1. Heat the panini press to medium high heat.

2. Lay out the eggplant slices on a cutting board. Brush olive oil on one side of each slice and season with salt and pepper. Place the eggplant slices, seasoned sides down, on the panini grill (you'll need to work in batches). Brush olive oil on the other side of each slice, season with salt and pepper, and close the lid. Grill the eggplant until it's tender and cooked through, 4 to 6 minutes. Set the eggplant aside and tent it with foil to keep it warm.

3. Unplug the grill, carefully wipe it clean, and reheat it to medium-high heat.

4. Combine the mozzarella and Parmigiano-Reggiano cheeses in a small bowl.

5. *For each sandwich:* Brush olive oil on two slices of bread to flavor the outside of the sandwich. Flip over one slice and layer the fillings as follows: cheese, marinara, eggplant, basil, more cheese, more eggplant, more marinara, and a final layer of cheese. Close the sandwich with the other slice of bread, oiled side up.

6. Grill two panini at a time, with the lid closed, until the cheese is melted and the bread is toasted, 4 to 5 minutes.

Black Bean Patty Melt Panini

Yield: 4 panini

For those who are keeping track, I've got four different recipes for patty melts in this cookbook—Cheeseburger Patty Melt Panini (page 136), Meatloaf Melt Panini (page 133), Portobello Patty Melt Panini (page 209), and now this Southwestern-inspired vegetarian version, made with black bean patties. It's true, I do enjoy a good patty melt. While I may not always have soft buns on hand to make traditional burgers, I almost always have bread I can slice and toast for melts on my panini press.

A recipe my friend Dara Michalski created for her blog, CookinCanuck.com, converted me into a black bean patty fan. Dara doesn't leave out one ounce of flavor in this healthier burger, seasoned with cilantro, lime juice, and cumin. Those flavors inspired these panini, which I make with avocado spread, plum tomatoes, red onions, and pepper Jack cheese.

BLACK BEAN PATTIES
1 (15-ounce) can black beans, rinsed and drained
1 large egg, beaten
½ cup plain bread crumbs
¼ cup minced fresh cilantro
1 shallot, minced
2 teaspoons freshly squeezed lime juice
1 teaspoon ground cumin
½ teaspoon coarse salt
½ teaspoon freshly ground black pepper
1 tablespoon extra-virgin olive oil

PANINI
4 tablespoons (½ stick) butter, at room temperature
8 slices sourdough bread, sliced from a dense bakery loaf
½ cup Avocado Spread (page 173)
2 plum tomatoes (such as Roma), thinly sliced and seeded
½ small red onion, sliced
4 ounces pepper Jack cheese, sliced

1. *Black Bean Patties:* Mash half of the black beans with a potato masher in a large bowl. Set aside the other half to mix in later.

2. Add the egg, bread crumbs, cilantro, shallot, lime juice, cumin, salt, and pepper to the mashed black beans. Mix all of the ingredients until they're well combined. Mix in the reserved whole black beans.

3. Heat the panini press to medium-high heat.

4. Divide the black bean mixture into four equal patties, about ½ inch thick. If your hands start to get too sticky, just moisten your hands with water—wet hands make it easier to form the patties.

5. Brush oil on top of each black bean patty. Carefully place the patties, oiled sides down, on the grill. Brush more oil on the other side of each patty and close the lid so that it's gently resting on top of the patties. Grill the patties until they're cooked through and browned, 7 to 9 minutes. Unplug the grill and carefully wipe down the grates while they're still hot.

6. *Panini:* Reheat the panini press to medium-high heat.

7. *For each sandwich:* Spread butter on two slices of bread to flavor the outside of the bread. Flip over one slice and spread a generous layer of avocado spread on the other side. Layer on a black bean patty, tomatoes, red onion, and cheese. Close the sandwich with the other slice of bread, buttered side up.

8. Grill two panini at a time, with the lid closed, until the cheese is melted and the bread is toasted, 4 to 5 minutes.

Grilled Peach Salad with Toasted Pecans, Blue Cheese, and Honey Balsamic Syrup

Yield: 6 servings

The only pregnancy craving I can remember having was for ripe, juicy, summer peaches. For my entire second trimester with my daughter, I was eating them by the crate. I've slowed my consumption since then, but peaches remain my all-time favorite fruit (with strawberries coming in a close second).

For this salad I caramelize fresh peaches on a searing-hot panini press, then arrange them over a bed of peppery baby arugula, and fill them with a few dabs (not too much!) of tangy, creamy, crumbled blue cheese and a smattering of toasted pecans. And at the end the peaches get a drizzle of honey balsamic syrup.

½ cup chopped pecans
½ cup honey
¼ cup balsamic vinegar
¼ teaspoon dried thyme
⅛ teaspoon black pepper

A pinch of coarse salt
1 tablespoon butter, melted
3 peaches, halved and pitted
5 ounces baby arugula
2 ounces blue cheese, crumbled

1. Heat the oven or toaster oven to 350°F. Spread the pecans on a baking sheet and toast in the oven until they are fragrant, 4 to 6 minutes. Set them aside to cool.

2. In a small saucepan, heat the honey, balsamic vinegar, thyme, black pepper, and salt over medium heat. Stir to dissolve the honey and bring the mixture to a boil. Reduce the heat to medium-low and simmer, stirring occasionally, until the mixture is slightly thickened and syrupy, about 10 minutes. Remove the pan from the heat and let the honey balsamic syrup cool a bit—it will continue to thicken as it cools.

3. Heat the panini press to high heat. If your panini press comes with a removable drip tray, make sure it is in place (see page 2).

4. Brush a little melted butter on the cut sides of the peaches. Place the peaches on the grill, cut sides down. Close the lid so that the upper plate is hovering just above the peaches, if possible, or touching them very lightly. Grill the peaches until they are softened and grill marks appear, 4 to 5 minutes.

5. Spread the arugula on a serving platter and top with the peaches, cut sides up. Fill the cavity of each peach half with toasted pecans and blue cheese and drizzle with honey balsamic syrup.

Grilled Smashed Potatoes

Yield: 4 to 6 servings

My husband and I fell in love with Smashed Garlic Fried Potatoes at Tom Douglas's restaurant Lola in Seattle on our babymoon, and I've been making my own version ever since. I've figured out what it is about these simple potatoes that makes them so irresistible: it's the smashed part. Once the little ball of a boiled potato gets pounded (gently) and its insides break out of the skin, it creates extra surfaces that get crisped up with salt and olive oil in the second tour under the heat.

1 pound small red-skinned potatoes
3 teaspoons coarse salt
2 tablespoons extra-virgin olive oil

1½ teaspoons dried rosemary
¼ teaspoon freshly ground black pepper

1. Place the potatoes in a large pot and fill the pot with enough cold water to cover them by an inch. Add 2 teaspoons of the salt. Bring the water to a boil. Continue boiling, uncovered, until the potatoes are fork-tender, 15 to 20 minutes more. Remove the pot from the heat and drain the potatoes into a colander.

2. Heat the panini press to high heat.

3. While they're still hot, carefully spread out the potatoes on a cutting board. Press down firmly on each potato with a potato masher or the bottom of a small skillet to flatten it into a round disc, like a little potato hockey puck. The potatoes should burst their skins but still remain intact.

4. Drizzle olive oil over the top of each potato. Season with the remaining 1 teaspoon salt, rosemary, and black pepper.

5. Place as many smashed potatoes as will fit on your grill (you may need to work in batches) and close the lid. Grill until the potatoes are crisp on top with golden grill marks, 4 to 6 minutes.

Grilled Fennel

Yield: 4 servings

When a preschooler eagerly eats a vegetable dish you've prepared and asks for more, you know it's a winner. My daughter proclaimed, "Fennel is my favorite!" for days after I prepared some for her on the panini press. When it's grilled, much of the licorice-like bite that fennel is known for in its raw form is replaced by a subtle sweetness, bolstered further by a drizzle of balsamic vinegar before serving.

Serve this as an easy side dish to accompany fish or chicken.

2 large fennel bulbs
1 tablespoon extra-virgin olive oil

Coarse salt and freshly ground black pepper
1 tablespoon balsamic vinegar

1. Heat the panini press to medium-high heat.

2. Cut off the stalks and fronds from the fennel. Reserve the fronds for a garnish and save the stalks for another use, such as chicken or vegetable stock. Slice each bulb in half lengthwise. Cut out the tough core—once you do this you'll need to carefully hold the layers together as they'll want to separate.

3. Drizzle or brush olive oil over both sides of each of the fennel halves and season with salt and pepper. Transfer the fennel to the panini press, cut sides down, and close the lid so that the upper plate rests on the fennel without pressing it. Grill the fennel until it's tender and golden grill marks appear, 6 to 8 minutes.

4. Arrange the grilled fennel on a serving platter, drizzle it with balsamic vinegar, and garnish it with some of the reserved fronds.

Grilled Acorn Squash with Cranberry-Ginger Maple Syrup and Toasted Walnuts

Yield: 4 servings

G rilling acorn squash on the panini press is much faster than roasting—this dish takes only 30 minutes, start to finish. Plus, I think the grill marks are kind of pretty, especially with the dark scalloped edges of the acorn squash. The cranberry-ginger maple syrup is sweet, fruity, and gingery all at the same time, and it dresses up the dish even enough to serve on your holiday table.

While it probably isn't harmful to eat the acorn squash peel, many people choose not to do so. Just cut away the flesh with your fork or go ahead and pick up the slices with your hands and eat 'em like melon—I won't judge!

1 acorn squash
2 tablespoons butter, melted
½ cup pure maple syrup
¼ cup dried cranberries

½ teaspoon grated fresh ginger or a pinch of ground ginger
¼ cup toasted chopped walnuts

1. Heat the panini press to medium-high heat.

2. Slice the acorn squash in half lengthwise, scoop out the seeds, and then slice the squash into ½-inch-thick scalloped crescent moons.

3. Working in batches as needed, brush melted butter onto one side of as many slices of squash as will fit on your grill. Place the squash on the grill, buttered sides down, and brush butter on the other side. Close the grill so that the lid rests on the squash without pressing it. Grill the squash until it is tender and dark grill marks appear, about 7 minutes. Transfer the squash to a serving platter and tent the plate with foil to keep the squash warm while you grill the remaining batches.

4. While the squash is grilling, bring the maple syrup, cranberries, and ginger to a boil in a saucepan over high heat. Turn down the heat to medium-low and let the syrup simmer for 2 to 3 minutes. Remove the syrup from the heat.

5. Drizzle the cranberry-ginger maple syrup over the squash and garnish with toasted walnuts before serving.

Grilled Herbed Vegetables

Yield: 6 to 8 servings

When I grill vegetables I like to make a large batch and then I use them for days, as a side dish, in sandwiches and salads, over pasta—you name it. They'll stay fresh for several days in the refrigerator. These fresh eggplants, zucchini, bell peppers, and onions get a good drenching in balsamic vinegar, olive oil, and herbs for robust Mediterranean flavor.

¼ cup extra-virgin olive oil
2 tablespoons balsamic vinegar
2 tablespoons dried parsley
2 tablespoons dried basil
1 tablespoon dried marjoram
1 teaspoon coarse salt
½ teaspoon freshly ground black pepper
6 garlic cloves, minced

2 Japanese eggplants, sliced lengthwise into ¼-inch-thick strips
2 small zucchini, sliced lengthwise into ¼-inch-thick strips
1 red bell pepper, cored, seeded, and sliced into ½-inch-thick strips
1 yellow bell pepper, cored, seeded, and sliced into ½-inch-thick strips
1 small red onion

1. In a large zipper-top plastic bag, combine the olive oil, vinegar, parsley, basil, marjoram, salt, pepper, and garlic. Place the eggplants, zucchini, and bell peppers in the bag (reserve the onion). Seal the bag, roll the vegetables around in the marinade to coat them, and let the vegetables marinate for 1 to 2 hours in the refrigerator.

2. Heat the panini press to medium-high heat. If your panini press comes with a removable drip tray, make sure it is in place (see page 2).

3. Remove the vegetables from the marinade and reserve 1 tablespoon of the marinade. Grill the vegetables in batches of the same type of vegetable (all of the eggplant together, all of the zucchini together, etc.), with the lid closed, until they are tender and grill marks appear, 4 to 6 minutes, depending on the type of vegetable. Arrange the vegetables on a serving platter as they come off the grill. Slice the onion into ¼-inch-thick rounds. Drizzle the reserved marinade over the onions and grill them, with the lid closed, until they are tender and grill marks appear, 4 to 6 minutes. Serve the vegetables immediately or at room temperature.

Grilled Herbed Vegetable Salad

Yield: 4 servings

On a whim I ordered a salad like this from a popular pizza chain one evening when I was out of time to make dinner. I wasn't much of a "salad person" at the time, but that day I was feeling like having something on the healthier side. When I read the long list of all the marinated vegetables and avocados (which I love), it seemed much more substantial than a lot of salads. Goodies like charred corn and sun-dried tomatoes sprinkled over the top quickly helped to make it a favorite of mine.

The restaurant oven-roasted its vegetables for this recipe, but I use the panini press to grill them in a matter of minutes per batch.

1 cup fresh or thawed frozen corn kernels
1 tablespoon chopped shallots
1 teaspoon Dijon mustard
¼ cup balsamic vinegar
½ teaspoon coarse salt
½ teaspoon freshly ground black pepper
¾ cup extra-virgin olive oil

5 ounces baby spinach
2 cups Grilled Herbed Vegetables (page 225)
1 (7-ounce) jar oil-packed sun-dried tomatoes, drained and thinly sliced
1 medium-size ripe avocado, pitted, peeled, and thinly sliced

1. Heat a medium-size skillet over medium-high heat. Place the corn kernels in the skillet and allow the corn to brown on one side, 3 to 5 minutes. The kernels will sizzle upon hitting the skillet (step back, they may start to jump a little!). Remove the pan from the heat.

2. Roll up a kitchen towel and wrap it around the base of a small bowl to keep it stable. Whisk together the shallots, Dijon mustard, balsamic vinegar, salt, and pepper until the salt is dissolved. While whisking constantly, slowly pour in the olive oil.

3. In a large bowl, toss the spinach in about 2 tablespoons of the dressing. Arrange the dressed spinach on a large serving platter or on individual plates. Add the grilled vegetables, sun-dried tomatoes, and avocado. Scatter charred corn kernels over the top. Drizzle on more dressing if you'd like (refrigerate the rest for later use). Serve immediately.

Grilled Cheese Panzanella Salad

Yield: About 4 servings

Panzanella is a true summertime treat. Chunks of day-old bread tossed with just-off-the-vine tomatoes, fresh basil, olive oil, and vinegar make up this traditional Italian salad. The dressing and juices from the tomatoes soak in and flavor the dry bread, which is where the real magic happens.

I had an idea one day . . . why not turn those chunks of stale bread into mini grilled cheese sandwiches? Traditionally, there's no cheese in panzanella, but there's no denying that mozzarella pairs perfectly with tomatoes and basil. I say food is food, so let's have fun with it. And nothing says fun, at least in the sandwich world, like teeny-tiny grilled cheese sandwiches in a salad.

GRILLED CHEESE CROUTONS

4 slices day-old sourdough or other rustic white bread, sliced from a dense bakery loaf

2 ounces (about ½ cup) shredded mozzarella or other semi-firm cheese

SALAD

4 medium-size ripe tomatoes, cut into bite-size chunks

½ small red onion, thinly sliced

¼ cup torn fresh basil leaves

1 recipe White Balsamic Vinaigrette (page 73)

1. *Grilled Cheese Croutons:* Heat the panini press to medium-high heat.

2. Place half the cheese on each of two slices of bread. Close each sandwich with a second slice of bread.

3. Grill both panini, with the lid closed, until the cheese is melted and the bread is toasted, 3 to 4 minutes. Transfer the panini to a cutting board. Trim the crusts from the panini and cut each sandwich into 1-inch squares.

4. *Salad:* Place the tomatoes, sliced onions, torn basil, and grilled cheese croutons in a large salad bowl.

5. Toss the salad with enough of the dressing to moisten the croutons without drenching them. Allow the flavors to meld at room temperature for 30 minutes before serving the salad.

Grilled Tomato Soup with Herbed Grilled Cheese Croutons

Yield: 4 servings

I knew I had a hit with this grilled tomato soup when I brought it to one of our local San Diego food blogger potlucks and, one by one, each person glanced up from her bowl and asked, "Who made the soup? I love it!" It intrigued them to learn that I'd actually grilled the tomatoes and onions for the soup on the panini press. It's another example of how you can use the panini press as a prep tool for all kinds of dishes.

2 pounds plum tomatoes (such as Roma), halved lengthwise
1 to 2 cups low-sodium vegetable broth
2 tablespoons extra-virgin olive oil
Coarse salt and freshly ground black pepper
1 medium-size yellow onion, sliced into ½-inch-thick rounds (rings intact)
1 red bell pepper, cored, seeded, and chopped

3 garlic cloves, minced
⅛ teaspoon red pepper flakes
1 teaspoon sugar
2 tablespoons chopped fresh parsley
1 sprig fresh thyme
1 recipe Herbed Grilled Cheese Croutons (page 232)

1. Heat the panini press to high heat. If your panini press comes with a removable drip tray, make sure it is in place (see page 2).

2. Place a strainer over a 2 cup liquid measuring cup. Scoop out the pulp and seeds from the tomato halves into the strainer and press down with a spoon to collect all of the tomato juice. Add enough vegetable broth to the measuring cup to bring the total amount of liquid to 2 cups. Set aside.

3. Drizzle the cut sides of the tomato halves with 1½ teaspoons of the olive oil and season with salt and pepper. In batches, place the tomatoes, cut sides down, on the grill. Close the lid, making light contact with the tomatoes without pressing them. Grill the tomatoes until they are soft and the outer skins are wrinkly, 8 to 10 minutes.

4. Drizzle the onion rounds with another 1½ teaspoons of the olive oil and season with salt and pepper. Place the onions on the grill. Close the lid, making light contact with the onions without pressing them. Grill the onions until they are tender and grill marks appear, 4 to 6 minutes.

5. Transfer the onions to a cutting board, let them cool a bit, and give them a rough chop.

(continued on next page)

6. Heat the remaining 1 tablespoon olive oil in a Dutch oven or large saucepan over medium heat. Add the red bell pepper and cook, stirring often, until it begins to soften, 4 to 5 minutes. Add the garlic and red pepper flakes and cook until fragrant, about 1 minute more. Stir in the grilled tomatoes, grilled onions, sugar, parsley, thyme sprig, and vegetable stock mixture. Bring the soup to a boil, reduce the heat, and simmer, uncovered, for 40 minutes. Remove the thyme sprig.

7. Puree the soup either with an immersion blender or in batches in a blender or food processor. Season with salt and pepper to taste.

8. Serve the soup hot with the croutons.

Herbed Grilled Cheese Croutons
Yield: 4 servings

I think these grilled cheese croutons are so cute. Obviously, they're nothing more than grilled cheese sandwiches that have been cut into small squares. I use fresh herb butter on the outside to make them extra-crisp and savory. We all love to eat grilled cheese sandwiches with tomato soup . . . so why not put them in the soup?

Add these croutons to any soup, chili, or stew that you might otherwise pair with a grilled cheese sandwich. You could also use them to top salads, such as the Grilled Cheese Panzanella Salad (page 228).

2 tablespoons butter, at room temperature
1 teaspoon chopped fresh basil
½ teaspoon chopped fresh chives
½ teaspoon chopped fresh thyme

4 slices sourdough bread, sliced from a
  dense bakery loaf
4 ounces semi-firm cheese such as
  cheddar, Colby, or Monterey Jack, sliced

1. Mix the butter and herbs in a small bowl.

2. Spread herb butter on one side of each slice of bread. Turn over two of the bread slices and top them with cheese. Close each sandwich with the remaining slices of bread, buttered sides up. Grill the panini until the cheese is melted and the bread is toasted, 3 to 4 minutes. Transfer the panini to a cutting board. Trim the crusts from the panini and cut each sandwich into 1-inch squares.

Grilled Tofu and Bok Choy Bowl

Yield: 4 servings

I love a good weeknight recipe that requires less than 10 minutes of active cooking time. Let the tofu drain its water and soak in the savory Asian-style marinade while you handle the things that need handling around your house. Then toss the tofu and baby bok choy on the panini press for just minutes to get a nice sear and serve it all over steamed rice. Fast, healthy, delicious—you'll keep coming back to this one.

1 (14-ounce) package extra-firm tofu
3 tablespoons reduced-sodium soy sauce
1 tablespoon vegetable oil
2 teaspoons rice vinegar
1 teaspoon toasted sesame oil
1½ teaspoons honey
1 teaspoon grated fresh ginger

1 small garlic clove, minced
¼ teaspoon red pepper flakes
2 baby bok choy, halved lengthwise
2 cups steamed brown or white rice, for serving
Chopped scallions and toasted sesame seeds, for garnish

1. Stack a few paper towels on a cutting board. Drain the water from the tofu package. Slice the tofu in half horizontally into two slabs, each about ¾ inch thick, and then cut each slab into 4 crosswise sections for a total of 8 pieces. Lay the tofu pieces side by side on the paper towels. Cover the tofu with more paper towels and set a heavy, flat object, like a baking sheet with a heavy skillet on it, on top to press the water out of the tofu. Press for 30 to 60 minutes.

2. While the tofu is being pressed, get the marinade ready. Whisk together the soy sauce, vegetable oil, vinegar, sesame oil, honey, ginger, garlic, and red pepper flakes in a glass pie plate. Lay the tofu pieces in the marinade and let them soak for 8 minutes. Flip them over and soak them for another 8 minutes.

3. Heat the panini press to high heat.

4. Transfer the tofu to the grill, reserving the remaining marinade. Close the lid and grill the tofu until grill marks appear, 2 to 3 minutes. Transfer the grilled tofu to a plate.

5. Pat the bok choy dry and place it, cut sides down, on the grill. Grill the bok choy until it's tender and grill marks appear, 2 to 3 minutes.

6. Meanwhile, pour the reserved marinade into a small saucepan and bring it to a boil. Simmer it for 2 minutes, then remove the pan from the heat.

7. Transfer the bok choy to a cutting board and slice it crosswise into bite-sized pieces.

8. Divide the rice among four bowls. Top the rice with tofu and bok choy and drizzle on the simmered marinade. Garnish with chopped scallions and toasted sesame seeds.

Spinach-Feta Quinoa Cakes with Lemon-Dill Yogurt Sauce

Yield: 4 servings (8 to 10 patties)

W e're meat-eaters in our house, without a doubt. But we don't mind a good veggie burger every now and then either—especially if it's got lots of great flavor. I like to make mine with quinoa (pronounced KEEN-wa). Even though many people consider quinoa to be a grain, it's actually a closer relative to beets, spinach, and Swiss chard. With its high protein content, it earns the status of a "superfood." And it happens to be very easy and versatile to cook with—even on the panini press.

These grilled quinoa cakes take on the zesty flavors of a classic Greek spanakopita. Spoon a little lemon-dill yogurt sauce over the top for a light, healthy lunch.

1 tablespoon extra-virgin olive oil
½ cup finely chopped onion
2 garlic cloves, finely chopped
5 ounces baby spinach, chopped
2 large eggs, beaten
1¼ cups cooked quinoa
2 ounces crumbled feta cheese

1 tablespoon chopped fresh dill
¼ teaspoon grated lemon zest
¼ teaspoon freshly ground black pepper
½ cup bread crumbs
1 recipe Lemon-Dill Yogurt Sauce (recipe follows)

1. Heat the olive oil in a large skillet over medium heat. Add the onion and garlic and cook, stirring often, until softened, about 4 minutes. Add the spinach and cook, stirring often, until wilted, about 3 minutes. Transfer the mixture to a medium-size bowl.

2. Add the eggs, quinoa, feta, dill, lemon zest, and black pepper and mix well. Mix in the bread crumbs and let the mixture sit for a few minutes to allow the bread crumbs to absorb some of the moisture.

3. Heat the panini press to medium-high heat.

4. Form quinoa patties about 2½ inches in diameter and ½ inch thick. Place the patties on the grill, in batches if necessary, and close the lid. Grill the patties until they're cooked through and browned on the outside, 4 to 5 minutes. Serve warm with lemon-dill yogurt sauce.

Lemon-Dill Yogurt Sauce

Yield: About ½ cup

This cool, creamy sauce brightens up all kinds of dishes, from salmon to falafel to raw vegetables. It tastes even better once the flavors have had a chance to meld, so make it at least 30 minutes before you need it, if possible.

½ cup plain Greek yogurt, reduced fat or whole
2 tablespoons finely chopped scallions
2 teaspoons freshly squeezed lemon juice

2 teaspoons chopped fresh dill
Coarse salt and freshly ground black pepper

Whisk together the yogurt, scallions, lemon juice, and dill in a small bowl. Season to taste with salt and pepper. Cover and refrigerate the sauce for at least 30 minutes to allow the flavors to meld.

Top Ten Surprising Uses for the Panini Press

Everyone knows that a panini press makes terrific sandwiches, but did you know that this versatile tabletop tool can do a whole lot more? With heat coming from both the top and bottom at the same time, there are endless possibilities for cooking food faster, more easily (no need to flip!), and without heating up the entire kitchen.

1. Ice cream cones. It works! Press out a spoonful of cone batter on the panini press, shape it around an easy DIY cone mold (see page 320 for the recipe and instructions), and serve ice cream in your own homemade cones all summer long.

2. Bacon. Just heat the grill, lay down as many strips as will comfortably fit on the grates, close the lid, and wait about 12 minutes to reveal perfectly crisped bacon. No more standing over a hot, spattering stove! (See page 115 for the recipe.)

3. Cakes. Yes, cakes. The trick: ramekins. Fill ramekins with cake batter, close the lid, and the individual-portioned cakes bake inside. (See pages 325 and 326 for recipes.)

4. Frittatas. Using the same ramekin approach, you can "bake" other dishes on your panini press as well. Whisk eggs and savory mix-ins together to make a Mini Frittata (page 307).

5. Corn on the Cob. Grill your fresh summer corn on the panini press and you only have to rotate the ears once—it grills two sides at the same time.

6. Hot Dogs and Sausages. Just as with corn on the cob, grilling hot dogs and other pre-cooked sausages (see Beer-Grilled Bratwursts, page 116) is made easier on the panini press because you only have to turn them one time to grill them on all sides.

7. French Toast. You love French toast but you don't love the task of flipping it in a skillet? Grill it on your panini press! With hot grates cooking the toast from the top and bottom at the same time there's no need to flip it, and you get a nice, lightly crisped exterior every time. (See page 293 for the recipe.)

8. Quesadillas. Speaking of foods that can be tough to flip, quesadillas were practically made for the panini press. Load your cheese, chicken, chiles, or whatever fillings you like between two tortillas, close the lid, and your melty treat is ready in minutes. (See page 58 for the recipe.)

9. Seafood. You can sear a fresh ahi tuna steak, sea scallops, or shrimp between the grates of a panini press in under 2 minutes. Dinner just doesn't get much faster than that.

10. Cookies. No oven in your dorm room? Bake cookies on your panini press. Frozen cookie dough often works well, or you can try my Peanut Butter Sandwich Cookies (page 333).

Grilled Tomatillo Guacamole

Yield: 8 to 10 servings

I finally put my finger on the not-so-secret ingredient that makes my favorite restaurant guacamole, from El Nopalito in Encinitas, California, especially fresh-tasting: tomatillos. The tart, green cousins of tomatoes are a staple in Mexican cuisine. They're nearly camouflaged by the avocados in the guacamole, but you can taste their presence in that *je ne sais quoi* kind of way. To dial down the tartness a little and coax out the sweetness, I grill the tomatillos for just a few minutes on the panini press before mixing them into the dip.

2 tomatillos, husks removed

2 teaspoons extra-virgin olive oil

3 medium-size ripe avocados, pitted, peeled, and chopped

¼ cup chopped red onion

½ jalapeño pepper, seeded and finely chopped

2 tablespoons chopped fresh cilantro

1 tablespoon freshly squeezed lime juice

½ teaspoon ground cumin

½ teaspoon coarse salt

¼ teaspoon freshly ground black pepper

1 recipe Grilled Tortilla Chips (page 238)

1. Heat the panini press to medium-high heat. If your panini press comes with a removable drip tray, make sure it is in place (see page 2).

2. Slice the tomatillos in half and drizzle olive oil on the cut sides. Place the tomatillos on the grill, cut sides down, and close the lid so that it's resting on the tomatillos without pressing them. Grill the tomatillos until they're softened and grill marks appear, 2 to 3 minutes.

3. Chop the tomatillos and place them in a large bowl. Add the avocados, onion, jalapeño, cilantro, lime juice, cumin, salt, and pepper to the bowl and mash it all together with a fork to a uniform but still chunky consistency.

4. Serve the guacamole with tortilla chips.

Grilled Tortilla Chips

Yield: 16 chips

After I grilled my first tortilla shells for Shrimp Tostadas (page 177) and felt their light, crisp crunch upon taking a bite, I realized I had the makings for some pretty easy tortilla chips as well. I brainstormed a bit and came up with three simple flavor combinations that would make these chips tasty for snacking on their own or as an elegant accompaniment for guacamole or cheeses: lemon–black pepper, chile-garlic, and coriander-lime.

2 tablespoons extra-virgin olive oil
⅛ teaspoon coarse salt

Additional seasonings (see below), optional
2 (8-inch) soft corn or flour tortillas

1. Heat the panini press to high heat.
2. In a small bowl, combine the olive oil, salt, and additional seasonings, if desired.
3. Brush each tortilla generously on both sides with the seasoned oil. With a pizza cutter or a sharp knife, cut each tortilla into 8 triangles.
4. Grill the triangles, with the lid closed completely, until they're browned and crisped, about 90 seconds for flour tortillas or 2 minutes for corn tortillas. Serve them warm or at room temperature.

Flavor	Additional Seasonings	Recommended Pairings
Lemon–Black Pepper	½ teaspoon freshly grated lemon zest ⅛ teaspoon freshly ground black pepper	Hummus, white bean dip, smoked salmon, goat cheese
Chile-Garlic	½ teaspoon chili powder ¼ teaspoon garlic powder	Guacamole, salsa, black bean dip
Coriander-Lime	½ teaspoon freshly grated lime zest ½ teaspoon ground coriander ⅛ teaspoon freshly ground black pepper	Guacamole, mango salsa, black bean dip

GOOEY GOODNESS

Grilled Cheese on the Panini Press

MORE FROM THE PANINI PRESS

Cheddar and Apple Butter Panini with Rosemary Candied Pecans

Yield: 4 panini

I really like cheddar and apples together, and this time I've brought fresh rosemary into the mix. Rosemary candied pecans, spiced with cayenne, add a sweet crunch and gentle heat to these cheddar and apple butter panini. I grill it all on buttered rosemary bread to bring in more of those subtle, woodsy rosemary notes.

It takes a little extra time to make the pecans, but it's well worth it—plus, you'll have an irresistible snack while you wait for the panini to grill.

4 tablespoons (½ stick) butter, at room temperature
8 slices rosemary bread or other rustic white bread, sliced from a dense bakery loaf

8 ounces sharp cheddar cheese, sliced
¼ cup Rosemary Candied Pecans (recipe follows)
4 tablespoons apple butter

1. Heat the panini press to medium-high heat.

2. *For each sandwich:* Spread butter on two slices of bread to flavor the outside of the sandwich. Flip over one slice and top the other side with cheese and some candied pecans. Flip over the other slice of bread and spread 1 tablespoon apple butter on the other side. Place it, buttered side up, on top of the sandwich to close it.

3. Grill two panini at a time, with the lid closed, until the cheese is melted and the bread is toasted, 4 to 5 minutes.

Rosemary Candied Pecans

Yield: 1 cup

Caution: These pecans are very addictive!

¼ cup sugar
2 teaspoons chopped fresh rosemary
½ teaspoon coarse salt
⅛ teaspoon ground cayenne pepper

1 large egg white
1 tablespoon water
1 cup chopped pecans

1. Heat the oven or toaster oven to 300°F. Line a baking sheet with foil and spray the foil with nonstick cooking spray. Place the sugar, rosemary, salt, and cayenne in a zipper-top plastic bag. Seal the bag and shake it well to combine it all.

2. In a medium-size bowl, whisk together the egg white and water until the mixture is slightly foamy. Add the pecans and toss to coat them well. With a slotted spoon, transfer the pecans to the bag with the sugar mixture. Seal the bag and shake it well to coat all of the pecans.

3. Transfer the coated pecans to the baking sheet and bake them for 30 minutes, giving them a stir with a fork after about 15 minutes. Set them aside to cool. The pecans should stay fresh in an airtight container for up to 2 weeks.

Cheddar, Apple, and Whole-Grain-Mustard Panini

Yield: 4 panini

Especially in autumn, during apple season, you're bound to have all the ingredients on hand to pull together these simple panini. The flavors are tangy, buttery, and a touch sweet—comfort in sandwich form.

4 tablespoons (½ stick) butter, at room temperature
8 slices rustic whole-grain bread, sliced from a dense bakery loaf
½ cup whole-grain mustard

8 ounces sharp cheddar cheese, sliced
1 medium-size apple, ideally a sweet-tart variety such as Gala or Jonagold, cored and thinly sliced

1. Heat the panini press to medium-high heat.

2. *For each sandwich:* Spread butter on two slices of bread to flavor the outside of the sandwich. Flip over both slices and spread a thin layer of mustard on the other sides. Top one slice with cheese, a single layer of apples, and more cheese. Close the sandwich with the other slice of bread, buttered side up.

3. Grill two panini at a time, with the lid closed, until the cheese is melted and the bread is toasted, 4 to 5 minutes.

Pimiento Cheese Panini

Yield: 4 panini

Pimiento cheese—a cheese spread made from sharp cheddar, diced pimientos, and mayonnaise—is real Southern comfort food. Don't knock it till you've tried it; that tangy flavor just might reel you in. It's most often served as a cold sandwich between two slices of white bread, but it also makes a pretty amazing—if a little oozy—grilled cheese.

¼ cup mayonnaise

2 tablespoons diced pimientos plus
  ¼ teaspoon of the juice from the jar

4 ounces (about 1 cup) shredded extra-
  sharp cheddar cheese

A pinch of cayenne pepper

4 tablespoons (½ stick) butter, at room
  temperature

8 slices rustic white bread, sliced from a
  dense bakery loaf

1. Blend the mayonnaise, pimientos, pimiento juice, and cheddar in a food processor until it's generally orange in color and has a semi-chunky consistency.

2. Heat the panini press to medium-high heat.

3. *For each sandwich:* Spread butter on two slices of bread to flavor the outside of the sandwich. Flip over one slice and spread a layer of pimiento cheese on the other side. Close the sandwich with the other slice of bread, buttered side up.

4. Grill two panini at a time, with the lid closed, until the bread is toasted and the cheese melts and starts to ooze out, about 3 minutes.

Honey Walnut–Crusted Aged Cheddar Panini

Yield: 4 panini

A visit to Beecher's Handmade Cheese, a small but renowned shop at Pike Place Market in Seattle, gave me a newfound appreciation for grilled cheese. Their basic grilled cheese sandwich—composed simply of their super-sharp, tangy Flagship cheese panini-grilled between two slices of rustic bread—compelled me to slow things down in my otherwise hectic day and savor every last gooey bite.

The day after I returned home I picked up a block of their cheese from my local grocery store so I could relive the experience on my own grill. I added a honey-walnut crust on the bread to lift the cheese onto a lightly sweet and crunchy pedestal. Any good-quality aged cheddar will work well in this recipe, but if you have the chance to try it with Beecher's, do!

¼ cup finely chopped walnuts
4 tablespoons (½ stick) butter, at room
   temperature
1 tablespoon honey

8 slices rustic white bread, sliced from a
   dense bakery loaf
8 ounces aged sharp cheddar cheese, thinly
   sliced

1. Heat the panini press to medium-high heat.

2. In a small bowl, mix the chopped walnuts, butter, and honey until well combined.

3. *For each sandwich:* Spread a layer of honey-walnut butter on two slices of bread. Flip over one slice of bread and top the other side with cheese. Close the sandwich with the other slice of bread, buttered side up.

4. Grill two panini at a time, with the lid closed, until the cheese is melted and the bread is toasted, 4 to 5 minutes.

Cheddar, Bacon, and Apple-Onion Panini
Yield: 4 panini

'm proud to say that I won a sandwich competition with this recipe. It was my concept for the ultimate autumn grilled cheese: sharp aged cheddar and smoky bacon with a sweet and tangy homemade caramelized apple–onion chutney on rye. Luckily, it was the ultimate in the minds—and taste buds—of the contest voters as well.

4 tablespoons unsalted butter, at room
  temperature
8 slices rye bread, sliced from a dense
  bakery loaf

8 ounces sharp aged cheddar cheese, sliced
¾ cup Caramelized Apple–Onion Chutney
  (recipe follows)
8 strips cooked bacon

1. Heat the panini press to medium-high heat.

2. *For each sandwich:* Spread butter on two slices of bread to flavor the outside of the sandwich. Flip over one slice and top the other side with cheese, a few spoonfuls of chutney, bacon, and more cheese. Close the sandwich with the other slice of bread, buttered side up.

3. Grill two panini at a time, with the lid closed, until the cheese is melted and the bread is toasted, 4 to 5 minutes.

Caramelized Apple-Onion Chutney
Yield: About 2 cups

This chutney is especially tasty with sharp-cheddar grilled cheese panini, but it also makes a flavorful condiment for roast pork or chicken.

1 tablespoon unsalted butter
1 tablespoon extra-virgin olive oil
2 medium-size onions, halved and thinly sliced
2 tablespoons minced shallots
½ teaspoon coarse salt
2 medium-size Granny Smith apples,
  peeled, cored, and thinly sliced

3 tablespoons cider vinegar
1 tablespoon freshly squeezed lemon juice
1 tablespoon light brown sugar
½ teaspoon mustard seeds
¼ teaspoon ground allspice
⅛ teaspoon freshly ground black pepper

Heat the butter and olive oil in a large skillet over medium heat. Once the butter melts, add the onions, shallots, and salt and cook, stirring occasionally, until they are tender, about 10 minutes. Add the remaining ingredients and cook until the chutney is golden-brown and caramelized, another 13 to 15 minutes. Refrigerate the chutney in an airtight container for up to 5 days.

Wine and Cheese Panini

Yield: 4 panini

Have you ever brushed wine inside a grilled cheese sandwich? I had never heard of such a thing until I read about the concept on a bakery chain's website one day. In a way, it's not so different from drizzling vinegar or vinaigrette on a sandwich—it just adds flavor. Come to think of it, wine and cheese are the most natural pairing on the planet. We should have been drizzling wine on grilled cheese sandwiches all along!

For these wine and cheese panini, I use *fromage fort*, the frugal French trick of combining odds and ends of whatever is left in the cheese drawer (you can imagine just how much cheese I have in my refrigerator on any given day) to make a flavorful spread. Go for a good balance of flavors and textures (for example, I once made an unbelievable cheese blend with extra-sharp cheddar, feta, raclette, Brie, Colby, and Asiago pressato). Include salty cheeses in moderation so as not to overwhelm the sandwich.

The French would add wine to the *fromage fort*, but in my grilled cheese version I apply wine directly to the bread itself to bring in the flavor of the wine without adding too much moisture. *C'est si bon!*

4 tablespoons (½ stick) butter, at room temperature
8 slices rustic white bread, sliced from a dense bakery loaf

2 tablespoons dry white wine
8 ounces (about 2 cups) shredded cheese, a combination of whatever you have on hand (see headnote)

1. Heat the panini press to medium high-heat.

2. *For each sandwich:* Spread butter on two slices of bread to flavor the outside of the sandwich. Flip over both slices and brush a little wine on the other side of each. Top one slice of bread with your cheese blend. Close the sandwich with the other slice of bread, buttered side up.

3. Grill two panini at a time, with the lid closed, until the cheese is melted and the bread is toasted, 4 to 5 minutes.

Jalapeño Popper Grilled Cheese Panini

Yield: 4 panini

t's not that spicy! I just wanted to put that out there from the get-go. I know when you see the word "jalapeño" you think this is going to be super-hot. If I were to use raw peppers, oh yes, there would be a fire in your mouth. But instead, I take the seeds out (where much of the heat comes from) and roast the peppers for a few minutes. Instead of an inferno, you get a milder, gently sweet heat.

What I also love about my panini version of the classic cheese-stuffed jalapeño popper appetizer is its tortilla chip crust spiced with cumin and cayenne. My friend Laura Werlin, a James Beard award–winning cheese expert, first introduced me to the brilliant idea of crusting a grilled cheese sandwich in tortilla chips (her Chips and Guacamole Grilled Cheese is out of this world). Here, that crunchy corn crust gives way to a lava of sweet roasted jalapeños and tangy melted cheese.

- 4 jalapeño peppers, halved lengthwise and seeded
- 2 ounces cream cheese, at room temperature
- 6 ounces (about 1½ cups) shredded sharp cheddar cheese
- 2 ounces corn tortilla chips (about 8 large chips)
- 4 tablespoons (½ stick) butter, at room temperature
- ¼ teaspoon ground cumin
- A pinch of cayenne pepper
- 8 slices sourdough bread, sliced from a dense bakery loaf

1. Set a rack on the top shelf of the oven or toaster oven and heat it to broil.

2. Place the jalapeños, cut sides down, on a baking sheet and broil until the skins are charred, 7 to 8 minutes. Transfer the jalapeños to a paper bag, close the bag, and let them steam until the skin of the peppers puckers and is easily removed, about 5 minutes.

3. Heat the panini press to medium-high heat.

4. Remove and discard the skins from the jalapeños, chop the peppers, and transfer them to a medium-size bowl. Add the cream cheese and sharp cheddar and mix them well.

5. Seal the tortilla chips in a zipper-top plastic bag and roll a rolling pin back and forth over the bag until the chips are crushed into fine crumbs. In a small bowl, mix the tortilla chip crumbs, butter, cumin, and cayenne until they're well combined.

6. *For each sandwich:* Spread a layer of tortilla chip butter on two slices of bread to flavor the outside of the sandwich. Flip over one slice and spread on a generous layer of cheese mixture. Close the sandwich with the other slice of bread, buttered side up.

7. Grill two panini at a time, with the lid closed, until the cheese is melted and the outside is toasted and crispy, about 5 minutes.

Gruyère, Apples, and Fig Preserves Panini

Yield: 4 panini

I keep a little file of tasting notes when I come up with new sandwiches. For this, I jotted down "Sweet, savory, and stretchy!" For some reason "stretchy" stands out in my mind as a desirable food trait. It must be the element of fun involved—you pull and pull and the strands of cheese just keep extending into a stringy pile of spirals. And then you get to pick them up and drop them into your mouth. Here's to playing with your food!

4 tablespoons (½ stick) butter, at room temperature
8 slices rustic whole-grain bread, sliced from a dense bakery loaf

4 tablespoons fig preserves
8 ounces Gruyère cheese, thinly sliced
1 Granny Smith apple, cored and thinly sliced

1. Heat the panini press to medium-high heat.

2. *For each sandwich:* Spread butter on two slices of bread to flavor the outside of the sandwich. Flip over both slices and spread a layer of fig preserves on the other side of each. To one slice add cheese, apple slices, and more cheese. Close the sandwich with the other slice of bread, buttered side up.

3. Grill two panini at a time, with the lid closed, until the cheese is melted and the bread is toasted, 4 to 5 minutes.

Gruyère and Pickled Sweet Onion Panini

Yield: 4 panini

t's most likely thanks to my fondness for French onion soup that I love the combination of melted Gruyère cheese and sweet onions on panini so much. Pickling the onions gives a powerful flavor boost to this classic pairing. Once you've got a batch of these quick pickles stored in your fridge, all you need to do is pile some inside a ciabatta roll and grill it with some nutty Gruyère for a flavorful, grown-up grilled cheese treat.

1 ciabatta loaf, cut into 4 portions, or 4 ciabatta rolls

8 ounces Gruyère cheese, sliced
½ cup Pickled Sweet Onions (recipe follows)

1. Heat the panini press to medium-high heat.

2. *For each sandwich:* Split a ciabatta portion to create top and bottom halves. On the bottom half, layer cheese, onions, and more cheese. Close the panini with the top ciabatta half.

3. Grill two panini at a time, with the lid closed, until the cheese is melted and the ciabatta is toasted, 5 to 7 minutes.

Pickled Sweet Onions

Yield: About 1 cup

There are few foods that will brighten up the flavor of a sandwich better than a pickle. They bring that big punch of acidity and, in the case of these quick pickled onions, a good dose of sweetness and spice. Try them in grilled cheese sandwiches, on hamburgers, or with pork chops.

1 medium sweet onion, such as Vidalia, Walla Walla, or Maui, halved and thinly sliced
½ cup cider vinegar

1 tablespoon packed brown sugar
1 teaspoon coarse salt
¼ teaspoon ground allspice

1. Bring a small pot of water to a boil over high heat. Add the onions, bring the water back to a boil, and let the onions cook for about 15 seconds (this will take away some of the onions' "bite"). Drain the onions and set them aside.

2. In a large nonreactive bowl, stir the vinegar, brown sugar, salt, and allspice until the sugar is dissolved. Add the onion slices and stir to coat them thoroughly in vinegar and seasonings. Cover the bowl and refrigerate the pickles for at least 1 hour before serving. Store any leftover pickled onions in the refrigerator, covered, for up to 10 days.

Gruyère and Red Onion Confit Panini

Yield: 4 panini

You know you've found a kindred spirit when you discover you both share the same taste in grilled cheese sandwiches. I was interviewing Gina Freize, owner of Venissimo Cheese, my favorite cheese shop here in San Diego, when she began to describe the staff's favorite panini: sweet, silky, ribbons of red onion confit layered on ciabatta with one of the best-melting cheeses out there, Gruyère. It sounded remarkably similar to my own prevailing favorite—Gruyère with Caramelized Onions (see PaniniHappy.com for this recipe)—except that the onions were more jam-like, sweetened further with sugar and simmered in red wine and thyme. In that moment, I couldn't think of anything else I wanted to eat.

Gina described Gruyère and Red Onion Confit Panini as "French onion soup on a bun," to which I would add "with a glass of wine."

1 ciabatta loaf, cut into 4 portions, or
    4 ciabatta rolls

8 ounces Gruyère cheese, thinly sliced
1 cup Red Onion Confit (recipe follows)

1. Heat the panini press to medium-high heat.

2. *For each sandwich:* Split a ciabatta portion to create top and bottom halves. Arrange enough cheese slices inside the bottom half to cover the surface. Top the cheese with a few tablespoons of red onion confit and more cheese. Close the sandwich with the top half of the ciabatta.

3. Grill two panini at a time, with the lid closed, until the cheese is melted and the ciabatta is toasted, 5 to 7 minutes.

Red Onion Confit

Yield: About 2 cups

It's worth the time it takes to make this red onion confit, and you won't mind at all about having some left over. You'll want to add these onions to everything—other panini, meats or poultry, pizzas, and pastas.

2 tablespoons butter
1 tablespoon extra-virgin olive oil
3 medium-size red onions, halved and
    thinly sliced
½ cup dry red wine, such as Cabernet
    Sauvignon or Malbec

2 tablespoons chopped fresh thyme
2 tablespoons sugar
3 tablespoons balsamic vinegar
Coarse salt and freshly ground black
    pepper

1. Heat the butter and olive oil in a large skillet or Dutch oven over medium heat until the butter is melted. Add the onions and cook, stirring often, until they're softened, 8 to 10 minutes.

2. Add the wine, thyme, and sugar and continue cooking, stirring occasionally, until the onions are very soft and tender, about 30 minutes more. Lower the heat, if necessary, to avoid scorching.

3. Pour in the balsamic vinegar and season the onions with salt and pepper to taste. Continue cooking and stirring for another 5 minutes to allow the liquid to absorb. The onions will be silky, glistening, and deep reddish-purple.

4. Use the onions right away or store them in the refrigerator, covered, for up to 5 days.

Brie, Basil, Bacon, and Blue Cheese Panini

Yield: 4 panini

Brie, basil, bacon, and blue . . . well, it's just a happy coincidence that all of these ingredients start with "B." They happen to combine into a pretty amazing grilled cheese sandwich.

Even if you're not a fan of blue cheese—I'm speaking to my husband here—you still have got to dab on just a little bit. The tangy flavor borders on sweet amidst the smoky bacon, bright basil, and creamy Brie.

1 French baguette, cut into 4 portions, or 4 mini baguettes

4 ounces Brie cheese (with or without the rind), sliced

2 ounces crumbled blue cheese

8 fresh basil leaves

8 strips cooked bacon

1. Heat the panini press to medium-high heat.

2. *For each sandwich:* Slice off the domed top of a baguette portion to create a flat grilling surface. Split the baguette to create top and bottom halves. Inside the bottom half, lay a thin layer of Brie slices and sprinkle about a tablespoon of blue cheese on top. Add 2 basil leaves, 2 bacon strips, more blue cheese, and more Brie. Close the sandwich with the top half.

3. Grill two panini at a time, with the lid closed, until the cheese is melted and the baguettes are toasted, 4 to 5 minutes.

Brie and Orange Marmalade Panini

Yield: 4 panini

'**ve** never seen a baked Brie appetizer survive to the end of a party—it's always the first to go. People love it for good reason. Warm, buttery Brie pairs so naturally with sweet condiments like honey, preserves, and marmalade. The combination also makes a pretty irresistible grilled cheese sandwich. I used orange marmalade in this recipe, but you could easily substitute any other sweet spread that you enjoy with Brie, such as fig preserves or raspberry jam.

1 multigrain baguette, cut into 4 portions, or 4 mini baguettes
½ cup orange marmalade

4 ounces Brie cheese (with or without the rind), sliced

1. Heat the panini press to medium-high heat.

2. *For each sandwich:* Slice off the domed top of a baguette portion to create a flat grilling surface. Split the baguette to create top and bottom halves. Spread 1 tablespoon marmalade inside both halves. Add a few slices of Brie to the bottom baguette half and close the sandwich with the top half.

3. Grill two panini at a time, with the lid closed, until the cheese is melted and the baguettes are toasted, 5 to 7 minutes.

Raclette and Honey Panini

Yield: 4 panini

The very first time that I asked PaniniHappy.com readers for sandwich suggestions, back in the early days of the blog, someone suggested that I try making grilled cheese with raclette. After a bit of Googling, I learned that raclette is a Swiss cheese—not the kind with big holes, but a semi-hard, buttery, easy-melting cheese that sounded perfect for a sandwich. Once I tasted raclette, I decided to play up its subtle sweetness a bit by adding honey to the mix. Don't let the simplicity of these panini fool you. This has become one of my favorite ways to enjoy grilled cheese.

1 seeded baguette, cut into 4 portions, or 4 mini baguettes

4 teaspoons honey
4 ounces raclette cheese, sliced

1. Heat the panini press to medium-high heat.

2. *For each sandwich:* Slice off the domed top of a baguette portion to create a flat grilling surface. Split the baguette to create top and bottom halves. Drizzle ½ teaspoon honey inside each baguette half. Add some cheese to the bottom baguette half and close the sandwich with the top half.

3. Grill two panini at a time, with the lid closed, until the cheese is melted and the baguettes are toasted, 5 to 7 minutes.

Sweet Corn Panini with Smoked Gouda, Scallions, and Chile Butter

Yield: 4 panini

t's not every day that we see corn kernels inside a grilled cheese sandwich, but maybe we should. Hot, sweet, and smoky corn chowder was my inspiration for these panini. As heavenly as these flavors are in soup form, they're even better surrounded by the crunch of chile-buttered and grilled sourdough.

4 tablespoons (½ stick) butter, at room temperature
1 teaspoon chile powder
A pinch of cayenne pepper
8 slices sourdough or other rustic white bread, sliced from a dense bakery loaf

8 ounces smoked Gouda or smoked cheddar cheese, thinly sliced
¼ cup cooked corn, ideally fresh from the cob
2 tablespoons chopped scallions

1. In a small bowl mix the butter, chile powder, and cayenne pepper until they're well combined.

2. *For each sandwich:* Spread chile butter on two slices of bread to flavor the outside of the sandwich. Flip over one slice of bread and top it with cheese, corn, scallions, and more cheese. Close the sandwich with the other slice of bread, buttered side up.

3. Grill two panini at a time, with the lid closed, until the cheese is melted and the bread is toasted, 4 to 5 minutes.

Spicy Grilled Cheese Sliders

Yield: 4 servings

learned this little trick from a local pizza place. One of the waiters divulged that the kick of flavor I couldn't get enough of in their pizza was actually a drizzle of chili oil on the crust. It's amazing what a difference the chili oil makes to the pizza—I knew it would be just as enlivening on grilled cheese sandwiches.

To spice things up even more for these sliders, I shred a blend of pepper Jack cheese along with some stretchy mozzarella. Stack up these sliders next to a nice warm mug of tomato bisque.

4 ounces (about 1 cup) shredded pepper
  Jack cheese
4 ounces (about 1 cup) shredded mozzarella cheese

1 large sourdough baguette (about 3 inches
  in diameter), sliced crosswise into 16
  ½-inch-thick slices
Chili oil for brushing (see Note)

1. Heat the panini press to medium-high heat.

2. In a medium-size bowl, combine the pepper Jack and mozzarella cheeses. Lay out half of the baguette slices. Drop a few spoonfuls of cheese on each baguette slice. Place the remaining baguette slices on top to form each slider. Brush a little chili oil on top of each slider.

3. Working in batches as needed, grill the sliders, with the lid closed, until the cheese is melted, 3 to 4 minutes.

NOTE: Look for chili oil, a spicy condiment that's been infused with chili peppers, alongside other oils or in the Asian foods section of your grocery store. The amount of heat can vary from brand to brand, so taste it first to gauge how much to use.

Rajas Grilled Cheese Panini

Yield: 4 panini

The word *rajas* in Spanish translates as "strips," as in strips of roasted chiles and onions that bring a punch of south-of-the-border flavor to all kinds of dishes. Grilling *rajas* is an easy job on the panini press—it takes just minutes to get them nicely charred. Pile them on a sandwich with pepper Jack for a spicy grilled cheese or, to tone down the heat, opt for Monterey Jack.

4 tablespoons (½ stick) butter, at room
   temperature
8 slices sourdough bread, sliced from a
   dense bakery loaf

8 ounces pepper Jack cheese, sliced
1 recipe *Rajas* (page 292)

1. *For each sandwich:* Spread butter on two slices of bread to flavor the outside of the sandwich. Flip over one slice and top the other side with cheese, a generous pile of *rajas*, and more cheese. Close the sandwich with the other slice of bread, buttered side up.

2. Grill two panini at a time, with the lid closed, until the cheese is melted and the bread is toasted, 4 to 5 minutes.

Goat Cheese and Pepper Jelly Panini

Yield: 4 panini

You peel back the cellophane on the gift basket a friend or coworker has sent you, and inevitably, amidst the crackers and dried fruit, sits a little jar of some kind of obscure spread that you have never heard of. You also have no idea what to do with it.

That was me with a jar of pepper jelly once. It must have sat idly on my pantry shelf for a year before I finally realized the perfect use for it: grilled cheese. Spreading a little pepper jelly inside the bread brings in that sweet heat that I love without adding too much moisture. This recipe calls for goat cheese, which is great for cooling things off, but you could also try this approach with cream cheese, Brie, or even cheddar.

4 tablespoons (½ stick) butter, at room temperature
8 slices rustic whole-grain bread, sliced from a dense bakery loaf

½ cup pepper jelly
4 ounces goat cheese, sliced into medallions

1. Heat the panini press to medium-high heat.

2. *For each sandwich:* Spread butter on two slices of bread to flavor the outside of the sandwich. Flip over both slices and spread 1 tablespoon pepper jelly on the other side of each. Top one slice of bread with goat cheese and close the sandwich with the other slice, buttered side up.

3. Grill two panini at a time, with the lid closed, until the cheese is softened and the bread is toasted, 3 to 4 minutes.

Marinated Mozzarella Panini with Artichokes and Roasted Red Peppers

Yield: 4 panini

Did you know you could marinate cheese? Mozzarella, in particular, soaks up flavor like crazy. You'll often see fresh mozzarella that's been soaked in garlic and herbs on an antipasto platter, but just think of the possibilities for grilled cheese sandwiches! Pizza-like aromas begin to emanate from the panini press as you're grilling these panini—get ready to get hungry.

MARINATED MOZZARELLA
2 tablespoons extra-virgin olive oil
1 garlic clove, minced
¼ teaspoon dried basil
¼ teaspoon dried oregano
¼ teaspoon dried thyme
A pinch of red pepper flakes
8 ounces fresh mozzarella cheese, sliced

PANINI
4 tablespoons (½ stick) butter, at room temperature
8 slices rustic white bread, sliced from a dense bakery loaf
½ cup sliced marinated artichoke hearts
½ cup sliced roasted red bell peppers

1. *Marinated Mozzarella:* Mix the olive oil, garlic, basil, oregano, thyme, and red pepper flakes in a medium-size bowl. Add the mozzarella and toss it around in the marinade to coat it well. Let the cheese sit in the marinade for 1 hour at room temperature to allow the flavors to seep in.

2. *Panini:* Heat the panini press to medium-high heat.

3. *For each sandwich:* Spread butter on two slices of bread to flavor the outside of the sandwich. Flip over one slice of bread and lay a few slices of marinated mozzarella on the other side. Top the mozzarella with artichokes, roasted red bell peppers, and more mozzarella. Close the sandwich with the other slice of bread, buttered side up.

4. Grill two panini at a time, with the lid closed, until the cheese is melted and the bread is toasted, 4 to 6 minutes.

Lemon-Basil Grilled Cheese Panini

Yield: 4 panini

For all of my fellow lemon lovers out there, this one is for you. Lemon zest and fresh basil make these about the most fresh-tasting grilled cheese sandwiches you're going to find. They're especially fabulous alongside a cup of roasted red pepper soup.

4 ounces (about 1 cup) shredded mozzarella
2 ounces crumbled feta cheese
2 teaspoons grated lemon zest

2 teaspoons chopped fresh basil
1 tablespoon extra-virgin olive oil
8 slices Italian or sourdough bread, sliced
 from a dense bakery loaf

1. Heat the panini press to medium-high heat.

2. Toss together the mozzarella, feta, lemon zest, and basil in a medium-size bowl.

3. *For each sandwich:* Brush olive oil on two slices of bread to flavor the outside of the sandwich. Flip over one slice and top the other side with a layer of the cheese mixture. Close the sandwich with the other slice of bread, oiled side up.

4. Grill two panini at a time, with the lid closed, until the cheese is melted and the bread is toasted, 4 to 5 minutes.

Green Chile Grilled Cheese Panini

Yield: 4 to 6 panini

Southerners who grew up on creamy, tangy pimiento cheese sandwiches (see page 245) may recognize these panini—they're my Southwestern spin on their regional specialty. Instead of mixing sweet red pimiento peppers into the cheese, I opt for the gentle heat of diced green chiles with sharp cheddar, Monterey Jack, and cream cheese. The bold flavor combination reminds me of cheese-filled jalapeño poppers. As you can tell from the photo, it's definitely a very oozy grilled cheese . . . just the type that I love most!

3 ounces cream cheese, softened
4 ounces (about 1 cup) shredded sharp cheddar cheese
4 ounces (about 1 cup) shredded Monterey Jack cheese
1 (4-ounce) can diced green chiles, drained

1 scallion, thinly sliced
4 to 6 tablespoons butter, at room temperature
8 to 12 slices rustic white bread, sliced from a dense bakery loaf

1. Heat the panini press to medium-high heat.

2. In a medium-size bowl, beat the cream cheese with an electric mixer or wooden spoon until it's soft and light. Mix in the cheddar, Jack, green chiles, and scallion.

3. *For each sandwich:* Spread butter on two slices of bread to flavor the outside of the sandwich. Flip over one slice and spread a generous amount of the cheese mixture on the other side. Close the sandwich with the other slice of bread, buttered side up.

4. Grill two panini at a time, with the lid closed, until the cheese is melted and the bread is toasted, 5 to 6 minutes.

NOTE: The total number of panini will depend on the size of your bread. Take care not to overfill each sandwich.

Green Goddess Grilled Cheese Panini

Yield: 4 to 6 panini

Bursting with bright, fresh green herbs and kicked up with the bold flavors of garlic and anchovies, Green Goddess salad dressing has been making a bit of a comeback in recent years. It was first created at the Palace Hotel in San Francisco back in the 1920s. Now it's again popping up at restaurants and being bottled commercially by major brands. As I toyed with ideas for making green panini for St. Patrick's Day one year, it struck me to invent grilled cheese panini based on this very green classic.

1 garlic clove, finely chopped

1 anchovy fillet, finely chopped

Zest of 1 lime (about 1 teaspoon)

3 tablespoons chopped fresh flat-leaf parsley

2 tablespoons chopped fresh tarragon

2 tablespoons chopped fresh cilantro

1 tablespoon chopped fresh basil

1 tablespoon finely chopped shallot

¼ teaspoon Dijon mustard

2 ounces cream cheese, cut into small cubes

4 ounces (about 1 cup) shredded mozzarella cheese

4 ounces (about 1 cup) shredded sharp white cheddar cheese

4 to 6 tablespoons butter, at room temperature

8 to 12 slices sourdough bread, sliced from a dense bakery loaf

1. Place the garlic and anchovies in a mini food processor and pulse a few times until they're very finely minced, almost a paste (if you don't have a food processor, just mince the ingredients as finely as possible with a knife).

2. Add the lime zest, parsley, tarragon, cilantro, basil, shallot, mustard, and cream cheese and pulse again until well blended. Transfer the mixture to a medium-size bowl and stir in the mozzarella and cheddar cheeses.

3. Heat the panini press to medium-high heat.

4. *For each sandwich:* Spread butter on two slices of bread to flavor the outside of the sandwich. Flip over one slice and spread a generous amount of the cheese mixture on the other side. Close the sandwich with the other slice of bread, buttered side up.

5. Grill two panini at a time, with the lid closed, until the cheese is melted and oozy and the bread is toasted, 5 to 6 minutes.

NOTE: The total number of panini will depend on the size of your bread. Take care not to overfill each sandwich.

Panini Pops

Yield: About 8 pops

We all love cute food, don't we? Pops of any kind qualify as cute to me, whether they're cakes, cookies, or even sandwiches. I was inspired by Bakerella, the immensely creative and talented blogger who popularized cake pops, to come up with Panini Pops. They're simply grilled cheese sandwiches cut into fun shapes, with minced goodies like bacon, herbs, or peppers mixed in, delivered on a lollipop stick. They're sure to go over well at your next children's birthday party or baby shower.

Depending on the cookie cutter shape you use, you may wind up with lots of grilled cheese scraps while making these pops. You can cut them up to use as grilled cheese croutons for soups and salads—or just pop them in your mouth as is.

8 ounces (about 2 cups) shredded semi-firm cheese (such as cheddar, Colby, or Swiss)

¼ cup finely crumbled or minced mix-ins (such as cooked bacon, herbs, or roasted red bell peppers)

4 tablespoons (½ stick) butter, at room temperature

8 slices rustic white bread, sliced from a dense bakery loaf

8 lollipop sticks (see Note)

1. Heat the panini press to medium-high heat.

2. Combine the cheese and your mix-ins in a medium-size bowl.

3. *For each sandwich:* Spread butter on two slices of bread to flavor the outside of the sandwich. Flip over one slice and top the other side with a generous amount of cheese (and any mix-ins) to ensure that there will be enough to hold the lollipop sticks in place. Close the sandwich with the other slice of bread, buttered side up.

4. Grill two panini at a time, with the lid closed, until the cheese is melted and the bread is toasted, 3 to 4 minutes.

5. Transfer the panini to a cutting board and immediately cut out shapes with large cookie cutters (if you're using a metal cutter it will get hot very quickly, so take care not to burn your fingers). Then insert the lollipop sticks, while the cheese is still hot and soft. Once the cheese cools for a minute or two it should firm up and hold the sticks in place.

NOTE: Look for lollipop sticks at craft stores or baking supply stores.

Grilled Brie with Honey and Toasted Pecans

Yield: 4 servings

For an easy, crowd-pleasing appetizer that you can pull together in just 10 minutes flat, look no further than grilled Brie. You just put the entire 8-ounce wheel right on the grill, then serve it drizzled with honey and toasted pecans. Keep these simple ingredients on hand and you'll be ready the next time unexpected guests show up at the door. If you don't happen to have a baguette on hand for dipping, offer crackers or apple slices.

½ cup chopped pecans
1 French baguette, sliced diagonally into
  ½-inch-thick slices

1 (8-ounce) wheel of Brie cheese
1 to 2 tablespoons honey

1. Heat the oven or toaster oven to 350°F. Spread the pecans on a baking sheet and toast them until they're aromatic, about 5 minutes.

2. Heat the panini press to medium-high heat.

3. In batches, arrange the baguette slices on the panini press, close the lid, and grill the slices until they're toasted and grill marks appear, about 2 minutes. Remove the baguette slices and set aside.

4. Place the entire wheel of Brie on the grill, close the lid so that it's touching the cheese without pressing it, and grill the cheese until it begins to melt (you'll see the cheese start to depress and flatten out a little), about 3 minutes.

5. Carefully lift the Brie with a spatula and transfer it to a serving platter. Drizzle honey over the Brie, scatter toasted pecans over the top, and serve it with the grilled bread.

ON THE MORNING MENU

Breakfast and Brunch on the Panini Press

MORE FROM THE PANINI PRESS

Granola-Crusted Pear, Almond Butter, and Honey Panini

Yield: 4 panini

We go through a ton of granola at our house, mostly as a healthy, crunchy topping for yogurt parfaits. Did you know that granola also makes a pretty terrific sandwich crust? All you do is crush the granola, mix it with butter, spread it all over the outside of your bread, and grill your sandwiches for an irresistibly crunchy exterior. It's an easy way to take these sweet panini to the next level.

¼ cup granola
4 tablespoons (½ stick) butter, at room temperature
8 slices rustic white bread, sliced from a dense bakery loaf

½ cup almond butter or peanut butter
1 ripe pear or apple, peeled, cored, and sliced
2 teaspoons honey

1. Pulse the granola in a food processor until the oats have been cut down to about ⅛-inch bits, but not completely ground up. Mix the chopped granola with the butter until it's well combined.

2. *For each sandwich:* Spread granola butter on two slices of bread to create the outer crust of the sandwich. Flip over both slices of bread and spread almond butter on each. Top one slice of bread with a layer of pear slices and a drizzle of honey. Close the sandwich with the other slice of bread, buttered side up.

3. Grill two panini at a time, with the lid closed, until the bread is toasted, 3 to 4 minutes.

Strawberry, Banana, and Nutella Panini

Yield: 4 panini

These sandwiches quickly became some of the most popular on PaniniHappy.com for one main reason: Nutella. To this day, I still feel sneaky whenever I dip into the Nutella jar—it just seems so wrong to eat spreadable chocolate by the spoonful. I even go so far as to store it in the back of my pantry to avoid temptation.

The truth is that I really do love the stuff. And when it's heated up with fresh strawberries and bananas between two slices of buttered and toasted whole-grain bread, it's irresistible! If you're among the many who unabashedly enjoy Nutella for breakfast, this will definitely make for a very happy start to your day.

4 tablespoons (½ stick) butter, at room temperature

8 slices rustic whole-grain bread, sliced from a dense bakery loaf

¾ cup Nutella chocolate hazelnut spread

4 to 6 strawberries, sliced

1 banana, sliced

1. Heat the panini press to medium-high heat.

2. *For each sandwich:* Spread butter on two slices of bread to flavor the outside of the sandwich. Flip over both slices and spread some Nutella on the other side of each. Top one slice with a single layer of strawberries and bananas. Close the sandwich with the other slice of bread, buttered side up.

3. Grill two panini at a time, with the lid closed, until they are heated through and the bread is toasted, 3 to 4 minutes.

Blueberry Ricotta Grilled Cheese Panini

Yield: 4 panini

They may remind you more of light, sweet blintzes than typical grilled cheese sandwiches, but don't let that stop you from experiencing these panini. Soft and almost fluffy, these sandwiches are one of those rare panini recipes where a softer bread, like thick-cut brioche, is the best accompaniment to the delicate fillings.

¾ cup ricotta
2 teaspoons honey, plus more for drizzling
1 teaspoon grated lemon zest

8 thick slices brioche, challah, or other soft enriched bread
½ cup fresh blueberries
1 teaspoon chopped fresh mint

1. In a small bowl, mix the ricotta, 2 teaspoons honey, and lemon zest until well combined.

2. Heat the panini press to medium-high heat.

3. *For each sandwich:* Spread a generous layer of the ricotta mixture on one slice of bread. Top the ricotta with blueberries and mint. Add a drizzle of honey and dot on another tablespoon of ricotta. Close the sandwich with another slice of bread.

4. If your grill allows you to adjust the height of the upper plate, adjust it so that it rests on top of the bread without pressing it (soft breads like brioche have a tendency to flatten under the weight of the panini press). Grill the panini, two at a time, until the bread is toasted, about 2 minutes.

Avocado and Bacon Toasts

Yield: 4 toasts

Avocado toasts are right up there with tomato sandwiches (see my Heirloom Tomato Panini recipe on page 198) as evidence of just how sublimely delicious the simplest sandwiches can be. Who would ever guess that smashing a creamy, ripe avocado onto grilled bread with a squeeze of lime juice and a sprinkling of salt could be so satisfying?

For me, a few slices of crisp, smoky bacon take these toasts up one impressive flavor notch, but if you prefer to leave off the bacon you'll still have something simply delicious. Many people enjoy avocado toasts for breakfast, but I think they're perfect any time of the day.

4 slices rustic white or wheat bread, sliced from a dense bakery loaf
4 teaspoons extra-virgin olive oil
8 strips cooked bacon

2 medium-size ripe avocados, pitted, peeled, and halved
1 lime, cut into 4 wedges
Coarse salt

1. Heat the panini press to medium-high heat.

2. Drizzle olive oil over each slice of bread and grill two slices at a time, with the lid closed, until they're toasted, about 2 minutes.

3. *For each toast:* Crisscross 2 bacon strips on a slice of grilled bread. Place an avocado half on top of the bacon and smash it with the back of a spoon to spread it around the toast. Squeeze the juice from 1 lime wedge over the top and season the avocado with salt to taste.

Bacon, Egg, and Cheddar English Muffin Panini

Yield: 4 panini

I f I had to choose my single favorite breakfast sandwich, this would have to be it: the classic bacon, egg, and cheese on an English muffin. It's the all-American breakfast in handheld form and it's simply perfect. While I love standard English muffins with all their "nooks and crannies," these sandwiches hold up better on the panini press with brands of muffins that are a bit thicker and denser.

2 teaspoons butter
4 large eggs
Coarse salt and freshly ground black pepper

4 thick English muffins
4 ounces sharp cheddar cheese, sliced
8 strips cooked bacon

1. One at a time, prepare the omelets. Melt ½ teaspoon of the butter in a small nonstick skillet over medium-low heat. Beat 1 egg very well in a small bowl, season it with salt and pepper, and pour it into the skillet. Once the egg has set slightly, pull in the sides with a rubber spatula to allow the runny egg to flow to the edges of the pan. When the egg is nearly set, carefully lift up one edge with the rubber spatula and fold it in half. Transfer the omelet to a plate and tent it with foil to keep it warm while you prepare the other three omelets in the same manner.

2. Heat the panini press to medium-high heat.

3. *For each sandwich:* Split an English muffin to create top and bottom halves. On the bottom half, layer cheese, an omelet (folded again, if necessary, to fit on the muffin), 2 bacon strips, and more cheese. Close the sandwich with the top English muffin half.

4. Working in batches if necessary, grill the panini, with the lid closed, until the cheese is melted and the muffins are toasted, 4 to 5 minutes.

Croque Madame Panini

Yield: 4 panini

I f you're among those who believe that adding a fried egg on top of a dish instantly makes it even better, I would like to introduce you to Croque Monsieur's better half, the classic Croque Madame. A grilled ham and cheese sandwich just like her husband—with a Parmesan crust for extra crunchiness—Mrs. Croque's sunny-side-up egg on top makes for an especially tasty brunch offering.

4 tablespoons plus 2 teaspoons butter, at room temperature

1 ounce (about ¼ cup) shredded Parmesan cheese

8 slices rustic white bread, sliced from a dense bakery loaf

4 tablespoons Dijon mustard

8 ounces Gruyère or Swiss cheese, thinly sliced

8 ounces sliced ham

4 large eggs

Coarse salt and freshly ground black pepper

1 teaspoon chopped fresh chives

1. In a small bowl, mix 4 tablespoons of the butter with the Parmesan cheese until well combined.

2. Heat the panini press to medium-high heat.

3. *For each sandwich:* Spread Parmesan butter on two slices of bread to flavor the outside of the sandwich. Flip over both slices and spread a thin layer of Dijon mustard on each. Top one slice with cheese, a few slices of ham, and more cheese. Close the sandwich with the other slice of bread, mustard side down.

4. Grill two panini at a time, with the lid closed, until the cheese is melted and the bread is toasted with a crispy crust, 4 to 5 minutes.

5. Once the first batch of panini is done, melt the remaining 2 teaspoons butter in a large nonstick skillet over very low heat, swirling the pan to distribute the butter evenly. One at a time, crack each egg into a small dish or bowl and then gently slide it into the skillet. Do your best to keep the eggs separate from one another, but don't worry if they run together—you can always separate them with the edge of your spatula at the end of cooking. Cover the skillet with a lid or foil and cook the eggs until the whites are set and the yolks are still runny, 3 to 4 minutes. Season the eggs with salt and pepper to taste.

6. Serve each sandwich with a fried egg on top and garnish with chives.

Monte Cristo Panini

Yield: 4 panini

For years, a ham and cheese sandwich was, to me, just that: ham, cheese, and bread (maybe a little mustard, definitely not mayo). If there's one thing I've learned since starting PaniniHappy.com, it's that there are about a million and one ways to make ham and cheese. My favorite of them all, thus far, has got to be the Monte Cristo. This is the savory French toast version of ham and cheese, where you dip the bread in an egg batter before grilling and serve the sandwiches with a sprinkling of confectioners' sugar and a side of sweet preserves. Just as with French toast, it's gently crisp on the outside and pleasantly spongy on the inside. When I'm feeling particularly "gourmet," I make these with prosciutto and Gruyère, but regular sliced deli ham and Swiss cheese work just as well.

2 tablespoons honey
2 tablespoons Dijon mustard
2 large eggs
¼ cup milk
½ teaspoon coarse salt
¼ teaspoon freshly ground black pepper
⅛ teaspoon ground nutmeg

8 slices rustic white bread, sliced from a
    dense bakery loaf
8 ounces Gruyère or Swiss cheese, sliced
8 ounces sliced prosciutto or ham
Confectioners' sugar, for dusting
Strawberry or raspberry preserves, for
    serving

1. Heat the panini press to medium-high heat.

2. In a small bowl, mix the honey with the mustard until they're well combined.

3. In a shallow bowl, whisk together the eggs, milk, salt, pepper, and nutmeg.

4. *For each sandwich:* Spread a few teaspoons of honey mustard on two slices of bread. On one slice of bread, layer cheese, prosciutto, and more cheese. Close the sandwich with the other slice of bread, honey mustard side down.

5. Just before grilling, dip both sides of the sandwich into the egg batter. Allow the bread to sit and soak up the liquid for several seconds.

6. Grill two panini at a time, with the lid closed, until the cheese is melted and the sandwich is browned and cooked through, about 5 minutes.

7. Dust the sandwiches with confectioners' sugar and serve them with preserves.

Egg White Omelet Panino with Spinach, Feta, and Sun-Dried Tomatoes

Yield: 1 panino (see Note)

I was waiting for a flight at the Atlanta airport when I noticed a young woman in her 20s who had just exited a plane. From afar, she gazed up at the familiar green-and-white logo of that ubiquitous Seattle-based coffee giant, stretched out her arms, and screamed, *"Sanctuary!"* I don't know where she'd been traveling or how long she'd been away, but I can relate to feeling a little perk in my mood when a branch of this particular establishment appears in my path just when I need it.

Beyond the coffee—mostly decaf for me these days—I've become a fan of the food at this coffee chain. One item in particular, a spinach and feta breakfast wrap made with egg whites, is so flavorful and satisfying that I easily forget that it's classed as a healthier option. The egg whites pack a lot of protein, feta is naturally low in fat, and the green, leafy spinach is loaded with nutrients. One day I ventured to make my own version of this fabulous wrap and it came together in a snap.

3 large egg whites
Coarse salt and freshly ground black pepper
2 slices sourdough or other rustic white
   bread, sliced from a dense bakery loaf

¼ cup loosely packed baby spinach
3 oil-packed sun-dried tomatoes, thinly
   sliced
1 ounce crumbled feta cheese

1. Spray a little nonstick cooking spray in a small skillet and heat it over medium-high heat.

2. Meanwhile, in a large bowl, whisk the egg whites until they're frothy. Season them with salt and pepper. Pour the egg whites into the skillet and let them cook until they're set on the bottom, about 1 minute. With a spatula, carefully lift up one side and fold it over, creating a half-moon shape. Continue cooking the omelet, flipping after another minute or so, until it's cooked through and set. Slide the omelet onto a plate and tent it with foil to keep it warm while you assemble the sandwich.

3. Heat the panini press to medium-high heat.

4. Create a little bed of baby spinach on one slice of bread and lay your egg white omelet on top of it. Arrange the sun-dried tomato slices on the omelet and sprinkle the feta on top. Close the sandwich with the other slice of bread.

5. Grill the sandwich, with the lid closed, until the cheese is softened and the bread is toasted, 4 to 5 minutes.

NOTE: You can easily scale up this recipe to make more servings; just be sure to cook the egg white omelets one at a time.

Panini vs. Paninis vs. Panino

In America it's common to hear people refer to a single grilled sandwich as "a panini" and multiple sandwiches as "paninis." These words have become part of the popular lexicon, but they drive linguistic purists absolutely crazy.

Technically speaking, there is no such word as "paninis." The word "panini" is already in the plural form—it's Italian for "sandwiches." Saying "paninis" is like saying "sandwicheses," And saying "a panini" is like saying "a sandwiches." Doesn't sound quite right, does it?

So what's the correct word to refer to just one grilled sandwich? The singular form of the word "panini" is "panino." One panino . . . two panini.

You're probably thinking to yourself, "Whoever heard of a panino?" Well, you're right, it's not a commonly used word here in the United States. Chances are you might be met with blank stares if you try to use it. To me, it's important to respect the integrity of a language, but it's also important to communicate and be understood. At the end of the day, as long as the sandwich tastes great, it doesn't matter to me what you call it!

Rajas, Steak, and Egg Panini

Yield: 4 panini

I
f you're looking for a lighter, healthier, simpler breakfast sandwich option, this ain't it—flip on over to the Egg White Omelet Panino (page 288) instead. These take some time to prepare, and they're hardly light—but they're fabulous. They're the ultimate steak and egg panini—cumin-grilled flat-iron steak, *rajas* (grilled red bell peppers, poblanos, and onions), an omelet, and sharp cheddar on sourdough. If cowboys ate panini, I could picture them going for these.

Short on Time? To save on prep time in the morning, grill the steak and *rajas* the night before. Quicker yet, just slice up any leftover steak you have on hand.

STEAK
1 (1-pound) flatiron or top blade steak
1 teaspoon coarse salt
1 teaspoon garlic powder
½ teaspoon ground cumin
½ teaspoon freshly ground black pepper

OMELETS
2 teaspoons butter
4 large eggs

Coarse salt and freshly ground black pepper

PANINI
4 tablespoons plus 2 teaspoons butter, at room temperature
8 slices sourdough or other rustic white bread, sliced from a dense bakery loaf
8 ounces sharp cheddar or pepper Jack cheese, sliced
1 recipe *Rajas* (page 292)

1. *Steak:* Heat the panini press to high heat. If your panini press comes with a removable drip tray, make sure it is in place (see page 2).

2. Season both sides of the steak with salt, garlic powder, cumin, and pepper. Grill the steak, with the lid closed, to your desired doneness, 5 to 7 minutes for medium (137°F).

3. Transfer the steak to a cutting board and let it rest for 10 minutes before slicing it very thinly across the grain. Meanwhile, unplug the grill and, while it's still hot, carefully scrape down the grates with a grill scraper to remove any stuck-on bits of meat. Allow the grill to cool and clean the grates.

4. *Omelets:* One at a time, prepare the omelets. Melt ½ teaspoon of the butter in a small nonstick skillet over medium-low heat. Beat 1 egg very well in a small bowl, season it with salt and pepper, and pour it into the skillet. Once the egg has set slightly, pull in the sides with a rubber spatula to allow the runny egg to flow to the edges of the pan. When the egg is nearly set, carefully lift up one edge with the rubber spatula and fold it in half. Transfer the omelet to a plate and tent it with foil to keep it warm while you prepare the other three omelets in the same manner.

(continued on next page)

5. *Panini:* Reheat the panini press to medium-high heat.

6. *For each sandwich:* Spread butter on two slices of bread to flavor the outside of the sandwich. Flip over one slice of bread and layer on cheese, steak, an omelet, *rajas*, and more cheese. Close the sandwich with the other slice of bread, buttered side up.

7. Grill two panini at a time, with the lid closed, until the cheese is melted and the bread is toasted, 4 to 5 minutes.

Rajas
Yield: About 2 cups

Even if you haven't heard the term *rajas* (pronounced RAH-has), chances are you've tasted them. They're simply bold-flavored strips of roasted chiles and onions, such as you might find served with fajitas. I grill them easily on the panini press, using mild poblano peppers, for use in all kinds of recipes—from sandwiches to tacos to pizzas.

1 poblano pepper (see Note)
1 red bell pepper
2 teaspoons vegetable oil

1 small white onion, sliced into ½-inch-thick rounds (rings intact)

1. Heat the panini press to medium-high heat.

2. Slice off the tops and bottoms of both peppers. Slice the poblano lengthwise down one side, spread it out flat, and remove the seeds. Cut the red bell pepper into three or four flat sections. Remove the seeds and trim any white ribs.

3. Lay the peppers, skin sides up, on the grill and close the lid. Grill the peppers until they're charred and blistered, 5 to 7 minutes. Transfer the peppers to a paper bag, close the bag, and let the peppers steam for 20 minutes to release their skins. One at a time, remove the peppers from the paper bag, peel off the skins (if they don't come off easily, try scraping them off with a paring knife), and slice the peppers lengthwise into strips. Transfer to a medium-size bowl.

4. While the peppers are steaming, drizzle both sides of the onion rounds with oil and grill them, with the lid closed, until they're tender and grill marks appear, 4 to 6 minutes. Separate the onions into rings and toss them with the peppers.

5. Use the *rajas* right away or refrigerate them, covered, for up to 3 days.

NOTE: Some grocery stores may label poblano peppers as "pasilla" peppers, which is a technically incorrect (but common) reference to the green pepper in its fresh state.

Grilled French Toast

Yield: 4 servings

The number one reason to cook French toast on a panini press instead of in a skillet: no need to flip! And the second-best reason is the lightly crisp, ridged surface created by the grill grates—it's perfect for holding maple syrup.

French toast works best on a panini press that allows you to adjust the height of the upper plate. It's one of those instances where a lighter-than-usual amount of pressure is required, to avoid squeezing the egg mixture out of the soft bread.

This is a wonderfully simple recipe for fluffy French toast made from day-old challah. For a slightly jazzed up, special-occasion version, try my Caramel Apple–Stuffed French Toast (page 294).

4 large eggs
1⅓ cups milk
¼ cup sugar
½ teaspoon ground cinnamon

¼ teaspoon pure vanilla extract
4 slices day-old challah, each about 1 inch thick
Pure maple syrup, for serving

1. Heat the panini press to medium-high heat.

2. In a large, shallow bowl, whisk together the eggs, milk, sugar, cinnamon, and vanilla. Soak two of the bread slices for about 2 minutes per side.

3. Place the eggy bread on the panini press and, if possible, adjust the top plate so that it lightly presses the bread. Grill the toast, with the lid closed, until it's browned, about 5 minutes. Soak and grill the remaining bread slices. Serve with maple syrup.

Caramel Apple–Stuffed French Toast

Yield: 4 servings

I was leafing through the pages of my favorite specialty cookware catalog when my eyes stopped on a photo of the most gorgeous, thick-cut, caramelized banana–stuffed French toast, created by chef Bryan Voltaggio. Better yet, it was grilled on a panini press! I, of course, had no choice but to try it out and I, of course, loved it.

Here, I've adapted Chef Voltaggio's recipe to feature caramelized cinnamon apples stuffed within the fluffy challah French toast. Once you drizzle the praline-like toasted pecan maple syrup down those lightly crisp grilled ridges—we're talking dessert for breakfast. Tell your family to have a little patience while you prepare this special-occasion French toast. It will be well worth the wait. (For a simpler, everyday version, see my Grilled French Toast, page 293.)

CARAMELIZED APPLES
3 tablespoons butter
2 tablespoons sugar
1 teaspoon ground cinnamon
A pinch of coarse salt
2 medium-size apples (about 1 pound), peeled, cored, and sliced (I like to use Gala)
⅓ cup heavy cream

FRENCH TOAST
4 slices day-old challah, each about 1½ inches thick
4 large eggs
1⅓ cups milk
¼ cup sugar
½ teaspoon ground cinnamon
¼ teaspoon pure vanilla extract
1 recipe Toasted Pecan Maple Syrup (recipe follows)

1. *Caramelized Apples:* Melt the butter in a large skillet over medium heat. Stir in the sugar, cinnamon, salt, and apples. Cook, stirring frequently, until the apples are brown and tender and a deep brown caramel forms, 7 to 10 minutes. Add the cream and simmer until the sauce thickens slightly, about 2 minutes. Transfer the apples to a medium-size bowl and let them cool.

2. *French Toast:* Using a small, sharp knife, create a pocket in each bread slice by cutting a 2-inch-long slit in the crust on one side of the bread and continuing to cut three-quarters of the way through the bread. Stuff the pockets with a few of the apple slices (this is a messy business!). Reserve the rest of the apples for serving.

3. Heat the panini press to medium-high heat.

4. In a large shallow bowl, whisk together the eggs, milk, sugar, cinnamon, and vanilla. Soak two of the bread slices for about 2 minutes per side.

5. Place the eggy bread on the panini press and, if possible, adjust the top plate so that it lightly presses the bread. Grill the toast until it's browned and cooked through, about 5 minutes. Transfer the toast to a plate and tent it with foil to keep it warm while you soak and grill the remaining two bread slices. Serve the French toast with more caramelized apples and the pecan maple syrup.

Toasted Pecan Maple Syrup

Yield: About 1 cup

A special French toast deserves a special syrup to go along with it. It takes less than 10 minutes to give ordinary maple syrup a nutty boost with butter-toasted pecans.

1 tablespoon unsalted butter
½ cup chopped pecans

A pinch of coarse salt
¾ cup pure maple syrup

Melt the butter in a small skillet or saucepan over medium heat and cook until it's lightly browned, a few minutes. Add the pecans and cook, stirring occasionally, until the pecans are lightly toasted and aromatic, about 3 minutes. Stir in the salt and maple syrup. Turn up the heat to medium-high and cook the syrup until it's slightly thickened, about 2 minutes. Transfer the syrup to a bowl and keep it warm while you prepare the French toast. If you've made the syrup in advance, reheat it on the stove or in the microwave.

Grill-Tarts

Yield: 6 tarts

We all know handheld, sweet-filled tarts like these by a more familiar (yet trademarked) name. Since we're grilling them rather than "popping" them from a toaster, I call them Grill-Tarts. You just cut some rectangles of puff pastry, fill them with jam, seal them up, and put them on the grill. In about 15 minutes you have perfectly puffed, flaky, golden homemade toaster-style tarts—complete with ridges to cradle some tangy lemon glaze.

GRILL-TARTS
1 (17.3-ounce) package frozen puff pastry
   sheets, thawed
¾ cup jam or preserves, such as strawberry,
   raspberry, or blueberry
1 large egg
1 tablespoon water

LEMON GLAZE
1 cup sifted confectioners' sugar
2 tablespoons freshly squeezed lemon
   juice

1. *Grill-Tarts:* Heat the panini press to medium-high heat.

2. On a lightly floured surface, roll out each sheet of puff pastry to a 9-inch square. Divide each pastry sheet into 6 equal rectangles, about 3 inches x 4½ inches each, for a total of 12 rectangles. Spoon 2 to 3 tablespoons of jam onto half of the rectangles, leaving a 1-inch border. Be careful not to overload them or the filling may ooze out during grilling.

3. In a small bowl, whisk the egg and water together to make an egg wash. Brush the egg wash around the edges of the rectangles that are topped with filling. Place the remaining rectangles on top of the filled rectangles, press to seal the edges, and crimp them with a fork.

4. In batches, carefully place the sealed tarts on the panini grill. Lower the lid until it's hovering about ¼ inch above the tarts *without actually touching them*. As the tarts bake they'll puff up and make contact with the upper plate—you want to give them a little room to expand. Grill until the tarts are puffed and golden, 12 to 15 minutes.

5. *Lemon Glaze:* While the tarts grill, whisk together the confectioners' sugar and lemon juice in a small bowl.

6. Drizzle the glaze over the tarts.

Maple Bacon Breakfast Sausage

Yield: 12 sausage patties

Why choose between smoky bacon and sausage if you don't have to? Make your own Maple Bacon Breakfast Sausage on the panini press and have both! Once you see how easy it is to make your own breakfast sausage, you'll never go back. With the panini press, you can grill a batch of homemade sausage in just 2 minutes—I don't think you can even defrost the frozen packaged stuff in that time!

1 pound ground pork
4 strips uncooked bacon, finely chopped
1 tablespoon pure maple syrup
¾ teaspoon coarse salt
¾ teaspoon freshly ground black pepper

1 teaspoon dried sage
1 teaspoon dried thyme
¼ teaspoon ground nutmeg
¼ teaspoon red pepper flakes

1. With a wooden spoon or your hands, mix all of the ingredients in a large bowl.

2. Heat the panini press to medium-high heat. If your panini press comes with a removable drip tray, make sure it is in place (see page 2).

3. Divide the sausage mixture into 12 equal portions. Form each portion into a ball and flatten it into a ½-inch-thick patty.

4. Working in batches, transfer the patties to the panini press and close the lid so that the upper plate is resting on the patties without actually pressing them.

5. Grill the patties until they are cooked through, about 2 minutes.

Egg Scramble Breakfast Quesadillas

Yield: 4 quesadillas

I n my busy house I don't always have a leisurely Saturday morning to prepare full-on breakfast burritos. Thankfully, it takes less time to pull together quesadillas—I just scramble eggs with peppers and onions and load them onto tortillas with pepper Jack cheese. And if I already happen to have cooked bacon on hand, which I often do, I'll go ahead and crumble it in. It's still not a "quick" recipe, but it'll get your weekend off to a tasty start in under an hour.

4 teaspoons vegetable oil
1 green bell pepper, cored, seeded, and
  chopped
½ medium-size onion, chopped
4 large eggs
¼ teaspoon coarse salt

⅛ teaspoon freshly ground black pepper
8 (8-inch) flour tortillas
8 ounces pepper Jack or sharp cheddar
  cheese, sliced
4 strips cooked bacon, crumbled (optional)
Salsa, for serving

1. Heat 2 teaspoons of the oil in a large nonstick skillet. Add the green bell pepper and onion and cook, stirring occasionally, until they've softened, about 5 minutes.

2. Beat the eggs in a medium-size bowl and season them with salt and pepper. Add the eggs to the skillet with the peppers and onions. Cook, stirring often, until the eggs are scrambled and set, about 3 minutes. Remove the pan from the heat.

3. Heat the panini press to medium-high heat.

4. *For each quesadilla:* Brush vegetable oil on two tortillas. Flip over one tortilla and top it with cheese, scrambled eggs, crumbled bacon (if you're using it), and more cheese. Keep about a 1-inch border around the edge of the tortilla so the fillings don't squeeze out when they're grilled. Close the quesadilla with the other tortilla, oiled side up.

5. Grill one quesadilla at a time, with the lid closed, until the cheese is melted and the tortilla is toasted, 3 to 4 minutes. Serve with salsa.

Bacon Breakfast Burritos

Yield: 4 large or 8 small burritos

Here in Southern California, breakfast burritos are as standard on restaurant break-fast menus as omelets or pancakes. My favorite breakfast burrito wraps up every-thing that would typically appear on a good Saturday morning breakfast plate—eggs, bacon, and potatoes—plus a few burrito-style extras like cheese, salsa, and sour cream. Grilling the burritos not only makes a crisp outer shell out of the soft tortilla, it also seals them closed, making these a true handheld meal.

Short on Time? Cook the bacon ahead of time, then substitute 1 tablespoon vegetable oil for the bacon drippings to cook the potatoes and peppers.

1 russet potato (about ¾ pound), peeled and diced

4 strips uncooked bacon

½ cup finely chopped bell pepper, any color(s) you like

¼ cup finely chopped onion

8 large eggs, beaten

Coarse salt and freshly ground black pepper

4 (10-inch) or 8 (8-inch) flour tortillas

4 ounces (about 1 cup) shredded sharp cheddar cheese

Salsa and sour cream, for serving

1. Place the diced potato in a large, microwave-safe bowl. Cover the bowl with plastic wrap and cook the potato on high for 4 minutes. It will be partially cooked and a bit tender.

2. Lay the bacon strips in a large nonstick skillet over medium heat. Cook the bacon, turn-ing it often with tongs, until it's cooked through and crisp. Transfer the bacon to a plate lined with a paper towel to drain.

3. Pour off all but about 1 tablespoon of the bacon drippings. Carefully add the potatoes to the skillet (they may sputter) along with the bell peppers and onions. Cook the vegetables, stirring occasionally, until they're browned and tender, about 10 minutes. Pour in the beaten eggs. Continue cooking and stirring until the eggs are scrambled and cooked through, another 3 to 4 minutes. Season with salt and pepper to taste.

4. Spoon the egg mixture into a large bowl. Crumble the bacon and toss it with the egg mixture.

5. Heat the panini press to medium-high heat.

6. *For each burrito:* Heat a tortilla in the microwave on High for 10 seconds to soften it. Place some egg mixture in the center of the tortilla and sprinkle some cheese on top. Fold the left and right sides of the tortilla over the filling, then roll it up from the bottom. Place the burrito, seam side down, on the panini press.

7. Grill two burritos at a time, with the lid closed, until the tortillas are toasted and golden grill marks appear, 4 to 5 minutes. Serve the burritos with salsa and sour cream.

Ham, Egg, and Cheddar Breakfast Crêpes

Yield: 4 rolled crêpes

first made these crêpes for a Valentine's Day post on PaniniHappy.com. The holiday fell on a weekend that year, which meant I could pull off a special family breakfast for the occasion: an omelet, sliced ham, and cheddar cheese rolled in a savory crêpe and grilled on the panini press. It sounds like a lot of work, but in reality the crêpes and omelets each take only a few minutes to make. The sun-dried tomato puree, aside from looking cute on the plate in its heart shape, adds a nice sweetness to the crepes.

Make It Ahead: You can prepare and refrigerate the crêpe batter up to 2 days ahead of time. Also, once you've cooked the crêpes, you can store them, cooled, separated by waxed paper, and wrapped airtight, in the freezer for up to 1 month. Defrost the crepes either in the microwave or overnight in the refrigerator.

CRÊPES
½ cup all-purpose flour
½ cup milk
¼ cup lukewarm water
2 large eggs
2 tablespoons butter, melted, plus 2 teaspoons butter for the pan
½ teaspoon coarse salt

OMELETS
Butter for the pan, if necessary

4 large eggs
Coarse salt and freshly ground black pepper

FILLING
4 ounces cheddar cheese, sliced
4 ounces sliced ham

OPTIONAL GARNISH
Oil-packed sun-dried tomatoes, plus some of the oil from the jar

1. *Crêpes:* Blend the flour, milk, water, eggs, 2 tablespoons melted butter, and salt in a blender or food processor until you have a smooth batter. Transfer the batter to a pitcher or liquid measuring cup. Let the batter stand, covered, at room temperature for 30 minutes.

2. Melt ½ teaspoon butter in a small nonstick skillet over medium heat. Give the batter a quick stir and pour about 2 tablespoons into the pan, swirling the pan around to create a very thin, even crêpe. Cook the crêpe until the top is set and the underside is golden brown, 30 to 60 seconds. Carefully flip the crêpe with a spatula or your fingers and cook the other side until it's lightly browned as well. Transfer the crêpe to a plate lined with waxed paper.

3. Cook the remaining crêpes in this manner, remembering to butter the pan and stir the batter before making each one. As each crêpe is done, add it to the stack, using waxed paper in between each one to prevent sticking.

4. *Omelets:* Make the omelets one at a time, ideally just prior to rolling them into the crêpes. In a small bowl beat 1 egg and season it with salt and pepper to taste. Pour the egg into the same small nonstick skillet that you used for the crêpes (melt more butter in the pan, if needed) and cook until the top is set and the underside is lightly browned. Flip it with a spatula and cook the other side until it's cooked through.

5. Heat the panini press to medium heat.

6. *Filling:* Place one crêpe on a work surface. Place one omelet on top of the crêpe (the omelet should be about the same size as the crêpe). Layer cheese and ham on top of the omelet. Carefully roll up the crêpe and place it, seam side down, on the panini press.

7. Grill two crêpes at a time, with the lid closed, until the cheese is melted and golden grill marks appear, about 2 minutes.

8. *Optional Garnish:* Puree sun-dried tomatoes and a small amount of the oil in a blender or mini food processor to create a paste. Spoon the puree into a small plastic bag, snip off one corner of the bag, and pipe the puree in a heart shape—or any other design you like—onto the plate alongside each crêpe.

Chorizo and Potato Grilled Hand Pies

Yield: 16 hand pies

A memorable moment from the summer my sisters and I spent at my grandparents' house in rural North Carolina was my introduction to hand pies. I was eight years old and my cousin Melissa, who was a worldly twelve, had the bright idea to goad our grandma into buying us each a glazed chocolate pie at the grocery store checkout. Even my pre-tween palate could detect more chemicals and gums than chocolate in the rubbery filling, but I was nonetheless delighted to be holding *a whole pie that fit in my hand*. This was an awakening.

With the help of puff pastry, your panini press can turn out all kinds of delicious homemade hand pies. These are some of the best, filled with spicy Mexican chorizo, Yukon gold potatoes, sharp cheddar cheese, chives, and a sweet kiss of dried apples. They make a great brunch alternative to the standard sausage or potato dish.

Make It Ahead: If you'd like, you can keep your prepared (but uncooked) hand pies in the refrigerator for a day or two and grill just a few at a time.

1 teaspoon vegetable oil
1 pound uncooked Mexican chorizo (not dry-cured)
1 to 2 Yukon Gold potatoes (about 8 ounces), peeled
2 (17.3-ounce) packages frozen puff pastry sheets, thawed

4 ounces (about 1 cup) shredded sharp cheddar cheese
$\frac{1}{3}$ cup chopped dried apples or golden raisins
4 teaspoons chopped chives, plus whole chives for garnish
Sour cream, for serving

1. Heat the vegetable oil in a large skillet. Cook the chorizo, breaking it up with a wooden spoon, until it's thoroughly browned. Set aside.

2. Meanwhile, bring a pot of salted water to a boil, add the potato, and cook until fork-tender, 15 to 20 minutes. Drain the potato, then return it to the pot. Smash with a potato masher; it doesn't need to be smooth, just crushed a little.

3. On a lightly floured surface, roll out each sheet of puff pastry to an approximately 12 x 15-inch rectangle. Cut 3-inch rounds out of the puff pastry—the rim of a drinking glass works well as a cutter.

4. Heat the panini press to medium-high heat and heat the oven to 250°F.

(continued on page 306)

5. On half of the pastry circles, place about 2 teaspoons potato, 2 teaspoons chorizo, 1 teaspoon cheese, ½ teaspoon dried apples, and ¼ teaspoon chives. Use your judgment—you want the pies to be full but not overstuffed. Have at hand a small bowlful of water. One at a time, pick up each remaining circle, dip your finger in some water and wet the outer edge of the circle. Place the circle, wet side down, on top of one of the filled circles. Stretch the pastry a little if necessary to cover the filling. Press around the edges to seal the pie. Crimp the edges with a fork.

6. Once you're done with 4 or 5 pies (or as many as will fit comfortably on your grill), carefully transfer the pies to the grill and close the lid so that it makes contact with the top of the pies without applying too much pressure. As the pastry bakes, it will puff up and become a more even disc shape. Grill until the pastry is puffed and fully baked (it will be quite brown in the center and pale golden around the edges), 10 to 12 minutes. Put the finished pies on a baking sheet and keep them warm in the oven while you grill the remaining pies.

7. Serve the hand pies with a dollop of sour cream and a few snips of chives.

Mini Frittata

Yield: 1 mini frittata (see Note)

My husband is notorious for saving two-bite leftovers in the fridge—a sliver of pizza, two grilled shrimp, broccoli florets the kids didn't eat. "I might want to eat 'em later!" he explains, and he usually does. But I found another way to use these little odds and ends: mini frittatas.

A lot of people bake individual frittatas like these in muffin tins, but you can do it just as easily—and perhaps even faster—in ramekins on your panini press. You just whisk an egg and some cheese with whatever mix-ins you have on hand. The mixture cooks in the ramekin and out pops a fluffy little crustless egg pie.

This recipe works best on a panini press that allows you to set a specific heat temperature.

1 large egg
2 tablespoons shredded cheese, such as sharp cheddar, Swiss, or Gruyère

Coarse salt and freshly ground black pepper
3 to 4 tablespoons mix-ins (see below)

1. Heat the panini press to 350°F. Spray a 6-ounce ramekin with nonstick cooking spray.

2. In a small bowl, whisk together the egg and cheese with a pinch of salt and pepper. Add your mix-ins.

3. Pour the egg mixture into the ramekin and set the ramekin on the grill. Close the lid so that the upper plate makes contact with the rim of the ramekin.

4. Grill the frittata until it is cooked through and set, 15 to 20 minutes. You'll know it's almost done when you start to hear sizzling, letting you know it has puffed up to the rim of the ramekin and is touching the upper plate. Let it brown on top for about 1 minute before carefully transferring the ramekin (with a potholder!) from the grill. Carefully remove the frittata from the ramekin and serve immediately.

NOTE: You can easily scale this recipe up to four ramekins on the grill to make breakfast for the whole family.

Frittata Mix-Ins

- Thinly sliced cherry tomatoes
- Crumbled cooked bacon or breakfast sausage
- Chopped leftover cooked vegetables
- Chopped green chiles
- Fresh herbs
- Leftover pasta

A LITTLE SOMETHING SWEET

Dessert on the Panini Press

PANINI

MORE FROM THE PANINI PRESS

Apple Pie Panini

Yield: 4 panini

What about a sandwich that tastes just like apple pie?" my sister Julie suggested to me in an email one day. I stopped what I was doing and, suddenly, I could think about nothing else besides apple pie panini. How dreamy would that be—tart apple slices layered with honey-whipped mascarpone on cinnamon raisin bread with a brown sugar crust on top? Well, here's the simple recipe for that dessert sandwich dream come true.

½ cup mascarpone cheese
2 teaspoons honey
4 tablespoons (½ stick) butter, at room
  temperature

8 slices cinnamon raisin bread, sliced from
  a dense bakery loaf
1 Granny Smith or other firm apple, cored
  and thinly sliced
2 tablespoons light brown sugar

1. Either in a small bowl with a whisk or in a mini food processor, whip the mascarpone and honey together until well combined and fluffy.

2. Heat the panini press to medium-high heat.

3. *For each sandwich:* Spread butter on two slices of bread to flavor the outside of the sandwich. Flip over both slices of bread and spread 1 tablespoon sweetened mascarpone on each. Top one slice of bread with a layer of apples and close the sandwich with the other slice, buttered side up. Sprinkle some brown sugar on top.

4. Grill two panini at a time, with the lid closed, until the fillings are warmed and the bread is toasted, with a sweet crust, 3 to 5 minutes.

PB & J Pound Cake Panini

Yield: 4 panini

Please don't be upset with me for suggesting this one. The first time I tried it, a coy smile emerged on my face, like a little kid up to mischief. This seemed so wrong, yet so right!

Pound cake that's a day or two old gets a new, crispy-edged life when you grill it. But don't stop there. Spread some peanut butter and jelly on your pound cake slices for just about the most decadent PB & J you ever had.

8 slices pound cake, each about ½ inch thick
4 tablespoons peanut butter

4 tablespoons jelly, jam, or preserves of your choice

1. Heat the panini press to medium-high heat.

2. *For each sandwich:* Spread 1 tablespoon peanut butter on one slice of pound cake and 1 tablespoon jelly on another slice. Close the sandwich.

3. Grill the panini, with the lid closed, until the pound cake is toasted and grill marks appear, about 2 minutes. Enjoy this treat right away with a fork.

Strawberries, Basil, and Lemon Curd Pound Cake Tartines

Yield: 4 tartines

Think of these easy-to-make tartines the next time you're looking for a crowd-pleasing dessert to bring to a spring or summer potluck. Not only do these open-faced pound cake sandwiches look pretty on display, they're incredibly quick to assemble. Make a few extras to keep at home because you'll be leaving the party with an empty tray!

4 slices pound cake, each about ½ inch thick
½ cup lemon curd, purchased or homemade (page 331)

½ cup sliced strawberries
1 tablespoon torn fresh basil leaves

1. Heat the panini press to medium-high heat.

2. Grill the pound cake slices, with the lid closed, until they're toasted and grill marks appear, 1 to 2 minutes.

3. Transfer the slices to a serving platter. Top each slice with a generous layer of lemon curd, strawberry slices, and basil.

Brie, Nutella, and Basil Panini

Yield: 4 panini

I have yet to meet someone who doesn't flinch uncomfortably when I mention the concept of chocolate, Brie, and basil panini. I have to admit, I had that same "uhh . . . no thanks" reaction when I first watched Giada De Laurentiis grill these sandwiches on TV. But I was also intrigued. I gave them a try one day and—wow!—Giada was right, it's a magical combination! The key ingredient, to my surprise, turned out to be the basil. It adds just the right amount of fresh, herbal flavor, much like mint (which we all know pairs very well with chocolate).

For my version, I've brought in Nutella to add the flavor of hazelnuts along with the chocolate. Bread is more of a supporting player in these panini than the star, but I'll tell you what, some buttery brioche is the perfect complement for these rich dessert sandwiches if you've got it!

4 ounces Brie cheese (with or without the rind), sliced

8 slices brioche, each about ½ inch thick

8 fresh basil leaves

½ cup Nutella or other chocolate hazelnut spread

1. Heat the panini press to medium-high heat.

2. *For each sandwich:* Lay a few slices of Brie on one slice of brioche and top them with 2 basil leaves. Spread 2 tablespoons Nutella on another slice of bread and place it on top of the basil, Nutella side down, to close the sandwich.

3. Grill two panini at a time, with the lid closed, until the cheese is melted and the bread is toasted, about 2 minutes.

Nutella S'mores Panini

Yield: 4 panini

I made my live TV cooking debut with this recipe. A producer from a local show in San Diego contacted me one day to see if I'd be interested in doing a cooking segment involving s'mores the following morning. My husband and I rearranged our schedules, I hit the grocery store, and the next morning I arrived at the station lugging three bags full of food, cutting boards, cooking utensils and, of course, a panini press. Ready or not, I was going to grill Nutella S'mores Panini on live TV!

Think classic s'more meets the Fluffernutter (see my Fluffernutter Panini recipe on page 316): Nutella and marshmallow crème on the inside, crunchy graham cracker crust on the outside. It's an oozy and over-the-top s'more in sandwich form. The TV segment went off smoothly, loud airplane flying overhead notwithstanding. Suffice it to say I was still out there grilling sandwiches for the crew after the cameras had stopped rolling.

4 tablespoons unsalted butter, at room temperature
¼ cup graham cracker crumbs
1 tablespoon sugar
8 slices rustic white bread, sliced from a dense bakery loaf
½ cup Nutella or other chocolate hazelnut spread
½ cup Marshmallow Fluff or other marshmallow crème

1. Heat the panini press to medium-high heat.

2. In a small bowl, mix the butter, graham cracker crumbs, and sugar until they're well combined.

3. *For each sandwich:* Spread a thin layer of graham cracker butter on two slices of bread to flavor the outside of the sandwich. Flip over both slices of bread. Spread 2 tablespoons Nutella on one slice and 2 tablespoons Marshmallow Fluff on the other. Close the sandwich with the other slice of bread, buttered side up.

4. Grill two panini at a time, with the lid closed, until the crust is crisped and golden and the Marshmallow Fluff has melted, 3 to 4 minutes.

Fluffernutter Panini

Yield: 4 panini

get why the people of Massachusetts sought to have the Fluffernutter—a peanut butter and marshmallow crème sandwich concoction—designated as their official state sandwich. But in reality, these things ought to be illegal, they're so decadent. Well, far be it from me to judge . . . or deny that this sandwich sounded pretty appealing to me. So I went ahead and dressed up my grilled version with nuggets of crunchy candied peanuts dispersed throughout the sandwich and added a cinnamon-sugar crust. Go big, right?

4 tablespoons unsalted butter, at room
   temperature
2 tablespoons sugar
2 teaspoons ground cinnamon
A pinch of coarse salt

8 slices white bread, each about 1 inch thick
½ cup peanut butter
½ cup Marshmallow Fluff or other marshmallow crème
¼ cup Candied Peanuts (recipe follows)

1. In a small bowl, mix the butter, sugar, cinnamon, and salt until they're well combined.

2. Heat the panini press to medium-high heat.

3. *For each sandwich:* Spread a layer of cinnamon-sugar butter on two slices of bread. Flip them over and spread a generous layer of peanut butter on one slice and a good amount of Marshmallow Fluff on the other. Scatter a small handful of candied peanuts over the peanut butter and close the sandwich with the other slice of bread, marshmallow side down.

4. Grill two panini at a time, with the lid closed, until the Marshmallow Fluff is melted and the bread is toasted, 2 to 3 minutes.

Candied Peanuts

Yield: 1 cup

If you find yourself with extra candied peanuts on hand, save them to top Grown-Up Grilled Banana Splits (page 324). Or keep them around for a sweet snack.

¼ cup sugar
¼ teaspoon coarse salt
1 tablespoon water

½ teaspoon pure vanilla extract
1 cup unsalted roasted peanuts

1. Lay out a large sheet of aluminum foil and coat it with nonstick cooking spray. Set aside.

2. Combine all of the ingredients in a large, heavy-bottomed skillet over medium-high heat. Cook, stirring constantly, as the mixture goes from syrupy to dry and sandy and finally to a deep brown, smooth caramel stage, 10 to 12 minutes. Carefully pour the candied peanuts onto the prepared foil and allow them to cool for 5 minutes. Transfer the peanuts to an airtight container, breaking the candy apart if needed, and store them at room temperature for up to 2 weeks.

Sprinkle Toasts

Yield: 4 toasts

Sprinkles are known as *hagelslag* in the Netherlands and are used on more than just birthday cakes and ice cream cones. The Dutch also enjoy their sprinkles with butter on bread. My childlike side can easily get behind this fun food tradition.

Maybe it's the frosting-like association, but my favorite way to enjoy sprinkle toast is with Nutella chocolate hazelnut spread. To me, this is dessert, but it would make a pretty terrific anytime snack as well.

4 slices white bread, each about 1 inch thick

½ cup Nutella or other chocolate hazelnut spread
Sprinkles

1. Heat the panini press to medium-high heat.

2. Arrange the bread slices on the grill, in batches if needed. Close the lid and grill the bread until it's toasted, 2 to 3 minutes.

3. Spread a generous layer of Nutella on top of each toast and adorn them with as many sprinkles as make you happy.

Homemade Ice Cream Cones

Yield: 14 ice cream cones

T his is worth screaming from the rooftops: *You can make ice cream cones with your panini press! Easily! With no special ingredients! And they're really, really good!*

Get ready for your inner child to leap with joy once that familiar sweet cookie smell from the ice cream parlor wafts about your kitchen. If you've ever watched the ice cream folks make cones, all they do is place some batter on a shallow waffle iron, press out the batter and shape the cone. It finally occurred to me . . . couldn't we do the same thing on a panini press? Absolutely!

I've adapted an easy, flavorful ice cream cone recipe created by pastry chef Gale Gand so it can be prepared on the panini press, with the help of a DIY cone mold. See the Note at the end of the recipe for instructions on how to make your mold.

This recipe requires a panini press that closes very tightly in order to make a wafer thin enough to turn into a cone.

1½ cups confectioners' sugar	1 tablespoon cornstarch
1½ cups all-purpose flour	1 cup heavy cream
¼ teaspoon ground cinnamon	1½ teaspoons pure vanilla extract
A pinch of ground nutmeg	

1. In a medium-size bowl, whisk together the confectioners' sugar, flour, cinnamon, nutmeg, and cornstarch. Set aside.

2. In another medium-size bowl, with a whisk or electric mixer whip the cream and vanilla together until it is mousse-like. Add the dry ingredients to the cream and stir to make a batter. Let the batter sit at room temperature for 30 minutes.

3. Heat the panini press to medium-high heat.

4. *For each ice cream cone:* Place a heaping tablespoonful of batter onto the grill and close the lid, completely pressing the batter. Grill until the pressed cone is browned but still malleable, about 90 seconds; it will be an oblong shape. Carefully transfer the pressed cone to a cutting board or piece of waxed paper. Position your cone mold (see the Note below) in the center of the pressed cone, leaving about ½ inch space between the long edge of the pressed cone and the pointed end of the cone mold. Working quickly and carefully (the cone will be very hot!), roll the pressed cone around the cone mold to shape it. Leave the cone on the mold for about 10 seconds to set the shape.

5. Enjoy your favorite ice cream in your freshly made cones! The cones are best enjoyed the same day that they are made, but they'll still be fresh the next day if stored in an airtight container at room temperature.

NOTE: To make a mold for the cone, mark a circle approximately 4⅝ inches in diameter on a piece of cardstock-weight paper. Use scissors to cut out the circle, then form the paper into a cone shape by overlapping two sides and twisting the circle until you've formed a point on one end. Tape the cone closed so that it retains its shape.

Grilled Pears with Honey-Whipped Greek Yogurt and Toasted Almonds

Yield: 4 servings

When fresh pear halves begin to sear on a hot panini grill, it smells as if someone is stirring up homemade caramel nearby. I like to drop these candy-like pears into a martini glass with cold, creamy Greek yogurt that I've whipped with a little honey and vanilla. A sprinkling of toasted almonds and an extra drizzle of honey are all that's needed to turn these simple ingredients into something special.

1 cup plain whole-milk Greek yogurt
2 tablespoons honey, plus more for drizzling
½ teaspoon pure vanilla extract

¼ cup blanched whole almonds
4 ripe pears, such as D'Anjou or Bosc
1 tablespoon butter, melted

1. Whip the yogurt, honey, and vanilla in a blender or mini food processor, or with an electric mixer, until it's creamy, smooth, and shiny, about 2 minutes. Transfer it to a small bowl, cover, and refrigerate while you prepare the other ingredients.

2. Heat the oven or toaster oven to 350°F. Spread the almonds on a baking sheet and bake until they're fragrant, about 5 minutes. Keep your eye on them to make sure they don't burn!

3. Heat the panini press to high.

4. Halve each pear lengthwise and remove the core (an easy way is to scoop out the core with a teaspoon). Brush a little melted butter on the cut sides.

5. In batches, place the pear halves, cut sides down, on the grill and close the lid so that it rests gently on top of the pears. Grill until dark grill marks appear and you can smell the aroma of burnt caramel, about 3 minutes.

6. Transfer the pear halves, cut sides up, to individual bowls or martini glasses. Top with a few dollops of the honey-whipped yogurt, sprinkle on a few toasted almonds, and drizzle with honey.

Grown-Up Grilled Banana Splits

Yield: 4 servings

Something pretty incredible happens when you grill a super-ripe banana in its peel. An already sweet treat turns near candy-like as the pulp softens, the juices are released, and it caramelizes inside the peel. Once you break it open, all you need is a spoon (and maybe a scoop of ice cream and some salted peanuts) to enjoy a very simple and—dare I say, grown-up—version of a banana split. If you're feeling very decadent, sub in my Candied Peanuts (see page 317) for the plain peanuts.

4 very ripe bananas (with lots of brown spots)
4 scoops vanilla ice cream

3 tablespoons chopped salted dry-roasted peanuts

1. Heat the panini press to medium-high heat.

2. Set the bananas directly on the grill (in their peels) and close the lid. Grill the bananas until they feel rather soft when you give them a poke, about 8 minutes. You'll start to hear sizzling as the moisture from inside the bananas seeps through the peel.

3. Using tongs, take the bananas off the grill and transfer them to serving plates or bowls.

4. Slide a sharp knife down the center of each banana and peel back the banana peel to expose the soft, hot pulp, which should be swimming in its own caramel. Dollop on a scoop of vanilla ice cream and sprinkle the chopped salted peanuts over the top. Enjoy the whole hot-and-cold, sweet-and-salty dessert right out of the banana peel.

Mini Yellow Layer Cake with Chocolate Buttercream

Yield: 1 to 2 servings

None of my friends could quite picture what I was talking about when I told them I had baked a layer cake on the panini press. "How . . . what . . . *why?*"

It's incredibly easy to do. You just fill ramekins with cake batter and close the grill lid. In less than 20 minutes you've got rich, delicious yellow cake ready to be cooled and frosted in chocolate. I adapted the small-batch cake recipe from the uber-talented Jessica Merchant of the blog HowSweetEats.com for these personal mini cake layers.

Since this recipe involves baking, I suggest that you prepare it on a panini press that allows you to set a specific temperature.

YELLOW CAKE
¼ cup all-purpose flour
A heaping ¼ teaspoon baking powder
A pinch of coarse salt
1 large egg
2 tablespoons sugar
2 tablespoons unsalted butter, melted
1 teaspoon pure vanilla extract
1½ tablespoons milk

CHOCOLATE BUTTERCREAM
3 tablespoons unsalted butter, melted
3 tablespoons unsweetened cocoa powder
1 cup sifted confectioners' sugar
1½ tablespoons milk
¼ teaspoon pure vanilla extract
Sprinkles (optional)

1. *Yellow Cake:* Heat the panini press to 350°F. Make sure that the grill sits flat on your work surface, not tilted. Spray two 6-ounce ramekins (3½ inches in diameter) with nonstick cooking spray.

2. In a small bowl, whisk together the flour, baking powder, and salt.

3. In a medium-size bowl, whisk together the egg and sugar until they are combined. Stir in the melted butter and vanilla. Add the dry ingredients and stir until the batter is smooth. Stir in the milk.

4. Divide the batter equally between the two ramekins. Set the ramekins on the panini grill and close the lid so that the upper plate makes contact with the rims of the ramekins. Bake the cakes until they are set and spring back when touched in the center, 17 to 19 minutes. Remove the ramekins from the grill and allow them to cool for 5 minutes, then invert the cakes onto a wire rack to cool completely.

5. *Chocolate Buttercream:* In a small bowl, whisk together the butter and cocoa. Add the confectioners' sugar, milk, and vanilla and whisk until the frosting is smooth.

6. Assemble the layers and frost the cake with chocolate buttercream. Sprinkles are optional, but they sure are fun.

Mini Carrot Layer Cake with Maple Cream Cheese Frosting

Yield: 1 to 2 servings

I f you have just one carrot on hand in your crisper, the healthiest thing to do with it would be to peel and eat it raw. A somewhat more indulgent approach would be to make yourself a mini carrot layer cake on your panini press.

After I posted my first mini layer cake on PaniniHappy.com, a consumer packaged-goods company approached me about creating another one for a "new take on cupcakes" feature they were putting together. This is the cake I came up with—classic carrot cake, full of walnuts and spices, and topped with an autumn-sweet maple cream cheese frosting. Without the egg yolk, this is a bit lighter in texture than the Mini Yellow Layer Cake (page 325) but just as rich and moist.

Since this recipe involves baking, I suggest that you prepare it on a panini press that allows you to set a specific temperature.

CARROT CAKE
¼ cup all-purpose flour
A heaping ¼ teaspoon baking powder
A pinch of coarse salt
A pinch of ground cinnamon
A pinch of ground ginger
A pinch of ground nutmeg
1 large egg white
2 tablespoons packed light brown sugar
2 tablespoons canola oil
1½ teaspoons milk
¼ teaspoon pure vanilla extract

⅓ cup packed shredded carrots (from about 1 carrot)
1 tablespoon raisins
1 tablespoon chopped walnuts

MAPLE CREAM CHEESE FROSTING
1 tablespoon chopped walnuts
2 ounces cream cheese, at room temperature
1 tablespoon unsalted butter, at room temperature
⅓ cup sifted confectioners' sugar
2 teaspoons pure maple syrup

1. *Carrot Cake:* Heat the panini press to 350°F. Make sure that the grill sits flat on your work surface, not tilted. Spray two 6-ounce ramekins (3½ inches in diameter) with nonstick cooking spray.

2. In a small bowl, whisk together the flour, baking powder, salt, cinnamon, ginger and nutmeg.

3. In a medium-size bowl, whisk together the egg white, brown sugar, oil, milk, and vanilla until they are combined. Add the dry ingredients and stir until the batter is blended. Mix in the carrots, raisins, and walnuts.

(continued on page 328)

4. Divide the batter equally between the two ramekins. Set the ramekins on the panini press and close the lid so that the upper plate makes contact with the rims of the ramekins. Bake the cakes until they are set and spring back when touched in the center, 17 to 19 minutes. Remove the ramekins from the grill and allow them to cool for 5 minutes, then invert the cakes onto a wire rack to cool completely.

5. *Maple Cream Cheese Frosting:* Spread the chopped walnuts in a small skillet. Cook the walnuts over medium-low heat, shaking the pan frequently to move them around, until they are fragrant and toasted, 10 to 12 minutes. Set the toasted walnuts aside to cool.

6. In a small bowl, beat together the cream cheese and butter with a hand mixer. Add the confectioners' sugar and maple syrup and beat until the frosting is smooth. Assemble the layers and frost the cake with the frosting.

7. Give the toasted walnuts an extra fine chop and sprinkle them on top of the cake.

Grilled Apple Turnovers

Yield: 8 turnovers

This is an updated version of the very first non-panini recipe I ever posted on PaniniHappy.com. I guess I figured out early on that there was more to this panini press machine than just sandwiches. Lots of familiar foods could be prepared just as well—perhaps even faster and better—on a panini press.

Oven-baked apple turnovers are always a treat. But if you grill them, the resulting ridges give you the excuse to fill those valleys with vanilla ice cream.

Make It Ahead: If you'd like to grill just a few turnovers at a time, you can wrap any assembled, uncooked turnovers tightly in plastic wrap and store them in the refrigerator for 2 to 3 days until you're ready to grill them.

3 medium-size apples (about 1½ pounds), a combination of sweet and tart, such as Gala and Granny Smith, peeled, cored, and thinly sliced
3 tablespoons freshly squeezed lemon juice
2 tablespoons sugar
1 tablespoon all-purpose flour
½ teaspoon ground cinnamon
⅛ teaspoon ground nutmeg
A pinch of coarse salt
A pinch of ground cardamom (optional)
1 (17.3-ounce) package frozen puff pastry sheets, thawed
1 large egg
1 tablespoon water
Ice cream, for serving

1. In a medium-size bowl, toss the apple slices with the lemon juice. Add the sugar, flour, cinnamon, nutmeg, salt, and cardamom (if you're using it) and toss to coat the apples.

2. Heat the panini press to medium-high heat (if your grill has a temperature setting, set it to 400°F).

3. On a lightly floured surface, roll out each puff pastry sheet into a 12-inch square. Divide each square into four 6-inch squares.

4. Spoon 6 or 7 apple slices onto the center of each pastry square.

5. In a small bowl, whisk the egg and water together to make an egg wash. One pastry square at a time, brush a little egg wash along the edges of the square and fold it over diagonally to form a triangle. Press the edges together with your fingers and then crimp them with a fork to seal them.

6. Carefully place two turnovers on the grill. Lower the lid until it's very lightly touching them (if your press allows you to fix the height so that the upper plate hovers about ¼ inch above the turnovers, that's even better). As the turnovers bake they'll puff up and make contact with the upper plate—you want to give them a little room to expand. Grill until the pastry is puffed, golden, and crisp on the outside, about 12 minutes. Repeat this step for the remaining 6 turnovers.

7. Serve the turnovers hot with a scoop of ice cream on top, running down into those crinkly pastry ridges.

Grilled Angel Food Cake with Lemon Curd

Yield: 4 servings

Something really cool happens when you grill angel food cake: the outside gets ever-so-gently crisped and practically dissolves on your tongue like cotton candy. It transforms an otherwise average, store-bought cake into something far more appealing—especially when you top it with some sweet-tart homemade lemon curd.

8 slices angel food cake, each about 1 inch thick (see Note)

1 cup Lemon Curd, purchased or home-made (recipe follows)
½ pint (about ¾ cup) fresh raspberries

1. Heat the panini press to high heat.

2. In batches, place the angel food cake slices on the grill. Close the lid so that the upper plate is resting on the cake without pressing it. Grill the cake slices until they're toasted and grill marks appear, about 1 minute. Alternatively, leave the grill open and grill the cake slices for about 90 seconds per side.

3. Serve the grilled angel food cake with a few spoonfuls of lemon curd and some fresh raspberries.

NOTE: If you bake your own angel food cake from scratch, save the yolks to make the lemon curd.

Lemon Curd

Yield: About 1½ cups

Chocolate lovers have their Nutella. If you're a lemon lover, then homemade lemon curd needs to be part of your repertoire. The silky-smooth citrus spread is a terrific topper for treats like angel food cake and pound cake and also makes an easy layer cake filling. It takes a little effort to make your own homemade lemon curd but, as with so many things, it tastes way better than store-bought.

5 large egg yolks
¾ cup sugar
2 tablespoons finely grated lemon zest

⅓ cup freshly squeezed lemon juice
5 tablespoons butter, cubed and chilled

1. Fill a medium-size saucepan with an inch of water and bring it to a simmer over medium-high heat (or, if you have a double boiler, heat an inch of water in the lower saucepan).

2. Meanwhile, whisk together the egg yolks and sugar in a medium-size heatproof bowl (or the upper saucepan of your double boiler) until smooth. Whisk in the lemon zest and juice until the mixture is smooth.

3. Once the water is simmering, turn down the heat to low and place the bowl on top of the saucepan; the bowl should not touch the water (if you're using a double boiler, assemble the upper and lower saucepans). Whisk the egg mixture continually until it thickens, about 15 minutes. It should be thick enough to coat the back of a wooden spoon.

4. Remove the bowl or upper saucepan from the heat and stir in one cube of butter at a time, incorporating each cube before adding the next. If you're using a double boiler, transfer the curd to a bowl. If you're not serving the curd immediately, press a layer of plastic wrap on the surface of the curd to prevent a skin from forming and refrigerate until you're ready to use it.

5. The lemon curd will thicken quite a bit in the refrigerator. To restore it to a spoonable consistency, set your bowl of curd inside a larger bowl. Fill the larger bowl with enough hot water to rise about halfway up the sides of the bowl of curd. Give the curd a stir every few minutes, refreshing the larger bowl with new hot water, until the curd is soft enough to serve. It will stay fresh in the refrigerator for up to 2 weeks.

Peanut Butter Sandwich Cookies

Yield: About 9 sandwich cookies

I had been mulling over ideas for how to parlay my grilled ice cream cones into some kind of filled cookie when my friend Kelly Senyei posted a revelation on her blog, JustATaste. com: Nutella Waffle Sandwich Cookies. She started with my grilled ice cream cones, cut circles out of them and filled them with Nutella. Ding-ding-ding! That was it.

Continuing the circle of inspiration, I borrowed Kelly's approach and changed it up a bit by adding peanut butter to the cone batter and whipping up some peanut butter buttercream for the filling. Get your tall glass of cold milk ready—these are rich! And oh so good.

COOKIES
1½ cups confectioners' sugar
1½ cups all-purpose flour
1 tablespoon cornstarch
¼ teaspoon coarse salt
¾ cup heavy cream
¼ cup creamy peanut butter
1 teaspoon pure vanilla extract

PEANUT BUTTER FILLING
¼ cup creamy peanut butter
2 tablespoons unsalted butter, at room temperature
½ cup sifted confectioners' sugar
A pinch of coarse salt
2 teaspoons heavy cream

1. *Cookies:* In a medium-size bowl, whisk together the confectioners' sugar, flour, cornstarch, and salt.

2. In another medium-size bowl, whip together the cream, peanut butter, and vanilla with a whisk or electric mixer until it is mousse-like. Add the dry ingredients to the cream mixture and stir to make a smooth batter. Cover the bowl and let the batter chill in the refrigerator for 30 minutes.

3. Heat the panini press to medium-high heat.

4. Place as many heaping tablespoonfuls of batter as will fit on your grill, with about 3 inches between them. Lower the lid until it's hovering about ¼ inch above the cookies *without actually touching them.* Grill the cookies until they are browned but still malleable, 2 to 3 minutes.

5. Carefully transfer the cookies to a cutting board and immediately cut out circles with a 2-inch cookie cutter. Set the cookies on a rack to cool.

6. *Peanut Butter Filling:* While the cookies are cooling, blend the peanut butter and butter in a medium-size bowl with a whisk or electric mixer until it's well combined. Mix in the confectioners' sugar and salt. Add the cream and continue whipping the filling until it's smooth and fluffy.

7. To assemble each sandwich, spread about 1 tablespoon of filling onto one cookie and close the sandwich with another.

Measurement Equivalents

Liquid Conversions

U.S.	Metric
1 tsp	5 ml
1 tbs	15 ml
2 tbs	30 ml
3 tbs	45 ml
¼ cup	60 ml
⅓ cup	75 ml
⅓ cup + 1 tbs	90 ml
⅓ cup + 2 tbs	100 ml
½ cup	120 ml
⅔ cup	150 ml
¾ cup	180 ml
¾ cup + 2 tbs	200 ml
1 cup	240 ml
1 cup + 2 tbs	275 ml
1¼ cups	300 ml
1⅓ cups	325 ml
1½ cups	350 ml
1⅔ cups	375 ml
1¾ cups	400 ml
1¾ cups + 2 tbs	450 ml
2 cups (1 pint)	475 ml
2½ cups	600 ml
3 cups	720 ml
4 cups (1 quart)	945 ml
(1,000 ml is 1 liter)	

Weight Conversions

U.S./U.K.	Metric
½ oz	14 g
1 oz	28 g
1½ oz	43 g
2 oz	57 g
2½ oz	71 g
3 oz	85 g
3½ oz	100 g
4 oz	113 g
5 oz	142 g
6 oz	170 g
7 oz	200 g
8 oz	227 g
9 oz	255 g
10 oz	284 g
11 oz	312 g
12 oz	340 g
13 oz	368 g
14 oz	400 g
15 oz	425 g
1 lb	454 g

Oven Temperature Conversions

°F	Gas Mark	°C
250	½	120
275	1	140
300	2	150
325	3	165
350	4	180
375	5	190
400	6	200
425	7	220
450	8	230
475	9	240
500	10	260
550	Broil	290

NOTE: All conversions are approximate.

INDEX